INTERNATIONAL DISPUTES: CASE HISTORIES 1945-1970

INTERNATIONAL DISPUTES

CASE HISTORIES 1945-1970

M. D. DONELAN

London School of Economics and Political Science

and

M. J. GRIEVE

University College, London

assisted by

P. C. FIELDER and H. R. WARNING

Published for

The David Davies Memorial Institute of International Studies

by

ST. MARTIN'S PRESS NEW YORK

AFFILIATED PUBLISHERS: Macmillan Limited, London;
also at Bombay, Calcutta, Madras and Melbourne

35954

Contents

Contents

Foreword

THIS book is the last of a series of three, each self-contained and standing on its own but all sponsored by the David Davies Memorial Institute of International Studies as related works on a single problem.

In 1966, the Institute published the Report of a Study Group on the Peaceful Settlement of International Disputes, Chairman Sir Humphrey Waldock. This has recently been enlarged and re-published under the title *International Disputes: The Legal Aspects* (Europa, London 1972). Subsequently the Institute invited us to act as co-chairmen of a further study group to advise Professor F. S. Northedge and Mr M. D. Donelan in writing *International Disputes: The Political Aspects* (Europa, London 1971).

In preparation for that book, the authors and their research assistants gathered facts on fifty disputes since the Second World War. It was suggested to the Institute that short historical accounts of these fifty disputes would make a further useful book. Mr M. D. Donelan and Miss M. J. Grieve were appointed to do the work. The Social Science Research Council made a grant of funds to supplement those of the Institute, for which we thank them. The present book is the outcome.

In making this suggestion to the Institute, we recognised the limitations which the book must have. The authors did not pretend to be experts on every one of fifty complicated disputes occurring in very diverse cultures at different junctures in world politics. Moreover, any short account is necessarily superficial and to that extent unsatisfactory to the specialist.

We believed, none the less, that the book should be useful to several kinds of people. It would be a work of reference on some of the most memorable disputes of the twenty-five years following the Second World War. It could help diplomatists, journalists and others who wish to reflect on how international disputes begin, develop and end, and who like to have matters presented to them in historical narrative form. It should provide a quarry of basic material for scholars undertaking research in this field. It might offer teachers and students one possible line of approach to the study of international politics in general.

Now that the book is finished, we recommend it to these kinds of reader and to all who are concerned in any way with the problem of international conflict. We hope that we are right in thinking that it will be of use to them in their work.

Caccia
Inchyra

Alphabetical List of Disputes

Preface

THE purposes of this book have been stated in the Foreword describing its origins. They are in brief to provide a moderately detailed reference work on some of the great episodes of world politics in the years 1945–70; and to offer a set of basic historical narratives to those interested in the study of international disputes whether as practitioners, theorists, teachers or students. Something further will be said of this purpose in the Introduction.

The limitations of the book were also noted in the Foreword but with a kindly brevity which the authors should amplify. Not only are they not experts in all the fifty disputes described; not only are short accounts necessarily superficial to anyone who remembers an affair or who knows it as a specialist; the very purposes of the book impose a style of writing which requires hard work on the part of the reader. The authors wished to present a full fifty disputes so that many different types should be represented; but within one book, this required compression. The narratives need to be fairly heavily loaded with names, titles, dates, lists of countries and similar details; but this does not improve readability. The aim has been to produce purely factual narratives as nearly neutral as possible; speculation on motives and interpretation of action and reaction have been kept to the minimum; but this does not make for a story which is instantly comprehensible.

The narratives also have what the authors would like to call the defect of a virtue. They are limited in depth and breadth. The approach throughout is to describe what was done by the antagonists in a dispute, individuals, civil factions, governments, states. Little attempt is made to delve into underlying movements in the societies in question. In this, the narratives reflect the approach adopted in the earlier study (mentioned in the Foreword) in which they originated. It was held there that the sociological method is a separate method of accounting for conflict and one, moreover, whose potential is not as yet fully developed. An approach which focuses on the statecraft of antagonists, on what they did and did not do and by implication on what they might and might not have done, has its own level of validity, and seems so far the most useful to those engaged in politics.

As important as the question of depth is the fact that these fifty narratives do not pretend to be a kind of history of world politics in the years 1945–70. On the contrary, they presuppose a fair knowledge of that history if they are to be fully understood. For in most of the disputes, the participants were influenced by ideas widely at work in the world, the ideas of nationalism,

ix

self-determination and anti-colonialism, changing attitudes to the use of force, general opinion on relevant international law, and so on. Again, in taking action in one dispute, participants seem usually to have paid much regard to any other disputes in which they were simultaneously engaged and to their other foreign policies. The course of many a dispute was also deeply affected by the attitudes of neighbouring states and the world powers, often springing from quite remote preoccupations of their own. In one way or another, the attention of the reader is drawn to these various wider influences on a dispute but necessarily without great elaboration and therefore with some appeal for assistance from his own knowledge.

Though there are thus drawbacks in isolating disputes from their context of national and international politics, there are also great benefits. This will be the theme of the Introduction. Meanwhile, mention of the wider context leads to the book lists appended to each narrative. The authors' aim has been to confine these to the specialised secondary works in English on which they have relied most heavily or which they believe will be most helpful to anyone seeking to go further into a particular dispute. (British editions are cited where the authors know of them.) Standard general works of reference useful for many disputes, for example, *Keesing's Contemporary Archives*, the Chatham House *Survey of International Affairs*, George Lenczkowski's *The Middle East in World Affairs*, are not cited each time. Foreign language works and memoirs have on the whole been excluded though with the hope that the works listed will carry the interested reader on to these. Footnotes in the text citing an author and page number refer to the book-lists. The temerity of the authors in making a selection from the great range of specialist literature did not extend to a general list of books on the wider setting of world politics and national foreign policies. They take refuge in the hope that the reader will have a favourite list of this sort on his own.

These remarks already indicate how deeply the authors are indebted to the books referred to above and in the pages which follow. They acknowledge this debt with gratitude. They thank the David Davies Memorial Institute of International Studies which sponsored their work, and for much encouragement and assistance, its director, Miss Mary Sibthorp. Members of the study group referred to by Lord Caccia and Lord Inchyra in their Foreword looked through many of the case histories, as did other specialists. If the authors thank them here generally and not by name, it is only because they do not wish to seem to attribute any responsibility to them. The authors are grateful to Miss Angela Hallett who typed their manuscript. Their debt to their research assistants, Mr Peter Fielder and Miss Hélène Warning, is signified on the title page. M. D. Donelan

M. J. Grieve

Introduction

HOW should we picture international society? Is it a world society of four thousand million people? Or an inter-state society of 140 separate states?

Those who see a world society stress aspects of human culture which have long transcended state frontiers regionally and which are now becoming world-wide: language, religion, secular beliefs, manners and life-styles, the sciences, technology and commerce. Above all, they say, there is nowadays one world economy. Rich countries and poor, over-populous countries and countries which plunder and pollute the environment – Sheffield, Santiago, Singapore, soon perhaps Sverdlovsk and Shanghai – are all caught up in a single system of material prosperity.

Yet those who believe in the novelty, importance and inevitable continuance of these developments are often the most vehement in stressing that one element is missing, politics. The political organisation of the world lags behind the changes in other aspects of its culture. Some believe that politics will necessarily follow, others that this is open for choice; but all believe that there is at present a discrepancy. The present reality is that politics is still conducted between nation-states. There is only the slowest movement towards amalgamation into regional states. There is not the slightest sign of a world politics that corresponds to a world society, a politics, that is, in which everyone everywhere in the world engages on his own account.

Admittedly, there are some qualifications to be made, now as in times past. There have been times in some regions of the world when politics burst through state frontiers. Such periods in modern Europe were those of the Thirty Years War and the French Revolution. Then politics were not just internal and inter-state but were one general *mêlée* of opinions in conflict. There was something approaching a European politics. Perhaps the present is also such a time on a world scale. As once in Europe religion and ideology were the great subjects of politics, so now everywhere, the economy. If the economy is not separate to each state but world-wide, if the accompanying social ills and conflicts are world-wide also, then each state is merely grappling in its politics with the local aspect of a common problem. There is, to this extent, a world politics.

It is only a very limited extent, however. Even if we concede that in some such general way the problem confronting politics is world-wide, the perspectives, the beliefs, the passions, the business of politics plainly are

1

not. All these centre on the state. There is no forum for world politics; only a hundred and forty states and the organisations in which they meet. Common observation is endorsed in this matter by theory. In the tradition of political theory, politics is the name we give to what goes on inside the state, that is, in a setting of community and authority. By courtesy (or lamentable confusion) dealings between states are called politics when they should properly only be called diplomacy. It may just be possible to theorise about these dealings, though in contrast with the internal affairs of states the element of the contingent and unpredictable is here so great as to make theory very difficult. But at all events there is nothing further. To speak of world politics, still more to attempt to theorise about it, is an absurdity. It will remain so until all human beings are members of one state, a world community with a world authority.

These are formidable points, perhaps even decisive. Yet, despite them, some people remain who desire to express their sense of the unity of mankind by talking of world politics. They are not content to wait patiently until mere events have created a world state; they may not indeed want to see any such consummation; in any case, they want to theorise about world politics now. For such people, the only solution is to look for world politics in a new direction. If politics is by definition confined within states, then of course there is no world politics. But suppose that politics should be defined more widely or, if you will, a wider word chosen.

Suppose, for example, that "politics" arises whenever there is any kind of association, a family, a tribe, a village, a club, a fire brigade, a business corporation, a state, an international organisation, a region or a world of states. Associations are very different, especially in the kind and degree of common purpose which they express, but all of them have one thing in common. They have an area of agreement and an area of difference, an area of rules and co-operation, and an area of freedom and conflict. Suppose that this basic characteristic of human life were a proper object of study, something first needing to be understood if one is serious in looking towards a world state, or something merely interesting to understand. It is a world-wide human characteristic, observable throughout world society, transcending state frontiers. If it is politics, it is world politics.

The implications of this for the shape of academic studies are worth indicating further. On this way of thinking, the study of politics or world politics, of the nature of human associations, their structure and conflict, is a whole; the family, the village, the industrial corporation, the church, the state, the world of states, considered under this aspect, are parts. At very least, the study of the state and the world of states belong together, separable by virtue of their different subject, but intimately linked. In recent years, students of the state (in university nomenclature students of "politics") have managed to proceed with little attention to the inter-state dimension. Whether or not this is satisfactory is for them to judge. Certainly the student of the world of states on his side finds the division uncomfortable and needs assistance from across it. If he is concerned with why states behave as they do, frontiers are an empirical fact but otherwise meaningless. If he is concerned with the theory of international society, the theory of the state is a necessary preliminary. A book such as the present one on international disputes necessarily contains some whose focus was within states as much as some whose focus lay between them. Empirically or theoretically, to drive a sharp division would be artificial.

Associations, whether a state or a world of states, are arrangements for the satisfaction of human concerns. It is these that require rules and co-operation, and from these that conflict springs. A little should next be said about what these concerns are.

The Western tradition has long been that, basic needs apart, the dominant concern for which men associate and conflict is "property", possessions. It is not acknowledged that they are equally concerned with activity as satisfying in itself and conflict about this also. A typical Western question about history is the purpose of Britain's rule of India and the answer is one word only: wealth. We are uneasy in looking beyond the abstraction "Britain" to the thousands of statesmen, soldiers, businessmen and workers to whom the India connection was a job, and with the cash, a satisfaction as a job. This same human concern must be remembered in any attempt to understand action on the world stage whether by Britain, China, the United States, the Soviet Union or any other state. Yet when we come to political analysis, we forget the meaninglessness of life without action, the fascination with action, beyond its alleged purposes, for its own sake. Western-received ideas no longer encompass delight in activity in their earnest, puritanical obsession with goals and results.

Because we are materialist, commercial, democratic, because we think the word "honour" aristocratic and old-fashioned, we are ashamed to acknowledge how deep is the concern for it in human affairs. No sooner do we hear of a quarrel over a patch of territory, no sooner do we learn that there is oil on it, than we instantly conspire together to pretend that we have the explanation of the quarrel, oil. But we know all the time that this is not the whole explanation, that things are quarrelled about as symbols as much as in themselves. In recent years, the word "status" has come into general use, at least in domestic politics, but it does not entirely cover the matter. For the desire for success which it mainly connotes, the desire to do or have a thing for superiority's sake, is closely connected with two other concerns which it does not so clearly signify: esteem, which requires the observance of an accepted code of conduct; dignity, which must be upheld against insult and oppression. These feelings enter as clearly into the conflicts of our own time as of any other, and with the close connection between them, are well expressed by the word "honour". Nor is this word markedly old-fashioned if we look beyond Anglo-Saxon culture. Even within that culture, even if a little shamefacedly, we still find that we must reach for the word when great national decisions are to be taken.

Next to possessions, "power" is the concept most widely favoured in the interpretation of human conflict. To picture public affairs and especially domestic or inter-state politics, as a struggle for power or mastery, summarises well enough the desire to be active, to possess, and to be seen as superior in the extent of action and possession. It is moreover a simultaneous reminder of another preoccupation, power as a means to these ends, and the deep concern of states as of anyone in an anarchic situation to maintain reputation for power.

On the other hand, to speak only of power blurs the crucial distinction in the conduct of human affairs between coercive and non-coercive means. It is better to contrast power with influence and bargaining. As a summary of ends or concerns, the concept is weak in that like "status" it covers only one of the aspects of honour. It does not fully explain why men and states act because they are expected to act; why, for example, they strive to avoid the shame of abandoning those who look to them for protection. It does not fully explain the great part played in human conflict by resentment of insult to personal or national dignity.

This point opens up a deeper weakness. The idea of a struggle for power takes no account of the existence of two very different situations in human affairs. In the one, men and states are competing for what they would like by way of activity, possessions, and the honour which arises from these. They work, they use influence, they bargain. If they fail, this is a setback. In the other situation, they are demanding what they consider is their due share of these things. They offer no return for it; it is their right. If they are denied, their feelings are of an altogether different and more bitter kind, the blow to their dignity felt most keenly of all. The interpretation of politics as a struggle for power dismisses this distinction, treating as superficial what is really profound, the sense that some things are due, the sense of legitimacy, the sense of justice and injustice.

With this we have returned in effect to the subject of associations. For, to put the point in other terms, we are merely insisting that human concerns are always social, related to others, pursued in associations. In associations, there is competition and co-operation, the acceptance of rules and ideas of what is just, and bitter dispute when it is held that something has been unjustly taken or denied.

Within states, the day-to-day business of politics is partly competition, partly co-operation. It is controlled by rules and results in a certain structure of society. There is dispute when the rules are breached or the structure challenged as unjust. Similarly, in the world of states, there is competition in activity, possessions, and honour. There is co-operation for the further-ance of these concerns in diplomacy towards common adversaries, in defence policies, economic policies and the like. All goes forward under treaties and organisational procedures and more fundamentally under ideas of what is justifiable in relations between states. Here too, when these limits are challenged, mere ordinary competition is transformed into dispute.

It would take too long here to try to elaborate this general picture of the nature of associations in terms of the many diverse kinds. Most difficult of all, the further dimension of unselfish feeling would need to be added: love, loyalty, public spirit, patriotism, humanity, the sense of a common good. Even as regards the two kinds of association which figure in this book, states and the world of states, we must focus on one aspect only, the distinction between competition and dispute.

This distinction is important not merely to the political theorist but to the statesman. This is plain enough in detailed situations; it is plainly one thing in diplomacy to be faced with competition or the offer of a bargain, and quite another to be faced with a unilateral action or a sheer demand; but the distinction also holds, if less precisely, over the whole history of relations between states. The fault, for example, in the policy of contain-ment of the Soviet Union and China pursued by the United States in the period covered by this book was that it countered two separate things with a single, inflexible vehemence: competitive expansion which is normal, tolerable and to be met with competition; and actions which go beyond these limits, which are intolerable and have to be disputed. This indis-criminate hostility to any advance in activity, possessions, and honour by the Soviet Union and China worked against the mellowing of these powers, buttressed their belief in the total enmity of the United States, and committed the United States to a scale of defensive action around the world which at length proved insupportable.

Admittedly, a statesman is always plagued by doubt and controversy in practice, since an expansion by a rival state which from one point of view is mere normal competition can assist it in a dispute or create an opening for a dispute. Herein lies the strength of the pessimists, the crisis-makers, the advocates of insurance against everything. Moreover, in the particular case of the United States, indiscriminate resistance could find an excuse in the propaganda of the communist powers. They, too, proclaimed the abolition of traditional inter-state relations and the onset of total hostility between capitalist and socialist states. Perhaps they truly believed this, perhaps to take detailed examples, they truly saw no difference of principle between the grant of Marshall Aid and the imposition of the Battle Act,[1] between American defensive agreements with South Korea and those with Taiwan. Certainly, as regards their own actions, they made little public acknowledgement of the idea of limits in Stalin's time. It was not until 1954 that his successors produced a crude version of the distinction between competition and dispute in their idea of competitive co-existence.

The example of American-Sino-Soviet relations to some extent forestalls a common objection to the distinction between competition and dispute in the analysis of world politics. Admittedly, it is said, the behaviour of civil factions and states manifests the distinction in that they usually say that they dislike an act or situation and only sometimes demand that it be redressed as unjust. This cannot be explained away as a mere matter of tactics. The difficulty remains, however, that there is no agreement on where the limits lie. At best, a merely formal list can be produced of what will be considered unjust in the contest for activity, possessions and honour. We can say that civil factions will be provoked by oppression, arbitrariness, disproportion in the scope allowed to various sections of the community, subjection of the state to foreigners. States will be provoked by unrequited alteration in the balance of activities, possessions and honour without merit or need. But who is to decide that a particular act or situation falls under these heads and is to be reckoned unjust? No conceivable refinement of the list could help us there. It is all a matter of opinion.

Certainly, it is all a matter of opinion, but it does not follow that the statesman need trouble himself no further. A dispute is a conflict of opinion on what is just. The most vital part of the statesman's job is to form reasoned opinions on what is just. We implicitly accept this when in current controversy we look back over the history of relations between China, the Soviet Union and the United States. We form opinions on which actions by the three powers were tolerable, which intolerable, which should have been taken, which not, which should have been resisted, which not. We do not confine ourselves to the other great aspect of political calculation, realistic assessment of the power to enforce or resist an action. If we think it worthwhile for us to make and argue such judgements in retrospect, how much more essential is it for the statesman in the act of making policy.

To say that disputes should be distinguished from competition is not to say that they can be understood without reference to it. Competition is the setting in which many a dispute arises. The same concerns are at stake, sometimes the very same objects; the difference lies in the conviction that

[1] This provided that aid to countries exporting "strategic" goods to the Communist bloc would cease.

tolerable limits have been breached and in the consequent eruption of the issue of justice. Inevitably, the statesman making policy appraises a proposed action or an action by the other side against the background of competition where this exists. The danger is that the competitive spirit easily makes him, and still more the public behind him, unwilling to try to do what is just. The action is adopted or denounced as unacceptable out of hand because the opponent is a competitor.

Still more serious is the problem of how far one dispute can or should be isolated from another. If disputes often arise out of excess of competition, they arise equally often out of the ill feeling created by past disputes. Possessions are seized when opportunity offers in revenge for old injuries; territory is seized, governments subjugated for security's sake in the light of bitter experience. All this is part of the background to the understanding of a dispute. In addition, the onset and development of one dispute is deeply affected by concurrent disputes between the parties and between influential outside powers. These too must be considered.

The danger here is that one dispute will not in fact cast light on the causes and manner of conducting another, but darkness. A first dispute creates ill feeling; when a second arises, little attention is paid to such merits as there may be in the opponent's case; by the time a third and a fourth arise, all are convinced that the opponent is a mere trouble-maker to be handled, not listened to. If the disputes are large, dangerous affairs, by the third or the fourth, the opponent is evil incarnate, each step is part of a single programme of limitless ambition, no concession can be made anywhere along the line.

In the 1930s the great powers were inclined to take Hitler's demands piecemeal; they realised too late that each demand was motivated by one malign ambition. In their post-war dealings with one another, they resolved not to repeat this mistake; from 1947 onwards, the many Western–Soviet disputes tended to become one single dispute. The particular, local and national aspect of any given affair was underestimated in a general, global, East–West perspective. Such was the fear created by this vast, terrifying vision that any suggestion of merit on the other side in any particular case, any discussion of concession was liable to be treated as absurd, even treacherous. It is conceivable, in short, that in the years 1930–70, the great powers went from one extreme to the other, their statesmen over-compensating at the end for the mistake of their predecessors at the beginning. Whether or not this is so, it is clear that such a danger exists all the time in statecraft. Disputes need to be connected and yet not amal-gamated. The effort must be made to consider each on its merits even if some-times those merits cannot be conceded in view of the motives of the oppo-nent or the power which would be given to him in relation to other disputes.

Sound though this may be, a statesman might still object to reading about disputes in separate case-histories as in this book. The sheer continuity of the narrative is unrealistic. The handling of a dispute in, say, Greece or Kashmir or Hungary or Cuba is in reality continually cut into by the press of other business. This is a difficulty encountered even by general histories of a nation's affairs, and, in ascending degree, by diplomatic histories and histories of international politics. Even these, however painstaking in connecting a wide variety of events, cannot fully recreate how discontinuity and the day-to-day accumulation of small fortuitous influences affected the course of policy on a particular matter. Still, it may be conceded that general histories, by proceeding on a broad front, capture more of what making policy actually felt like.

In defence of the separate case-history there are two things to be said. First, it is not too far from reality at the lower levels of responsibility. What we have just said is certainly relevant to foreign ministry officials but on the whole far more so to the politicians. Much more important, a case-history and all the further study of the case in amplification is not primarily concerned with experience but with reason. Its purpose is not to recreate life but to permit reflection on principles. It is not intended as history for its own sake but as material for political theory.

For the statesman, the value of studying narratives of civil or inter-state disputes lies in the strengthening of his sense of how a given action tends to be met by a certain kind of reaction. In any particular case, this reaction may have come about through extraneous circumstances, perhaps not even mentioned in the narrative; equally, it may have failed to come about through such influences. The impact of the fortuitous, the contingent, the personal, the trivial, the organisational in any particular case is undoubtedly great and may be decisive. But what is none the less needed in statecraft is a sense of how politics tend to work on the whole, luck and chance apart. What is needed for the handling of disputes, amidst the distracting muddle and confusion of other business and the din which any dispute generates, is a grasp of how such affairs tend in general to unfold, a sense of the likely and the possible. Such understanding is mostly derived from practice but something may be added by reflection, not just on history, but on case by case history. What is lost in richness of detail is gained in the clarity of essentials.

The understanding of disputes of some statesmen will not be further improved by the case-history method, and it is worth considering whether something more detailed might be possible in the future. This might take the form of case studies of problems which arise time and again in diplomacy. Many statesmen have faced case after case of much the same problem in the course of their careers; but they do not write their memoirs in this form. Many a diplomatist spends months in a protracted negotiation in which familiar problems have to be surmounted; but what he learns is not systematically recorded and accumulated. Perhaps a way should be found of doing this, or perhaps from general case histories, instances of particular problems should be culled and studied and put together and written up as briefs of a new kind. These could never achieve the form of a set of standard techniques for automatic application. They might never rise above an account of what was done in a number of cases. They might none the less be suggestive to a statesman approaching a new negotiation.

Whether considering the course of disputes or the problems of diplomacy which arise, the aim of the statesman is to strengthen his sense of how politics work. The aim of the academic theorist, in contrast, is to formulate propositions. At the lowest, his concern is to produce an artificial but none the less helpful order in the bewildering complexity of events by classifying. In the case of disputes, all sorts and sizes of human conflicts are loosely given that same name in everyday speech. As the basis for this book, we have made use of the broad distinction between the pursuit of things wanted, which we call competition, and the demand for things considered due in justice, which we call dispute and which alone is included. Within that boundary, the fifty cases given are still very diverse but we have not attempted to impose our classificatory ideas upon the reader. The disputes are merely set out in a rough chronological order, the dates indicating in a workaday fashion when the affair "started" and when it or a fairly clear phase "ended" or the terminal date of 1970 supervened.

Any attempt at more elaborate classification soon runs up against the point that a dispute is a complex of aspects and that classification is therefore by the aspect selected as particularly significant or interesting. No doubt we can often say roughly that a dispute as a whole was about a transfer or that it was about a distribution, that it was an internal dispute or that it was inter-state, but after that we must break it down into aspects. To take inter-state disputes, we can classify, for example, according to what we take to be the main thing at stake, a piece of territory, an installation, control of the government of a state or the like, or, on deeper analysis, the promotion or security of activities or possession or honour. Alternatively, we can focus on the protagonists, the kind of state involved or whether the dispute is bilateral or multilateral; or we can look at the dispute as a set of component disputes between protagonists, between protagonists and interveners, between interveners.

This reference to interveners raises the further point that a dispute is not merely a complex of aspects but a dynamic affair, divisible into phases of origin, development, and solution, during which any of its aspects may change profoundly. With this in mind, we can see that some of our fifty disputes might best be called episodes or incidents or crises or phases in other disputes, for example, Quemoy and Matsu, Berlin, the U-2 affair, Vietnam. Some of our fifty might be considered "situations of friction" rather than disputes, for example, the Chinese in Indonesia or the affair in Hong Kong in 1967. But, as we say, we have not sought to impose an answer to such questions by our selection of disputes or their arrangement. We have sought simply to provide a quantity of raw material for the theorist to classify and to use as he wishes.

Beyond classification, lies explicit exposition of this or that aspect or phase of disputes. Here the theorist offers generalisations about how states behave derived from a scrutiny of a number of cases, and increasingly nowadays, ideas on the handling of disputes. All such propositions are the theorist's equivalent of the statesman's unarticulated sense of how politics works, neither better nor worse. Since they are general and abstract whereas the practice of politics is always particular and concrete, they easily strike the statesman as vague and jejune. They can never be completely valid propositions. Each is partial only and needs to be weighed against others in a particular situation. None the less they are helpful as providing a systematic reminder of a range of considerations and possibilities which the statesman might otherwise overlook. Taken together as a body of thought about politics, they are also the basis on which the theorist, the citizen, the journalist, the observer of any sort debates with the responsible practitioner. Though only he knows the full facts of any given situation, though the ideas and criticisms of the observer are irritatingly general, such debate is vital.

At the highest, the concern of the theorist is with reason in politics. He is concerned with what an association is, what its purposes are in relation to its members, its structure, the conditions of its continuance, its obligations to outsiders. From a consideration of smaller associations, the theorist comes to the state and to international society, trying even here in the deepest obscurity to say something about what reason is in relations between states or in any form of organisation of humanity. It is no reproach to such theory that it can never be conclusive but is an endless discussion. Nor is it a reproach that it is always ideal and subject in practice to a multitude of exigencies and confusions. Without constant confrontation with the ideal, practice becomes shallow pragmatism. In disputes between states, statesmen and citizens are tempted to dismiss the behaviour of the other side as entirely attributable to its personalities or particular internal condition. Without the reminder that disputes are also public acts of world society they will not look for the element of reason and acknowledge the conflict of justice.

Though reason is not the same as history, though the ideal is different from the practical, still the rift between them is not total. Human behaviour is flawed and twisted, not finally corrupt and chaotic. Reasoning about politics can therefore proceed by continual reference to the actual and observable, and indeed must do so if it is not to drift into cranky realism or idealism. The material to be used for this purpose can take many forms and among them, case histories of disputes have a traditional place.

Thinking about international relations has always taken the harsh fact of conflict between states as its starting point, reasoning about the methods which they use in pursuing their demands on each other. Moral ideas about the treatment of "barbarians" gave place to religious doctrines and ecclesiastical and secular codes on the use of force; and these in turn to the phase of legalism and nowadays to a new casuistry of the management of power. Case histories of disputes also reveal for scrutiny what the demands of states are, and so provide a basis for reasoning about what justice between states is and about the whole nature of the association of states which at present constitutes international society. Many theories of the past and present generations about this society and the solution of its disputes do not survive a reading of such narratives. They thus do something to prepare the ground for more secure theory in the future.

The final aim of the case histories in this book is to serve as material for university teaching of International Politics. It may be helpful to give in conclusion an indication of one way of using them to this end in brief practical terms.

The way envisaged and used for some time by the authors is that of a continual confrontation of theory with history. A group of students comes to the university with certain notions about international politics and foreign policy. In each week of the course they are given a case history or some phase of it for study. All are asked to master the basic narrative. One (or more) is asked to make use of the bibliography to go deeper into some aspect. Group discussion takes the form in the first weeks of an invitation to the students to try their hand at explaining why the antagonists acted as they did and why the interaction unfolded as it did. The response at first is necessarily only more elaborate history but in time general ideas begin to form about the concerns of states, the constraints on aims and methods, the difference between competition and dispute, the multiplicity of pressures which in either case go to the making of policy and of the interaction. The more elaborate explanatory theories of various writers can then be brought forward and the degree to which they are helpful or redundant to explanation assessed.

Later discussion consists of an inquiry into the justice of what is done in disputes. The students are asked to consider what necessity is in statecraft and what it means to say that a statesman could not avoid acting as he did at a given juncture in a dispute. They discuss, to the degree that an action seems to have been freely chosen, how far it could benefit the state or its members and how far it was consistent in aim and method with obligations to other states and their members. This entails discussion of the reasons with which states justify the demands they make in disputes. It raises in the end the purposes of the state, its obligations, the nature of its association with other states, the consequences of the imperfection of that association, and the relationship between justice and prudence.

Throughout such a course the part of the teacher is to lead by continual questioning and suggestion on the basis of his own knowledge and ideas of theory. This is no doubt obvious. What is not obvious, even controversial, is the idea that he should be ready to lead the discussion ultimately into the area of reason and justice in international politics. Few of us are well equipped to do this. Fear of the relapse of the study of international politics into vague personal moralising is strong. The temptation to remain at the level of the observable behaviour of states is overwhelming.

None the less, it is in the area of reason and justice that the great questions of international politics lie. Thought or the lack of it in this area are in the end decisive for the handling of world affairs. To teach only the behaviour of states runs the risk of leaving the student with nothing but a crude and dissatisfying realism. How his country should act, how he as a citizen should try to influence it to act is what the student wants and needs to decide. The questions must be raised in his time at the university, the thought and discussion must be promoted which will help him in this responsibility.

Assistance to clear and objective reasoning in this area is to be found in both historical and theoretical literature. Some of it is directly concerned with the world of states. The student needs concurrent study of general international history and foreign policy if he is to understand separate case histories of disputes. He needs to know and to draw on the tradition of thought on international society and on statecraft, the idea of a community of states, realism and *raison d'État*, idealism and legalism, doctrines of intervention and the morality of power and force. But behind this lies the wider literature of politics. International Politics though separate by virtue of its subject cannot proceed in isolation. Study of the nature of associations, of co-operation and conflict, in any manifestation right down to the least is helpful to the study of the greatest, the world of states. Reasoning about international society and its present organisation in states needs the tradition of theory about the state, what it is, what it does for its members, and what it alone cannot do.

Poland 1941-47

IN the late eighteenth century, the kingdom of Poland was extinguished in three successive partitions by Austria, Prussia and Russia. Revived in a truncated form by Napoleon, it was again dismembered by these Powers. The modern Polish state came into being in 1918. It was ruled for most of the interwar period as a dictatorship, first by Marshal Josef Pilsudski and later by army officers of similar views.

For the Polish–Soviet border, the Allied Supreme Council proposed in 1919 the Curzon Line, roughly the ethnic frontier, but after warfare between the two countries, the Poles secured a line a hundred and fifty miles to the east in the Treaty of Riga, 18 March 1921. The Soviet–German Treaty of 23 August 1939 promised the Soviet Union the Curzon Line in the south and more in the north. On 1 September, the Germans invaded Poland, followed by the Russians on the 17th, and, for the fifth time Poland was partitioned.

On 22 June 1941, Germany invaded the Soviet Union. The Soviet Union annulled the Soviet–German Treaty (30 July) and recognised the Polish government-in-exile in London headed by General Wladyslaw Sikorski as prime minister. Friction immediately developed, however, the Russians insisting that the Curzon Line should be the frontier, the Poles adamant for the interwar boundary.

On 13 April 1943, the Germans stated that they had discovered mass graves at Katyn near Smolensk where "the Bolsheviks had murdered 10,000 Polish officers" at the time of their occupation of eastern Poland. The Soviet Union subsequently countercharged the Germans with this crime. Sikorski's response was to propose that the International Red Cross should investigate (16th). The Soviet Union retaliated by breaking off relations with the Polish government-in-exile (25th).

Sikorski was killed in an air crash at Gibraltar on 4 July 1943 and was succeeded by Stanislaw Mikolajczyk. When Stalin raised the Polish frontier question at the Teheran Conference (28 November–1 December) Roosevelt made no definite commitment but Churchill agreed to roughly the Curzon Line, with compensation for Poland at Germany's expense in the west. In the following months, he pressed the Polish government-in-exile to accept this formula but they would not. United States policy remained unsettled and ambivalent.

Meanwhile, in Poland, two resistance movements against the Germans had developed. The government-in-exile was in contact with a Home

13

Council and a Home Army there; the Soviet Union with the Polish Workers' Party (Communist, established in January 1942) and its fighting organisation, the People's Guard.

On 21 July 1944, the Red Army offensive against the Germans reached the Curzon Line, and on the following day a Committee of National Liberation was inaugurated, consisting of members of the Workers' Party and other "left-wingers", and claiming to be the sole legal executive power in the country. When the Germans had been further driven back, it established itself at Lublin, south-east of Warsaw.

On 1 August, the rival organisation, the Home Army, rose against the Germans in Warsaw, hoping to liberate it before the Red Army arrived. The Red Army halted its advance temporarily, whether by necessity or design, the Germans reacted powerfully, and in bitter fighting which lasted until 2 October destroyed the Poles. Afterwards, the Red Army resumed its advance and took the city.

Two days after the beginning of the rising, on 3 August, Mikolajczyk achieved an interview with Stalin in Moscow but received little satisfaction. It seemed only that the Soviet Union might make minor concessions on the Curzon Line if the government-in-exile would take the Committee of National Liberation into a strong position in a coalition. Churchill, during his own visit to Moscow that October, redoubled his pressure on Mikolajczyk to settle with the Soviet Union and negotiate with the Lublin Committee. Mikolajczyk now accepted the need for some concession but his colleagues in London and Poles with the Allied forces were unyielding. He made a last appeal to Roosevelt, then engaged in the presidential election in which the Polish vote had some significance. Roosevelt merely replied (17 November, after his re-election) that if the Polish, Soviet and British governments could reach an agreement on the eastern frontier, the United States would offer no objection. Beyond this, the United States urged the Soviet Union not to take unilateral action regarding the Lublin Committee. On 24 November, Mikolajczyk resigned and was succeeded by Tomasz Arciszewski.

In December, the Lublin Committee proclaimed itself the Provisional National Government and came to Warsaw where it was recognised by the Soviet Union on 5 January 1945. The Soviet Union, by this time fighting in Germany, subsequently justified this action to its allies on the grounds that it needed a secure government behind its lines in Poland.

The Polish question was the most lengthy issue at the Yalta Conference of 7–12 February 1945. Roosevelt now endorsed the agreement reached by Stalin and Churchill at Teheran that Poland's eastern frontier should be roughly the Curzon Line with compensation to Poland in the west at Germany's expense. The precise western frontier would be determined at the eventual peace conference. The governmental question was more difficult. In the end, the three said in the conference communiqué of 11 February that "a new Polish Provisional Government" should be set up. "The Provisional Government which is now functioning in Poland should therefore be reorganised on a broader democratic basis with the inclusion of democratic leaders from Poland itself and from Poles abroad." This government would hold free elections in the country as soon as possible.

From 24 February to 2 April, a three-man commission of the three allies sought to implement this agreement, but fruitlessly. The United States and Britain wanted a "new" government, the Soviet Union a "reorganised" Lublin government. Moreover, the representatives of the Lublin government would only share power with Poles who accepted the Curzon Line, thus excluding most of the London Poles. This stalemate and other episodes, such as the arrest on 28 March on charges of spying of fifteen representatives of the Home Council who had come to Warsaw on safe conduct, led Roosevelt in his last days to adopt a stronger tone with Stalin.

On 12 April, Roosevelt died. On 22–23 April, President Truman talked in Washington with the Soviet Foreign Minister, Molotov, then on his way to the San Francisco Conference on the United Nations. Truman spoke sharply. The Soviet Union should "carry out its agreements". After further talks in Moscow in May between Stalin and Harry Hopkins, Truman's special representative, the three-power commission set to work again. Eventually, from 17–28 June, a group of Poles from Lublin, elsewhere in Poland and London, mostly in fact Lubliners or sympathisers, held a conference in Moscow. A Provisional Government was announced headed by Edward Osobka-Morawski, the Lublin premier, with Mikolajczyk and Wladyslaw Gomulka as deputy premiers, and containing in all five non-communist members and sixteen Lubliners (28th). The United States and Britain, against the protests of the government-in-exile, recognised this government (5 July).

Meanwhile, the Soviet Union had allowed the Polish Government to take administrative control of Danzig, and in the west, as far as the Oder-Western Neisse rivers, including Stettin. At the Potsdam Conference, 17 July–2 August, Polish representatives, sponsored by Stalin, gave the arguments in favour of so drastic an extension of Poland westwards: the German inhabitants had fled and Poles had taken possession; four million Poles, displaced in the east, and three million who, they said, could be expected to return from abroad, needed territory. Churchill countered with arguments about the displaced Germans and about the effect on Germany of losing this agricultural territory; Truman, with arguments about the effect on Germany's ability to pay reparations; but to little effect. In the communiqué of 2 August, with renewed Soviet reassurances on free elections in Poland, the three powers accepted that the territory up to the Oder-Western Neisse should be under Polish administration, though the final delimitation of this frontier was to await the peace settlement.

In the event, amid the East–West conflicts of subsequent years, no further advance was made regarding the western frontier. The eastern frontier, a line roughly the same as the Curzon Line, was settled in the Soviet–Polish treaty of 16 August 1945. Inside Poland, the Workers' Party organised the lesser parties into a Democratic Bloc in the course of 1946 to contest the elections eventually held on 19 January 1947 against Mikolajczyk's Polish Peasant Party. According to the official returns, the Democratic Bloc won overwhelmingly. The United States and Britain protested that these elections could not be taken as a free expression of the popular will. In October, Mikolajczyk fled from the country, with American assistance, to London.

*　　　*　　　*

V. Benes and N. Pounds: *Poland*, Ernest Benn, London 1970.

D. Clemens: *Yalta*, Oxford University Press, 1970.

H. Feis: *Churchill, Roosevelt, Stalin*, Princeton University Press 1957.

E. Rozek: *Allied Wartime Diplomacy, A Pattern in Poland*, Wiley, New York 1958.

Greece 1944-49

FROM 1924 to 1935, Greece was a republic. From 1936, it was ruled under a restored monarchy, by a dictator, General Ioannis Metaxas. In October 1940 Italy invaded Greece but the Greeks were victorious and so avoided the need to take up the British offer of ground troops which, the Greeks feared, might bring Germany down upon them. Metaxas died in January 1941 and in April Germany attacked Greece anyway. A British force was sent to its aid but the Germans rapidly overran the country and the force had to be evacuated. King George II and the Greek Government went into exile.

Metaxas had suppressed the Greek Communist Party but some of them had escaped the dragnet and at the beginning of 1942 they organised a National Liberation Committee, EAM, including several other left-wing groups. EAM built up a guerrilla army, ELAS, and this achieved considerable success. By the middle of 1943 it controlled about a third of the Greek mainland.

This left-wing success was not entirely palatable to the British Government. It decided not to back EAM–ELAS but instead to support General Napoleon Zervas and his rival guerrilla army, the National Republican Greek League, EDES. In addition to fighting the Germans, EAM–ELAS and EDES fought each other and eventually the latter were pushed back into the Epirus region and dwindled to about 6,000 men.

The Allied Military Mission negotiated an armistice between the two forces in Plaka on 29 February 1944. During the summer, it became evident that the Germans were preparing to evacuate Greece. EAM agreed (2 September) to take six ministries in a Government of National Unity under Giorgios Papandhreou, a Democratic Socialist. Later the same month, it was agreed that the two armies, ELAS and EDES, should come under the orders of a British commander of a liberation force, General Ronald Scobie.

On 18 October, the British force of some 5,000 men escorted Papandhreou's National Unity Government to Athens. Neither in government nor country was there in fact unity. In the confusion, many murders and atrocities took place as personal scores were settled. Politically, there was intense suspicion and rivalry. The Left called for the punishment of wartime collaborators; the Right feared that this would be used to decimate them. The Left feared that the British were planning to reimpose the monarchy. Many more in Greece opposed George II personally in view of his association with Metaxas.

17

The tension came to a head over the future of ELAS. In the Greek context, it was now a powerful and victorious army, strengthened by abandoned German equipment. Papandhreou proposed that ELAS together with EDES should be dissolved and that a new national army should be formed around one brigade from each of them and one formed from Greek units overseas. The EAM ministers agreed to this with the rest of the Greek cabinet on 27 November but the agreement immediately broke down. On the 30th, ELAS groups were ordered to converge on Athens. During the night of 1–2 December, the six EAM ministers resigned from the Papandhreou government and EAM issued a call for a general strike and a mass demonstration in Athens on the 3rd.

The demonstration led to violence and the situation degenerated into armed revolt against the Government. General Scobie informed the EAM leaders that the ELAS units must withdraw from Athens not later than midnight on the 6th. Papandhreou offered to resign but the British dissuaded him. EAM announced that it would set up an alternative National Unity Government and the ELAS military commanders refused to withdraw.

By 4 December armed clashes were taking place between British and ELAS patrols in Athens and early on 5 December Churchill ordered Scobie to use all measures including force to stop the revolt. ELAS tried to take over key government buildings on the night of 5–6 December. Scobie's troops prevented this but their position was precarious and reinforcements were sent in from Italy and Egypt.

Churchill was deeply concerned about the Greek situation not merely because he was determined to prevent a communist *coup d'état* but also because United States public opinion was hostile to British policy. The view commonly taken was that the British were suppressing the Greek people in favour of a reactionary monarchy. On 25 December, Churchill arrived in Athens for a conference on Greece's future. At the conference on 26–28 December, the ELAM–ELAS representatives would not accept terms agreeable to the British and the other Greeks, and attempts to achieve a cease-fire were in vain. The others agreed that Archbishop Damaskinos of Athens should be made Regent with a mandate to appoint a caretaker government excluding Communists. The Archbishop had a notable record for anti-Nazi resistance and was popular in Greece. The Government was to hold office until tension subsided and a plebiscite could be held on the monarchy. It took office on 1 January 1945, with General Nicholas Plastiras as Prime Minister.

These arrangements undercut the appeal of EAM–ELAS which was further reduced by reports of daily executions of right-wing hostages. The British forces, which were built up to some 75,000, pressed ELAS hard.

EAM was weakened by the secession of its leading socialist members. The result was an armistice under which hostilities were to cease from midnight on 15 January. Military engagements gradually petered out. ELAS evacuated Athens, Salonica and central Greece. On 12 February, the two sides signed the Varkiza Agreement. The Government pledged itself to an amnesty for political acts; guaranteed civil rights; and promised a plebiscite on the monarchy and the holding of elections for an assembly to draft a new constitution. The ELAS units were to hand in their arms and disband.

In the event, some old weapons were handed in but new material, especially that abandoned by the Germans, was retained. Some ELAS units regrouped in camps in northern Greece, Albania, Bulgaria and Yugoslavia. In June, Nikos Zakhariadis returned from Dachau concentration camp to be secretary-general of the party, determined, it seems, on a new offensive. Surrounding countries were being taken over by the Communists. The condition of Greece continued favourable to the Communist cause. In addition to the constitutional question, there was discontent with the Government's handling of the economic situation. Because of the destruction of the war and the civil war, much United Nations Relief and Rehabilitation Agency relief was needed to prevent starvation.

In December 1945, the Greek Communists held a meeting at Petich in Bulgaria with members of the Bulgarian and Yugoslav general staffs. The hostility of Bulgaria and Albania towards the Greek Government was increased in the following year by the territorial claims which it loudly urged against them. At Petich, agreement was reached on co-operation to put a new Greek Communist army into the field, eventually known as the Democratic Army of Greece, popularly, the "Andartes".

The Soviet Union apparently approved the planned new offensive but gave little practical support. In the preceding years, it seems to have given little assistance to EAM–ELAS in the struggle with the Germans; it was not until mid-1944 that Soviet liaison officers were parachuted to their headquarters. The willingness of EAM to join the Papandhreou government in September 1944 rather than try to seize power at that time may perhaps have been at Moscow's orders. At the Moscow Conference of October 1944 when Stalin and Churchill divided up responsibility for the liberation of the Balkans, Greece was allotted to Britain. Thereafter, Stalin remained passive on Greek affairs. The Soviet Union complained at the first meeting of the United Nations Security Council in January 1946 of the continued presence of British troops in Greece, but this seems to have been in retaliation for the raising of the Iran question.[1] Stalin now in 1946

[1] See p. 88.

apparently urged Albania, Bulgaria and Yugoslavia to aid the Andartes and promised Soviet supplies, but these, it seems, never appeared.

In March 1946, governmental elections were held in Greece. EAM appealed for a boycott but about 60 per cent of the electorate voted and a Populist government took office under Constantine Zaldaris. The first armed clashes between Government and Communist troops began. In September, the plebiscite on the monarchy was held; 89 per cent voted in favour of restoration, and King George II returned. That month, the second round of the civil war began in full force.

General Markos Vafiades took command of the Andartes in October and by the following spring had an army of some 13,000, later rising to some 23,000. His guerrilla tactics scored great successes and the Greek Government's area of control shrank daily until in the course of 1947, it controlled little more than the area around Athens and Salonica. The already weak Greek economy well-nigh collapsed under the strain. Refugees streamed into government-held areas. International distress aid had to be increased.

Britain was in a poor position to shoulder the military and economic burden, whereas the development of East–West relations had changed United States attitudes to the affairs of Greece. The problem was therefore largely handed over by Britain to the United States, although Britain kept troops in Greece until 1950. The Greek Government requested United States aid on 3 March 1947, and a few days later, on 12 March, President Truman enunciated the "Truman doctrine". "It must be the policy of the United States to support free peoples who are resisting attempted subjugation by armed minorities or by outside pressures." The United States now gave massive economic and military aid to Greece.

The United Nations debated the Greek crisis on several occasions. In August 1946, the Ukraine complained about the aggressive nature of the Greek Government as indicated by frontier incidents but no action followed. The Greek Government argued on 3 December 1946 that the Bulgarian and Yugoslav aid for the Greek Communists constituted a threat to the peace. The Security Council responded by setting up a Committee of Investigation on 19 December, but in the confused circumstances of the time, this committee made little headway.

In view of the Soviet veto, the Greek question was taken from the agenda of the Security Council on 15 September 1947 and transferred to the General Assembly. On 21 October, the Assembly established the UN Special Committee on the Balkans (UNSCOB) with a brief to attempt conciliation between the parties and observe border incidents. UNSCOB set up its headquarters at Salonica and its interim reports confirmed the passage of supplies to the Greek Communist forces from Yugoslavia and Bulgaria.

As the conflict between the Andartes and the Greek National Army continued, the Communists took a series of fateful decisions. Zakhariadis and Vafiades had always differed in their style of Communism, the former Moscow-trained, the latter national. Zakhariadis moreover pressed continually for regular warfare whereas Vafiades insisted on continuing the guerrilla technique. Vafiades was dismissed and later murdered on orders, it seems, from Moscow. Regular tactics were adopted and defeats followed at the hands of the now well armed and trained Greek National Army.

Equally serious, despite the fact that the Soviet Union had given little practical assistance, and despite the fact that it had struck a serious blow at morale by failing to recognise the Communist rebel government set up on 24 December 1947, Zakhariadis led the Greek Communists in taking the Soviet and not the Yugoslav side when Tito of Yugoslavia broke with Cominform on 18 June 1948. This meant that the most important supply-lines of the Andartes were cut. Zakhariadis further antagonised Tito and also many members of the Greek Communist Party when he broadcast on 1 March 1949 in favour of an independent Macedonia.

Public opinion both in Greece and abroad was alienated by large-scale kidnapping of Greek children who were carried off to Communist states. Signs of disaffection began to multiply among the Andartes, evidenced by the need for pressed recruitment. The Greek National Army had become skilled at breaking up the communications system on which the Communist forces depended. Vigorous pressure was maintained against the Andartes and by April 1949 the Peloponnese was securely under the control of the Athens government. Military action continued in the Grammos range of mountains in north west Greece but by August 1949 it was clear that the Communists were defeated.

On 15 August 1949, the rebel government sent a message to the UN Secretary-General indicating that they were willing to make a settlement. On 26 August, Albania announced that in future armed Greeks found in the country would be disarmed and interned and shortly afterwards it cut off supplies to the Greek Communists. Zakhariadis and the Greek Communist Party apparently intended to carry on the struggle from their bases in Bulgaria but received orders from the Soviet Union to announce a cease-fire. On 16 October, Radio Free Greece announced that the Andartes would stop fighting in the interests of Greece. The rebels finally admitted defeat on 4 November and dispersed across the borders to Bulgaria and Rumania.

*   *   *

J. K. Campbell and P. Sherrard: *Modern Greece*, Benn, London 1968.

E. C. W. MYERS: *Greek Entanglement*, Rupert Hart-Davis, London 1955.

E. O'BALLANCE: *The Greek Civil War 1944–49*, Faber, London 1966.

C. M. WOODHOUSE: *The Story of Modern Greece*, Faber, London 1968.

S. XYDIS: *Greece and the Great Powers 1944–47*, Institute for Balkan Studies, Salonika 1963.

Trieste 1945-54

WHEN the Austro-Hungarian empire was dismembered in 1919–20, Trieste and its hinterland, Venezia Giulia or Julyska Krajina, were given to Italy. On the collapse of Germany in the spring of 1945, the Italians of the city rose to free themselves (29 April); the Yugoslav partisan forces having overrun Venezia Giulia, arrived on 1 May and the New Zealanders on 2 May. Then followed tense discussions, the Yugoslavs claiming the city, the Western Allies insisting that nothing should be done in advance of the peace settlement. They would if necessary expel the Yugoslavs by force. In the end, the Yugoslavs agreed to withdraw from the city, influenced apparently by warnings from the Soviet Union that it would not support them in a fight.[1] By the Belgrade Agreement of 9 June, they were to administer the area to the east of a line proposed by General William Morgan, Chief of Staff to Field Marshal Alexander (the Morgan Line), and the Supreme Allied Commander, the area to the west, including Trieste itself, pending the peace settlement.

In claiming Trieste and Venezia Giulia, all Yugoslavs, including the royal government-in-exile, felt that they were reclaiming something of theirs by right. The population of Venezia Giulia was largely Slav. As to the city, predominantly Italian, they argued that this was a just reward for their war effort, that Italian promises to respect minority groups were untrustworthy, and that the city was economically inseparable from the hinterland. They feared that the Italians would use control of the city to exert economic pressure on the hinterland as they had done in the interwar years, and more generally, as a springboard for renewed eastward expansion. The deep-water port at Trieste was a particular concern; the Italians, they feared, would contrive to deny its benefits to them.

Italian arguments were the mirror image of these. They felt that in view of their declaration of war on Germany in 1943, they should pay no territorial penalty. They feared Yugoslav control of the area as a first step in Communist expansion. They not only feared that they would lose the benefits of the port but stressed the importance to their economy of access to the mineral resources of the area.

Both countries no doubt saw the strategic importance of the territory, controlling the lower passes between central Europe and the Mediterranean, and felt the prestige significance of the dispute. In both of them, public opinion was deeply stirred. "From the point of view of emotional

[1] Novak, p. 198.

involvement and public concern, the Trieste issue has been the single most important foreign policy problem in the history of the Italian Republic. Surveys indicate that it is the only foreign policy issue that has ever penetrated the villages and countryside."[2] These feelings focused on Trieste itself but appear also to have extended more diffusely to the whole Istrian peninsula, especially the coastal towns, predominantly Italian. Awareness of public feeling was a major determinant of Italian Government policy through the dispute. As to the Yugoslavs, Tito's strength in 1945 lay in a tacit alliance between the Communists and the peasants. The latter were determined not to lose access "to the big city's resources"[3] and, in the early years of the dispute, were a powerful force against dropping the claim to it.

The responsibility for deciding the conflicting claims lay with the Allied powers. The Council of Foreign Ministers took up the problem at its September 1945 meeting and ordered the setting up of a four-power expert commission to recommend a boundary between Italy and Yugoslavia which would leave a minimum of people under alien rule. Their report in April 1946 contained four different proposals. The Soviet line gave Yugoslavia almost all the territory including the city; the French line, conforming most closely to the ethnic situation, gave Italy the city and a strip of hinterland extending half-way down the Istrian peninsula; the British line extended the strip to the end of the peninsula; and the American line widened it.[4]

After heated discussions, the Council of Foreign Ministers announced on 3 July that the French line was to be the Italo-Yugoslav frontier but that the southern part of the area which this gave to Italy (that is, the city and the immediately surrounding country) was to be placed under a special regime as the Free Territory of Trieste.[5] These decisions were incorporated in the Italian Peace Treaty of 10 February 1947, Annex VI containing the Permanent Statute for the FTT. This charged the United Nations with responsibility for ensuring the observance of the Statute. The territory was to be demilitarised and neutral, and a constitution was envisaged with a governor appointed by the Security Council.

Until the Statute was implemented, the FTT was to be administered by the "Allied Military Commands within their respective zones", namely Zone A, the northern half including the city itself, by the Allied Military Government (AMG), composed of United States and British units, and Zone B by the Yugoslavs. The Security Council failed to agree on a

[2] N. Kogan, *The Politics of Italian Foreign Policy*, Pall Mall Press, London 1963, p. 117.
[3] Anon., p. 161.
[4] Maps: Novak, p. 243; Duroselle, end papers.
[5] Maps: Novak, p. 261; Eden, p. 176.

governor, the Russians and the Western powers each vetoing the other's nominees. Consequently the temporary arrangement remained in force.

The Peace Treaty's solution was immediately denounced by both sides, their attention focusing on the FTT, each determined to have the whole of it. In the FTT itself, the AMG in the northern zone regarded its task as care and maintenance but in the southern zone the Yugoslavs introduced administrative, legal, economic and fiscal reforms, bringing it into line with Yugoslavia.

On 20 March 1948, the three Western powers issued a Tripartite Proposal according to which the Peace Treaty should be modified; the FTT should be given to Italy. Their prime motive was to influence the Italian elections of 18 April against the Communists, who felt obliged to follow the Soviet line in the dispute. The initiative was successful in this respect. For the longer term, it strengthened Italy's determination to have the whole of the FTT. Meanwhile, the AMG began to allow the reintegration of the northern zone into the Italian economy.

On 28 June 1948, Yugoslavia, quarrelling over other matters with the Soviet Union, was expelled from the Cominform. The effect of this on the Trieste dispute was twofold. The Soviet Union stopped helping Yugoslavia, became equally hostile to both sides, and, as they saw it, merely obstructive. In Security Council debates it continually insisted that the next step was to appoint a governor for the FTT even though both sides had denounced the whole FTT idea. Conversely, the Western powers gradually began to see Yugoslavia differently and to be less warm in their support for Italy. The Italians tried to persuade the United States to put pressure on Yugoslavia, considering this their due as a member of the West and, after 1949, of NATO; but the United States was unwilling.

In April 1951, prompted by rumours of an impending Soviet attack on Yugoslavia, the United States offered it military aid (agreement signed, November). Simultaneously, the Western powers began to present their declaration of March 1948 in a rather new light. They pointed out that it had been a proposal to the Soviet Union and argued that, since it had proved unacceptable, it no longer had much practical value. The Italians should negotiate with the Yugoslavs.

Italian–Yugoslav contacts began in Rome on 18 July 1951 and negotiations followed in Paris from 21 November. The Yugoslavs put forward various compromise proposals including the partitioning of the FTT with Trieste as a free port or a condominium, but these were unacceptable to the Italians. The talks ended in March 1952 without success. That month, riots in Trieste led to a Memorandum of Understanding of 9 May (1st London Agreement) between Italy, Britain and the United States whereby the Italian Government was to be given a greater share in administering the northern zone. Yugoslavia responded by further steps to incorporate the southern zone into Yugoslavia. Each side protested vehemently against the other's action.

In September 1952 Britain got some Yugoslav response to a plan, the gist of which was that the northern zone would go to Italy, the southern to Yugoslavia. In March 1953 the United States offered to press Yugoslavia if Italy would be content with the northern zone. This was unacceptable to Alcide de Gasperi's government, especially in view of the elections to be held on 7 June.

That summer, the dispute entered a critical phase. In August, the new Italian Prime Minister, Giuseppe Pella, then seeking to establish support for his government, made speeches reaffirming Italy's adherence to the tripartite proposal of 1948 (i.e. that Italy should have the whole FTT). On 28 August, the Yugoslav news agency, Yugopress, stated that Belgrade thinking was that the whole question of the FTT would have to be reconsidered. This, together with planned Yugoslav manoeuvres in Slovenia, was taken by the Italian Government to mean that Yugoslavia was considering annexing the southern zone. Italy moved army and naval units towards the FTT, a minor frontier violation was alleged, heated notes were exchanged. Tito declared that the only possible solution was to make Trieste an international city, giving the hinterland to Yugoslavia, while Pella demanded a plebiscite throughout the FTT.

In this crisis the United States and Britain, in some conflict and compromise over tactics, took the initiative again. They announced publicly on 8 October that they had decided to hand over the administration of the northern zone to Italy. In a secret communication to the Italian Government alone, they said that they would not object if Italy annexed the zone and Yugoslavia the southern. The crisis deepened. The Italian public, and the Government as well, greeted the decision as a first step towards getting the whole of the FTT. Yugoslavs reacted furiously to the announcement and to the manner of proceeding, a *diktat* by the great powers. They moved troops to the frontier and announced that if Italian troops entered the northern zone, so would theirs.

The United States and Britain postponed implementing their decision and there was a welter of diplomacy looking to a conference. Riots against the postponement followed in Trieste in the early days of November but Yugoslavia, pacified, withdrew its forces from the frontier in December and so did Italy. On 2 February 1954 in London, American and British representatives began to thrash out a plan with the Yugoslav Ambassador, Dr Vladimir Velebit, and this was completed on 31 May. From 1 June to 14 July, the two representatives discussed the plan with the Italian Ambassador, Signor Manlio Brosio. Finally, from 14 July to 5 October,

Velebit and Brosio negotiated directly down to the last inch of territory, with the two representatives and their governments behind them acting as intermediaries, making available on two occasions economic assistance to Yugoslavia.[6]

The Memorandum of Understanding of 5 October 1954 (2nd London Agreement) between the United States, Britain, Italy and Yugoslavia, laid down that the northern zone (A) was to come under the civil administration of Italy, the southern zone (B) under Yugoslavia's. There was to be a marginal adjustment of the zone boundaries, slightly in Yugoslavia's favour. The Italian Government undertook to maintain the free port at Trieste in accordance with Articles 1–20 of Annex XIII of the Italian Peace Treaty, and provision was made for the protection of minorities and free migration between the zones for a limited period. In addition it was stipulated that no person was to suffer discrimination on account of his past political activities concerning Trieste.

The settlement was similar to that rejected before the crisis of 1953. Known factors making for a settlement now were first that in Italy the Mario Scelba government, which replaced Pella's in February 1954, was popular because of the energy with which it embarked upon social reform; it had more room for manoeuvre over Trieste. Moreover, time seemed to be working against Italy. Since 1949 Yugoslavia's position had been steadily strengthening, largely with United States aid; in 1953 it joined the Balkan Pact with Greece and Turkey, converted by the Treaty of Bled of 9 August 1954 into a military alliance; its relations with the Soviet Union were now also improving. As to Yugoslavia's attitudes, it was conscious of subtle United States economic pressures and inducements to settle on the basis of the existing position and was more ready to accept the 1954 solution than the 1953 one because in the negotiations leading up to it, it had been treated as an equal party; there was no *diktat* by the great powers.

The Memorandum of Understanding spoke only of civil administration and said nothing of sovereignty. Nonetheless, the settlement was not questioned in the following years. The Soviet Union issued a statement welcoming it. The provisions were carried out rapidly. Italian–Yugoslav relations improved greatly.

*   *   *

J.-B. Duroselle: *Le Conflit de Trieste 1943–1954*, Institut de Sociologie de l'Université Libre de Bruxelles, Brussels 1966.

Anthony Eden: *Memoirs, Full Circle*, Cassell, London 1960.

B. C. Novak: *Trieste, 1941–1954*, University of Chicago Press, 1970.

Anon.: Trieste Diary, *The World Today*, October 1945.

[6] Eden, pp. 186–7.

Berlin 1945–49

AT the Moscow Conference of October 1943, the United States, Britain and the Soviet Union established a European Advisory Commission to plan for the postwar situation in Europe. This drew up a draft for the unconditional surrender of Germany, envisaging a total Allied occupation of the country by zones. By mid-September 1944, the three zones had been agreed. Berlin, some 110 miles inside the proposed Soviet zone, was treated as a special entity and was divided into three sectors. Later, the French were given a zone in Germany and a sector in Berlin.

It was not expected that the Allied zones and sectors would be sealed off from one another. Agreement was reached by November 1944 on an Allied Control Council to govern Germany jointly. In Berlin, the commanders of the forces occupying the sectors were, as Military Governors, to act together in a Kommandatura.

The war in Europe ended in May 1945, and in June, final arrangements were made between the Allied Military Commands for withdrawal of Western forces to their respective zones and for the entry of United States and British forces into Berlin. No written agreement on Western rights of access to the city was concluded. General Lucius D. Clay, at that time United States Deputy Military Governor, was wary of accepting specific routes across the Soviet zone as these might later be interpreted as a denial of unlimited access rights. Instead, as a temporary measure, the Western allies accepted Russian verbal assurances on the use of the railway via Magdeburg, the autobahn from Helmstedt, and two air corridors. The right to reopen the matter in the Allied Control Council was reserved.

By the time the Western Military Governors arrived in Berlin in July, the Soviet Military Administration had set up a new city government largely composed of German Communists. The Western Military Governors confirmed the arrangements made, to their later regret. Over the next months they were willing to make concessions for the sake of good relations and the four-power machinery, although beset by disagreements, worked adequately. On 30 November an agreement was approved which provided three air corridors to link Berlin with the Western zones, through which Western aircraft could fly without advance notice.

In August 1946 a temporary constitution for the city was approved and on 26 October elections were held. The Communists suffered a heavy defeat. From this time, relations rapidly worsened. The Russians were determined to keep as many key positions of the city government in

Communist hands as possible. The Western powers stopped making concessions which were not reciprocated. Disputes occurred over the city
police and over alleged Russian kidnappings and intimidation. Four-power
administration became a fiction and instead a struggle developed on two
levels, "that of inter-Allied relations, which centred in the Kommandatura,
and that of Allied relations with the city population, which centred in the
party political battle".[1]

The wider background to these developments was the breakdown of
co-operation over Germany as a whole. Throughout 1947, with the
Truman Doctrine and the Marshall Plan, the East–West conflict deepened.
After the failure of the London meeting of the four-power Council of
Foreign Ministers in November 1947, the Western powers began to
discuss the future of Germany on their own.

In February 1948, to the accompaniment of the Communist *coup d'état*
in Czechoslovakia, the London Conference of the three powers and the
Benelux countries began. In March, it announced that Western Germany
would be brought into the Marshall Plan for economic reconstruction; and
that, as an essential adjunct, its currency would be reformed; and finally,
on 4 June, that steps towards the formation of a federal constitution and
government for Western Germany were to begin.

These successive actions evoked increasing Soviet protests and reactions
in Berlin. In January, the Western powers began to experience difficulties
in military transport access to the city. In March, the Soviet representative
left the Allied Control Council. In April, the Western powers had to begin
a small-scale airlift to supply their personnel. In June, the Soviet Military
Governor left the Kommandatura and their zone authorities began to hold
up civilian as well as military supply trains.

On 20 June, the Western powers introduced their reformed currency
in their zones, while announcing that they were prepared to accept the
proposed Russian Ostmark in their sectors of Berlin, provided it was subject
to four-power management. On the 23rd, the Russians, rejecting this
proviso, introduced the Ostmark into their zone and into Berlin. The
Western powers countered on the 24th by introducing their reformed
currency into West Berlin.

On the same day, the Foreign Ministers of the Soviet Union and its
eastern European associates, meeting in Warsaw, issued a long statement
condemning the London Conference as a violation of the Potsdam principle
of four-power control of Germany and its decisions as, among other things,
creating favourable conditions for the resurgence of German aggression,
consummating the division of Germany and frustrating the conclusion of
a peace treaty. The statement called instead for joint four-power action to

[1] Windsor, p. 52.

complete the demilitarisation of Germany, to prevent the redevelopment of Germany's war potential, to form a democratic all-German government, to conclude a peace treaty, and to ensure the discharge of Germany's reparations obligations.[2] On this same day also, all rail traffic between the Western zones and Berlin was halted because of "technical difficulties". This soon extended to canal and road links and by 4 August Berlin was completely blockaded.

In this crisis, the Western powers began a full-scale airlift to supply the city. They also halted all rail transport to the Soviet zone as a counter-measure. There was some fear of war. Already in the weeks after the Czechoslovakian *coup d'état* (February), General Clay, by this time US Military Governor, had said that he sensed a "subtle change" in Russian attitudes and had warned that war might come with a "dramatic suddenness".[3] On 30 June Ernest Bevin, the British Foreign Secretary, speaking in the House of Commons of the decision to remain in Berlin and to supply it from the air, recognised that "a grave situation might arise"; but "Her Majesty's Government and our Western Allies can see no alternative between that and surrender, and none of us can accept surrender".[4]

The Western powers at first saw the airlift as a temporary stop-gap response. In July, they considered the idea of breaking the blockade with an armoured column but dismissed it. They offered to negotiate with the Soviet Union at any level, if it would life the blockade. During August, there were talks between representatives of the three powers and Molotov, the Soviet Foreign Minister, and on two occasions, the 2nd and the 23rd August, with Stalin. These talks concluded with a four-power directive to the Military Governors in Berlin to lift the blockade and to make the Ostmark the sole currency there, subject to agreement among them on practical implementation. In September, negotiations began between the Military Governors, but these quickly reached deadlock.

At this point, the Western powers raised the matter in the UN Security Council. The Soviet Union, citing Article 107 of the Charter, contested the Council's competence. Their protests were overruled and the Council debated the issue, though without progress. Proposals by the smaller powers on the Council, Argentina, Belgium, Canada, China, Colombia and Syria, one of which involved "a committee of experts", also failed. The Secretary-General, Trygve Lie, suggested that senior United States and Soviet officials on his staff should act as intermediaries and work out a solution without formal negotiations, but this too was unacceptable to the parties.

[2] Ruhm von Oppen, pp. 300–7.
[3] Walter Millis (ed.), *The Forrestal Diaries*, Viking Press, New York 1951 p. 387.
[4] Hansard, 30 June 1948, col. 2233.

From September to the following January, four-power contacts continued but still made no progress. Dr Philip Jessup, US representative to the General Assembly and also (in 1949) ambassador-at-large, said: "We discovered that the talks we were holding were serving as an excuse to prolong the blockade rather than as a method of removing it."[5] Meanwhile, the formation of the Anglo-American Combined Air Lift Task Force in October indicated that the Western powers were prepared to develop the airlift into a long-term arrangement.

The deadlock began to break in January 1949. By this time, the airlift had proved itself even in winter conditions. Despite the hazards, the daily average tonnage flown in January reached 5,000 and was still climbing. (The figure reached 8,000 in the spring, the amount ordinarily brought in by rail and water; in the whole 11 months blockade, 1.4 million metric tons of supplies were flown in, with planes landing and taking off at the peak at 30-second intervals). This success confirmed the steady determination of the Berliners and the self-confidence of the Western powers.

The Russians now began to appear conciliatory and on 30 January 1949, in reply to questions submitted by a United States press correspondent, Stalin indicated that he might lift the blockade if the Western powers raised the counter-blockade and postponed the establishment of a West German government pending a new meeting of the Council of Foreign Ministers. He did not mention the currency question.

Dr Jessup was able to confirm from the Soviet representative on the Security Council, Mr Jacob Malik, that this omission had been deliberate. Secret negotiations by Jessup and Malik followed, and on 5 May, it was announced that the blockade and counter-blockade would end on 12 May.

The Foreign Ministers met in Paris on 23 May and reaffirmed the lifting of the blockade but without agreement on Berlin or Germany. The Western mark remained the sole legal currency in West Berlin, the Ostmark in East Berlin. The Basic Law drawn up by the West German Parliamentary Council was approved by the Western powers (May) and on 21 September, while maintaining the existing status of Berlin, they recognised the establishment of the Federal Republic of Germany. On 7 October, the German Democratic Republic was proclaimed in the Soviet zone.

* * *

W. P. DAVISON: *The Berlin Blockade, A Study in Cold War Politics*, Princeton University Press, 1958.

M. GOTTLIEB: *The German Peace Settlement and the Berlin Crisis*, Paine-Whitman, New York 1960.

[5] Davison, p. 239.

H.M. STATIONERY OFFICE: *Berlin and the Problem of German Reunification*, H.M.S.O., London 1970.

E. PLISCHKE: *Government and Politics of Contemporary Berlin*, Nijhoff, The Hague 1963.

B. RUHM VON OPPEN (ed.): *Documents on Germany under Occupation 1945–1954*, Oxford University Press, London 1955.

P. WINDSOR: *City on Leave, A History of Berlin, 1945–62*, Chatto & Windus, London 1963.

Austria 1945-55

IN the Moscow Declaration of October 1943, the United States, Britain and the Soviet Union stated that Austria, "the first free country to fall victim to Nazi aggression, shall be liberated from Nazi domination" as a "free and independent state". They added, however, at Russian insistence, that "Austria . . . has a responsibility which she cannot evade for participating in the war on the side of Hitlerite Germany". The Moscow Conference also established the European Advisory Commission to draw up occupation arrangements. Progress on Austria was slow.

Russian troops entered Vienna in early April 1945 and on the 24th the Russians announced the formation of a provisional government, under the veteran right-wing socialist Karl Renner, consisting of representatives of the Socialists, the People's Party and the Communists. The key Ministry of the Interior and the Education Ministry went to Communists, but Renner reduced their influence by appointing two under-secretaries drawn from different parties to that of the minister for each major Cabinet post. The United States, Britain and France withheld recognition from this government, considering it unrepresentative of political feeling in the country and of the interests of the provinces.

In July 1945, agreement was finally reached in the EAC. There was to be an Allied Commission consisting of the four occupying powers (USA, USSR, Britain and France) with an Allied Council as the deliberating body assisted by an Executive Council. The country was to be divided into four occupation zones. Vienna, in the Russian zone, was to be similarly divided but with a jointly occupied international zone in which the Allied administration and the Austrian Government was to be situated.

At the Potsdam Conference in late July, Stalin reported that Russian forces were being withdrawn from the area allotted to the Western powers. On 23 August, the Western powers were able to enter Vienna. In September, Renner's provisional government was broadened and the following month received four-power recognition. Free elections throughout Austria were to be held before the end of the year.

The elections, held on 25 November, were followed by a rapid worsening of relations between the Austrians and the Russians. The Austrian Communist Party had been optimistic about the outcome, expecting to win 25–30 per cent of the votes and to join a coalition government. In the event, they won only 5.42 per cent. Leopold Figl, the People's Party leader, formed a new coalition government with the Socialists in which, as a gesture of

33

propitiation, the Communists were given a newly created Ministry of Power and Electrification, although their share of the votes did not warrant this. The Russians henceforth restricted the freedom of the Austrian Government within their zone and gave greater privileges to Communist Party members. Friendly relations with the Austrian authorities changed to antagonism.

On the highest level of policy, a major issue was that of reparations. It had been agreed at the Potsdam Conference that, while no reparations were to be demanded from Austria, the Russians might claim Germany's external assets in eastern Austria. The Russians gained considerably from interpreting "German assets" to include those seized by the Germans after the *Anschluss* of 1938. At first they followed a policy of removals to the Soviet Union but in the spring of 1946, this was changed; remaining "German assets" were kept in Austria but were worked by Russians for the benefit of the Soviet economy. A special organisation, the Administration of Soviet Property in Austria (USIA), was set up for this purpose.

The Austrian Government was seeking at this time to increase its control over the country's affairs while acting circumspectly towards the occupying powers. A new Control Agreement in June 1946 gave it the right to make agreements with any of them without Allied Council approval, although this body had to be informed. All laws, except constitutional laws, were to come into force unless disallowed by the Council within thirty-one days. Since to disallow a bill the Council had to act unanimously, this prevented any occupying power from interfering unilaterally in the country's domestic affairs.

The Austrians sought, at the same time, to avoid provoking the Russians needlessly. However, in July 1946, they made a desperate attempt to check the Russian seizure of "German assets" by passing nationalisation laws. This was criticised by the Russians and disregarded by them, causing an almost complete rupture of relations.

Meanwhile, relations between the Western occupying powers and the Soviet Union had also grown tense and they were making little progress towards a State Treaty regulating the future of Austria and ending the occupation. (A peace treaty was not required because of Austria's incorporation into Germany in 1938.) This was attributable partly to differences over Austria and partly to differences over other aspects of the European settlement. The Western occupying powers disliked Russian actions in Austria; the two sides had different hopes about the future internal political complexion of the country; the Soviet Union benefited economically from the continued occupation and there were also strategic considerations. Concern for a *cordon sanitaire* around the Soviet Union appears to have dominated Stalin's thinking about 1945 and this gave reason to stay in Austria. The Western powers, for their part, would not contemplate a withdrawal unless the Soviet Union did likewise.

Possibly more important than all this, the Russians may simply have been in no hurry to withdraw from anywhere they had occupied, including eastern Austria, until a general European settlement, and particularly a German settlement, had been arrived at. They may have taken the view that their policy on Austria should depend on the development of the German question and that the Austria issue could be used to exert leverage in the German question. Certainly, on several occasions, the Soviet Union sought the postponement of negotiations on Austria on the grounds that the German question should be solved first.

In 1946, the United States tried to raise the Austria issue at the Foreign Ministers' meetings but with little success. Not until December 1946, when consideration of the Italian Peace Treaty was complete, did the Soviet Foreign Minister, Molotov, consent to the German and Austrian treaties coming before the Foreign Ministers. The Moscow Conference of 10 March–24 April 1947, which an Austrian delegation attended, considered the issue and established a Four Power Commission to negotiate outstanding points and to draw up a draft treaty. This met regularly but for some time made little progress.

The two most contentious points were frontiers and reparations. Other matters were raised, such as denazification, but gave relatively minor difficulty. On frontiers, the Soviet Union until 1948 supported Yugoslavia's claim to a small part of Styria and a larger part of South Carinthia, totalling over a thousand square miles and including Villach and Klagenfurt. The Western powers, on the other hand, supported Austria's claim to retain its 1938 frontiers unaltered. After the breach between the Soviet Union and Yugoslavia in June 1948, this issue faded in importance.

On "German assets", the Soviet Union insisted that it had the right to make its own definition. Eventually the search for a common definition was abandoned. The French "Cherrière Plan" sought rather to arrive at an agreed list of assets to go to the Russians and of assets to go to the Austrians with compensation to the Russians. On these lines, progress was made. At the Paris Conference of 23 May–20 June 1949, the Foreign Ministers instructed their deputies to reach agreement on a draft treaty by 1 September. It was at this conference that Vyshinsky, the Soviet member, abandoned the Yugoslav territorial claim. Although the September deadline was not met, the points still at issue in the negotiations were small at the end of the year and, so far as this went, the completion of the treaty seemed in sight.

In the event, the Soviet Union proved determined to delay the treaty. Negotiations continued but it repeatedly raised new issues, including the demand that the Trieste problem should be settled first. Wider events probably reinforced its determination to hold on to what it had: the failure of the Berlin blockade, the formation of NATO, the outbreak of the Korean War, full-scale Western rearmament.

Within Austria, there had been Communist-inspired disturbances from time to time and these came to a climax in 1950. In the 1949 elections, the Communist Party had again received only some 5 per cent of the votes. Now, against a background of economic difficulties caused by inflation and cutbacks in Marshall Aid (much to the Soviet Union's displeasure, Austria had joined in the Marshall Plan from its inception in 1947) and taking as an immediate issue the Government's new wage-price policy, the Communists called for a general strike on 26 September. In the Soviet zone, all USIA factories closed and intimidation was used against other workers. Demonstrations occurred in Vienna and disturbances in various industrial towns in the rest of Austria.

The Government, at first unsure of itself, appealed to the Allied Council for assistance but this was refused. The Socialist Party and the Trades Union Federation declared their opposition to Communist actions. In the Russian zone, the Communists increased their efforts, and strikes and disruptions were renewed on 4 October. However, the great majority of workers, even in the Russian zone, not only refused to support the strike but actively repelled Communist attempts to enforce it. By the 6th it was clear that the strike was a failure.

On the external front, Austria and the Western occupying powers mounted a campaign in 1952 to ensure that the question of State Treaty should remain fully alive. In March, the Western powers proposed a new "Short Treaty" under which the occupying powers would hand back all property held to the Austrian Government and withdraw their forces. The Soviet Union, as expected, refused. In July, Austria (not itself a member of the United Nations) sent a memorandum on the subject to all member states and the issue was debated at the autumn General Assembly. Brazil introduced a resolution calling on the great powers to take the necessary measures to bring about a quick completion of an Austrian Treaty and this was adopted unanimously on 20 December, the Soviet bloc states being absent. The Austrians recognised that this did little to advance the problem but sought to counteract apathy. They feared a gradual weakening within eastern Austria of opposition to "Sovietisation" and a general acceptance of Soviet "ownership through a lapse of time".[1]

The Austria dispute remained in this frozen state until the unexpected Russian *volte-face* of 1955. This was first evident in Molotov's speech to

---

[1] Karl Gruber, *Between Liberation and Liberty*, trans. L. Kochan, London 1955, p. 205.

the Supreme Soviet on 8 February in which he offered to sign a State Treaty independent of any settlement of the German question, provided guarantees could be worked out to prevent a future *Anschluss*. This statement was followed by talks between Molotov and the Austrian ambassador in Moscow on 25 February, 2 March and 14 March 1955. In April, an Austrian delegation, headed by Chancellor Julius Raab, arrived in Moscow and on 15 April the Moscow Memorandum was signed. Austria, in return for a Russian promise to sign "without delay" an Austrian Treaty, reaffirmed an undertaking "to join no military alliances and to permit no military bases on its soil". "The Austrian Federal Government will make a declaration in a form which will obligate Austria internationally to practice, in perpetuity, a neutrality of the type maintained by Switzerland." This agreement was acceptable to the Western powers and, on 15 May 1955, the Austrian State Treaty was signed in the Belvedere Palace in Vienna. On the following 26 October, the Austrian constitution was amended to establish permanent neutrality.

There has been much speculation on the reasons for the Russian *volte-face*. It seems that the fate of Austria was a point of controversy in the struggle within the Soviet Union for the succession to Stalin. Krushchev favoured a neutral Austria and his emergence as the Russian leader opened the way to this. "Molotov himself announced the new Austrian course on the very day the Krushchev era began with the resignation of G. M. Malenkov."[2]

Possibly the Krushchev party reckoned that stubbornness on Austria had lost value as leverage in relation to the German question; the rearmament of West Germany, its entry into NATO and the setting-up of a Federal Republic had already been decided; a milder line on Austria and on European and world affairs generally might nowadays be more influential. The Austrian settlement was part of a pattern. The Soviet Union improved its relations with Finland, Yugoslavia and West Germany in a general atmosphere of East–West *détente* and became a supporter of Afro-Asian neutralism.

Strategically, while Stalin may have been deeply concerned to protect the Soviet Union against conventional warfare, his successors may have reassessed the need to maintain forward troop positions in eastern Austria in the nuclear age. By the Warsaw Treaty of 14 May 1955, the Soviet Union converted its bilateral defence treaties in Eastern Europe into a multilateral security organisation and this provided an alternative justification for keeping troops in Hungary and Rumania after the withdrawal from Austria. In the confrontation between NATO and the Warsaw Pact, there was no doubt value to be found in ensuring that Austria remained neutral.

[2] Bader, p. 202.

W. B. BADER: *Austria Between East and West, 1945–1955*, Stanford University Press, 1966.

C. J. GRAYSON: *Austria's International Position 1938–1953*, Librairie E. Droz, Geneva 1953.

R. HISCOCKS: *The Rebirth of Austria*, Oxford University Press, 1953.

G. SHEPHERD: *The Austrian Odyssey*, Macmillan, New York 1957.

H. STEAMAN: *The Soviet Union and the Occupation of Austria*, Siegler, Bad Godesberg 1961.

P. E. MOSLEY: The Treaty with Austria, *International Organisation*, May 1950.

South Tirol 1945–69

ON the dismemberment of the Habsburg empire in 1919, Italy gained the part of the Tirol which lies south of the Brenner Pass. This consisted of the Province of Bolzano (South Tirol in the narrower usage of the term and called by the Italians, Alto Adige), two-thirds of whose population spoke German and were similar in culture to the Austrians across the border; and the Province of Trento whose population was mainly Italian.

During the interwar period, the Fascist regime in Rome initiated a policy of Italianisation and this widened the gulf between the two communities. The policy was endorsed by the Hitler–Mussolini agreement of 1939. The German-speaking Tirolese were given the choice either to accept Italianisation or to leave for the Reich into which Austria had been absorbed by the Anschluss. A large number chose to leave but by September 1943, only half of these had actually done so. In that month Italy surrendered to the Allied powers and Germany annexed the territory.

On the defeat of Germany in May 1945, the fate of the South Tirol lay in the hands of the Council of Foreign Ministers of the United States, the Soviet Union, Britain and France. Austria immediately requested a plebiscite in the Bolzano Province; Italy argued against this a strategic need for the Brenner frontier and the economic importance of the province to its economy. Notably, Bolzano contributed a large surplus of electric power to the rest of Italy.

Austria's claim roused some sympathy in Britain and France especially, but it was Italy that proved to have the margin of favour within the governments of the "Big Four". The United States attached greater importance to Italy and received assurances from it of respect for minority rights. The Soviet Union also endorsed the Brenner frontier. The meeting of the Council of Foreign Ministers of April 1946 made clear that a plebiscite was not contemplated; all that Austria could hope for was minor frontier changes. This decision provoked some disturbances in the South Tirol, but after renewed discussions in which Austria was asked to state its case, the Council decided even against frontier changes. The Council became increasingly aware as work on the Italian peace treaty went forward that several of its terms, reparations, military limitations, losses of territory to France, Greece and Yugoslavia, would cause much resentment in Italy, as they eventually did. They felt it wise to allow Italy to retain South Tirol untouched.

Faced with this attitude, Austria had little alternative but to negotiate with Italy. Bilateral discussions began in London in June 1946 between Dr Karl Gruber, Austrian Foreign Minister, and Signor Nicolo Carandini, the Italian ambassador, and continued later in Paris. Carandini raised the possibility of an Austro-Italian customs union, while Gruber proposed a condominium over the South Tirol, but neither side could accept the other's idea.

The outline of a more modest agreement did, however, emerge and this was completed in talks between Gruber and the Italian Prime Minister, Alcide de Gasperi, in Paris, and adopted by them on 5 September 1946. Austria succeeded in spite of Soviet opposition in getting the agreement attached to the Italian Peace Treaty of February 1947 (Annex IV) and in getting the signatories to take note of it (Article 10).

The Paris Agreement, a very short document, provided that the "German-speaking inhabitants of the Bolzano Province and of the neighbouring bilingual townships of the Trento Province will be assured of complete equality of rights with the Italian-speaking inhabitants within the framework of special provisions to safeguard the ethnical character and cultural and economic development of the German-speaking element. . . ." Article 2 said: "The populations of the above-mentioned zones will be granted the exercise of autonomous legislative and executive regional power. The frame within which the said provisions of autonomy will apply, will be drafted in consultation also with local representative German-speaking elements."[1]

The Italians now set to work on a Statute to implement this agreement. The formula eventually arrived at, and endorsed notably by the Sudtiroler Volkspartei (SVP), was that the whole South Tirol (Trento and Bolzano) should become the Trentino-Alto Adige Region with regional autonomy and that each province should have a degree of provincial autonomy. The effect of this was that the German-speaking Tirolese would be in a minority on the Regional Council but in a majority on the Bolzano Provincial Council. Detailed provisions were also made safeguarding their culture, language, education, economic opportunity and access to public employment.[2] The Statute was approved by the Italian Constituent Assembly on 29 January 1948 and came into effect on 14 March.

Over the next decade the Italian authorities, whether for reasons centring on the South Tirol or through wider anxieties about regionalism in Italy, were slow to make the necessary legal and administrative decrees to implement the detailed provisions of the Statute. Frustration gradually sharpened among the German-speaking population. Their fears also grew for their majority position in Bolzano Province in view of the immigration

[1] Alcock, Appendix 1, pp. 473–4.
[2] *Ibid.*, Appendix 2, pp. 475–92.

of Italians, mainly from southern Italy, and there were economic resentments. The industrialisation of the area emphasised the difference between the Italian urban, industrial population and the mainly German-speaking countryside. It tended to raise the living standard of the former in relation to the latter. On the constitutional side, the German-speaking Tirolese gradually became convinced that they suffered more from their minority position in the Regional Council than was compensated by their majority in the Bolzano Provincial Council. They began to say that by creating a joint region for Bolzano and Trento, the Italians had tricked them out of the autonomy promised in the 1946 Agreement. They began to wish for greater autonomy for Bolzano on its own.

As early as 1948, an organised movement led by the SVP, which had only reluctantly abandoned such aims in the discussions leading to the Statute, began to agitate in this sense. This movement had little overt support for some years but in the early 1950s it became important, largely because of developments abroad.

In the summer of 1953, an Italian–Yugoslav crisis was gathering over Trieste and the Italian Prime Minister, Giuseppe Pella, demanded (11 September) that a plebiscite be held throughout the Free Territory of Trieste as the best method of settling its future.[3] Although this proposal came to nothing, it roused many among the German-speaking Tirolese to demand a plebiscite to settle their future.

A still more significant event was the signing of the Austrian State Treaty in May 1955. Sovereign once more, and no longer hampered by the great problem of the Soviet occupation, Austria could act more vigorously. The revival of West Germany and its incorporation of the Saar following the October 1955 plebiscite further encouraged the German-speaking Tirolese.

A month after the State Treaty, the Austrian Foreign Minister, Leopold Figl, assured Tirolese representatives that the Treaty and Austria's neutral status did not prevent it from concerning itself with the South Tirol question (24 June 1955). The next major event was the appointment on 29 June 1956 of Professor Franz Gschnitzer, an outspoken champion of their cause, as Under-Secretary of State for Foreign Affairs with special responsibility for the South Tirol. On 8 October, after some preliminary exchanges, Austria sent a full-scale memorandum to Italy which, while moderate in tone, said that Italy had not fully implemented the 1946 Agreement and proposed a Mixed Commission to examine the question.

Italy replied on 9 February 1957 with a detailed rebuttal of Austria's arguments. Meanwhile, in the region itself in the last months of 1956, terrorist incidents had begun. These, the dynamiting of installations,

[3] See p. 26.

especially electrical, increased over the next few years. It seems that organisations operating from Innsbruck aided this violence with a view not merely to greater autonomy for Bolzano Province but to its eventual union with Austria.

The Austrian Government itself accepted throughout the validity of the 1946 Agreement, questioning only its interpretation and implementation. In discussions which opened in Vienna on 22 February 1958 and continued for two years, it claimed that the German-speaking Tirolese had never been properly consulted in the framing of the Statute as required by Article 2 of the Agreement and that the proper interpretation of the Article required regional autonomy for Bolzano Province by itself. The Italians rejected this interpretation and no progress was made on this or on the issues of language equality and ethnic proportions in public employment. The Italians moreover resented Austria's intervention. They insisted that the discussions were not negotiations; the affair was a purely domestic one. They suspected and especially resented Austrian Government complicity in the more drastic political actions of the SVP, as when in February 1958, the SVP presented a new draft statute to the Italian Parliament whereby Bolzano Province should become an autonomous region by itself; and when in February 1959, they provoked a crisis by resigning *en bloc* from the Provincial Council.

In September 1959, the dispute was brought before the Council of Europe which recommended that it be taken to the International Court of Justice, an idea acceptable to Italy but not to Austria. In October 1960, Austria raised the issue in the United Nations General Assembly, an action which Italy resented since it denied the UN's competence. The General Assembly debate showed little support for Austria's case. A compromise resolution was adopted urging the resumption of bilateral negotiations and, if these failed, resort to the ICJ or any other method of peaceful settlement in Article 33 of the Charter.

The issue was discussed again in 1961; Austria still found little support; and a similar resolution was passed. Leaving aside their views on the merits of the case, most Western countries favoured Italy because of its membership of NATO and because, it seems, they accepted that the Brenner frontier was strategically important. The United States, for example, had rejected an Austrian request in 1959 for mediation. A factor in Soviet passivity was no doubt the fear of encouraging German nationalism in any way. The African and Asian countries were primarily interested in anti-colonial self-determination and were moreover wary in their own interests of secessionist ideas.

None the less, the desire to retain international good opinion appears to have played some part, along with the wish to have done with the dispute, in a certain softening of Italian attitudes from this time. Italian–Austrian negotiations in accordance with the 1960 UN resolution began in January 1961. Italy offered to increase the powers of the Bolzano Province and to take other steps to ensure the rights of the German-speaking Tirolese. In September 1961, the Italian Government set up a commission of nineteen, including seven SVP members, under Signor Paolo Rossi to report on the problems of the province.

Austria in 1961 stuck to its support for the SVP view that only regional autonomy for the province by itself would do. In this year, terrorism reached a peak and killings began to be added to the bombing of installations. Now, however, in revulsion against this and the general waste and disruption caused by the dispute, a strong movement of moderate opinion developed rapidly among the German-speaking Tirolese. In response, on 2 August 1962, the SVP stated that it would withdraw its demand for a separate Bolzano region if genuine increased powers were given to the province.

On 10 April 1964, the Rossi Commission reported. It proposed additional powers for the Bolzano Province and a series of measures on language, education, housing, economic opportunity and public employment. The SVP declared these inadequate, especially as regards the powers of the province in economic affairs, and in negotiations on the basis of the Report which began in Geneva in May, Austria said the same. An Italian–Austrian Committee of Experts was agreed and, in the summer, recommended the stages of an eventual settlement but there was still little progress on substantive issues, especially the powers to be given to the province. Discussions continued for a further five years. Finally, in the summer of 1969, the two governments reached agreement.

Probably a major factor now influencing Austria was the development of the European Community. In particular, in 1967, Italy had vetoed discussions of Austrian association with the Community on the grounds that it had failed to act energetically to suppress terrorist organisations. As regards the agreement, it consisted of a 137-point "package" of measures along the lines of the Rossi Report, and an "Operational Calendar" for putting these into effect over four years. As each point was effected, Austria was to make formal acknowledgment, and, at the end, to declare the dispute settled. The SVP Party Congress accepted the agreement (by a narrow majority) on 22 November, the Italian Parliament on 4–5 December, and the Austrian on 16 December. The Calendar began to be implemented forthwith.

*　　*　　*

A. ALCOCK: *The History of the South Tyrol Question*, Michael Joseph, London 1970.

A. Fenet: *La Question du Tyrol du Sud, Un Problème de Droit International*, Pichon et Durand-Auzias, Paris 1968.

H. Siegler: *Austria, Problems and Achievements since 1945*, Siegler, Bonn 1967.

M. Toscano: *Storia Diplomatica della Questione dell'Alto Adige*, Laterza, Bari 1967.

Palestine 1945-49

THE first Zionist Congress, organised by Theodor Herzl at Basle in 1897, resolved to seek "a home in Palestine" for the Jews. In November 1917, a letter from the British Foreign Secretary, Arthur Balfour, to Lord Rothschild was made public in which he said that: "His Majesty's Government view with favour the establishment in Palestine of a national home for the Jewish people, and will use their best endeavours to facilitate the achievement of this object, it being clearly understood that nothing shall be done which may prejudice the civil and religious rights of existing non-Jewish communities in Palestine, or the rights and political status enjoyed by Jews in any other country."

Then followed in the course of the First World War the defeat and division of the Turkish empire by Britain and France in which Palestine fell to Britain's share. The Allied Supreme Council offered it to Britain as a League of Nations mandate in April 1920 and Britain formally accepted this arrangement on 22 July 1922.

The Jews wanted free immigration but Arab nationalist sentiment was also strengthening, demanding an end to Jewish immigration and of land sales to them by Arabs, and self-determination for the Arabs. As Jewish immigration increased in the 1930s under the pressure of Nazi persecution, the Arabs launched a campaign of strikes and terrorism against the British and Jews, known as the Arab Rebellion (1937–39).

In 1937, a British Royal Commission (the Peel Commission) recommended partitioning the country between Jews and Arabs but the Arabs rejected this, and after an abortive Round Table Conference early in 1939, the British announced their own decision in a White Paper of 17 May 1939. Jewish immigration would be limited to 75,000 in the next five years and then end; sale of land to Jews would be restricted; within ten years, Palestine would become an independent state in treaty relationship with Britain.

Though the Arabs rejected this plan as inadequate, it none the less represented a British swing towards them under the exigencies of approaching war with Germany. This, combined with the presence of large British forces during the war, kept the Arabs quiescent for its duration. The Jews were disappointed but, supporting the Allied cause, they too officially maintained a truce so long as the war lasted.

The two main developments of the war period were, first, that Jewish extremists did not accept the truce and, gaining wider sympathy from the tragic plight of would-be immigrants turned away by the British, launched

45

terrorist attacks against the British from 1942 onwards. The two principal groups attacking the British were Irgun Zvai Leumi and Lehi, called by the British, the Stern Gang.

The second main development was that the official Jewish organisations began to look less to the British and more to the United States for support for their cause. On 11 May 1942, the American Zionist Association, meeting in the Biltmore Hotel, New York, adopted a programme proposed by the head of the executive committee of the international Jewish Agency, David Ben Gurion, calling for a Jewish state of the whole of Palestine, unlimited immigration, and the creation of a Jewish Army. The Biltmore Programme was endorsed as the official policy of world Zionism the following November.

This was the situation when the war against Germany ended in May 1945 and a Labour Party Government took office in Britain on 26 July. Ten days later, Ben Gurion asked the British Government to admit 100,000 Jewish immigrants, an appeal endorsed by President Truman in a public speech at the end of the month (31 August). The British reply to Ben Gurion was that the 2,000 unused certificates left over from 1939 should be used first and that then the Jews should try to compromise with the Arabs on an entry of 1,500 immigrants per month. The Arabs refused any compromise and the British Foreign Secretary, Ernest Bevin, feared serious trouble in Palestine if they were overruled. He made it clear to the United States that he would only allow 100,000 immigrants to enter Palestine if the Americans were willing to help the British keep law and order. This meant deadlock since President Truman did not wish to send American troops to Palestine.

However, in October, to the accompaniment of increasing Jewish terrorist activity, the United States accepted a British proposal for a non-official Anglo-American Committee of Enquiry, consisting of six men a side, to study the situation. They visited Palestine and "displaced person" camps in Europe. In their report of 30 April 1946, they recommended that British mandatory (eventually UN trusteeship) rule continue, that 100,000 victims of Nazi and Fascist persecution be immediately admitted, and that the restrictions on land sales be ended.

Making no formal comment on this solution, the British Government set up with the United States Government an official Anglo-American Commission to consider the problem further. Meanwhile, British relations with the Arabs and Jews continued to worsen. In May 1946, the Mufti of Jerusalem, who had played a large part in the prewar Arab Rebellion, arrived back in the city. Official Jewry was dismayed by Britain's recognition of the related mandatory territory of Transjordan as an independent sovereign state on 22 March. The Jewish terrorist groups heightened their campaign, including the blowing up on 22 July of the King David Hotel in Jerusalem, the headquarters of the British security forces, killing 91 British, Arabs and Jews and wounding 45.

On 30 July 1946, the Anglo-American (Grady-Morrison) Commission produced its plan for a federal structure of Arabs and Jews in Palestine under British trusteeship, with immigration to depend on their joint consent. This did not go far enough for the Arabs and bitterly disappointed the Jews. The British and United States governments were still at odds, moreover. The British wanted United States support in policing the proposed new arrangements, but this was not forthcoming. President Truman (in October) repeated his appeal for the admission of 100,000 Jews.

From September 1946 to January 1947 negotiations went on in London to try to get some form of Arab–Jewish compromise but as on earlier occasions the parties would not meet together and would not even refer directly to each other. Under these circumstances the separate discussions which the Colonial Office conducted with the Jewish Agency members and the Foreign Office held with the Arabs could make little progress. In the end, it was clear that while the Zionists would settle for a partition of Palestine, the Arabs wanted the whole of it as an independent Arab majority state. Within this state, the Jews would be granted minority rights (for instance, a third of the legislative seats) but would have their rights of immigration and land purchase strictly controlled.

On 7 February 1947 Bevin offered the two sides a final compromise. Palestine would be divided into Jewish and Arab provinces which would have local autonomy while Britain would remain to police the state for another five years under the higher authority of the UN Trusteeship Council. Immigrants totalling 96,000 would be allowed in over the next two years at the rate of 4,000 per month and later quotas would be fixed by the Mufti, representing the Arabs, and the Jews.

This plan was a modification of the Grady-Morrison scheme and was similarly rejected by both Jews and Arabs. Bevin was exasperated by their intransigence and angered by the loss of British lives; it was also clear that Britain found the economic cost of policing Palestine too high. On 14 February 1947 Bevin stated that the Mandate would be referred back to the UN by Britain without any particular recommendation. The British delegate to the UN requested (2 April) a special session of the Security Council on Palestine. This opened on 9 May, and resulted in a UN Special Committee on Palestine (UNSCOP) charged with preparing a report. The Arab Higher Committee boycotted UNSCOP. The Zionists may have organised the famous incident of the immigrant ship *Exodus* to coincide with UNSCOP's presence in Palestine.[1]

[1] Sykes, p. 381.

UNSCOP's report was issued on 1 September 1947. The majority plan (put forward by members from Canada, Czechoslovakia, Guatemala, the Netherlands, Peru, Sweden and Uruguay) proposed partition into two states, each consisting of three segments of Palestine. Jerusalem would remain under international trusteeship. The minority plan (supported by India, Iran and Yugoslavia) provided for a federal state of two states, each having autonomy in local affairs, though Jewish immigration was to be controlled by an Arab–Jew–UN committee of three men apiece. The whole Committee agreed that there should be an economic union under which the Jewish areas would aid their poorer Arab neighbours. Independence was to be granted after the economic union treaty had been signed.

The Jews accepted the majority plan, the Arabs the minority plan. Britain announced (26 September) that it would relinquish its mandate by 1 August of the following year and that it would not implement any plan not agreed by both sides. The General Assembly voted on 29 November 1947 by a two-thirds majority including both the United States and the Soviet Union (Britain abstained) in favour of the majority plan.

The resolution also established a UN Palestine Commission to implement the plan, but on the following day the Arab League states declared that they would fight to prevent the establishment of a Jewish state. In view of this, the British refused to co-operate with the Commission. The Commission called for a UN force to maintain law and order after the end of the mandate (which the British had now brought forward to 15 May) but suspicions and reluctance to become embroiled prevented agreement. The United States urged a temporary UN trusteeship but the Soviet Union called for the implementation of partition and eventually (May 1948) the General Assembly agreed only on the appointment of a UN mediator and a UN Commissioner for Jerusalem.

By this time, fighting between Jews and Arabs was developing fast. In January, Arab units had begun to enter Palestine. Haifa and Jaffa were seized by Zionist forces and by May 1948, perhaps as many as 300,000 Arabs had fled or been evicted from Jewish Palestine (a number which may have more than doubled in the course of the following year). On 15 May, the British formally relinquished their mandate and the Jewish State of Israel was proclaimed. It received United States *de facto* recognition on the same day and that of the Soviet Union and various other states in the following days.

The armies of Egypt, Iraq, Jordan, Lebanon, Saudi Arabia and Syria immediately attacked and full-scale fighting ensued. The UN mediator, Count Folke Bernadotte, President of the Swedish Red Cross, managed to persuade the two sides to accept a truce for four weeks from 11 June, during which time he sought to negotiate exchanges of territory and to form joint councils, but in vain. A second cease-fire was arranged on 18 July and Bernadotte continued his mediation, including proposals to the UN for alterations in the partition plan. On 17 September, he was assassinated by Jewish terrorists.

Bernadotte was succeeded as UN mediator by Dr Ralph Bunche. Heavy fighting began once more (mid-October) and in the following weeks the Israelis won a series of victories over their opponents. The Egyptians and the Israelis, with Bunche as mediator, began armistice negotiations in Rhodes on 12 January 1949, resulting in an agreement on 24 February. Separate negotiations were held with Lebanon and Jordan, and agreements were reached on 23 March and 3 April. Negotiations with Syria followed later. Iraq and Saudi Arabia signified their acquiescence.

It was understood that the armistice lines, which broadly speaking reflected the results of the fighting, and which left more, and more coherent, territory in Israeli hands than the partition plan, were provisional pending a political settlement. This, it was hoped, would develop from talks to be held under UN auspices at Lausanne in April 1949. At this conference between the UN Conciliation Commission, composed of American, Turkish and French representatives, and the Arabs and Israelis, irreconcilable differences emerged. The Israelis wanted a comprehensive peace settlement, including the problems of boundaries, the status of Jerusalem and refugees. The Arabs considered that these three matters should be cleared up before negotiations for a general settlement. Under United States pressure, the Israelis agreed to take back 100,000 of the Arab refugees but specified that they must be able to determine where the refugees were settled. About 500 Jews per day were arriving in Israel at this time. The Arabs contended that the refugees must be allowed to return to their own homes and land. Neither side would alter its view and many thousands of the refugees remained in their camps in Egypt and Jordan dependent on aid through the UN Relief and Works Agency for Palestinian Refugees (UNWRA), the UN Children's Fund (UNICEF) and the World Health Organization (WHO).

When the UN General Assembly met in the autumn of 1949 much attention focused on the status of Jerusalem. A resolution of the General Assembly of 9 December called for the internationalisation of Jerusalem but neither the Jews nor the Arabs responded. Jerusalem remained a two zone city, divided between the Jordanians and the Israelis. The year 1949 ended with Israel possessing greater and more coherent territory than that allocated to it by the UN, but unrecognised and unaccepted by its Arab neighbours.

*   *   *

B. HALPERN: *The Idea of a Jewish State*, Harvard University Press, Cambridge 1961.

J. C. HUROWITZ: *The Struggle for Palestine*, W. W. Morton, New York 1950.

W. LAQUEUR: *A History of Zionism*, Weidenfeld and Nicolson, London 1972.

E. MONROE: *Britain's Moment in the Middle East*, Chatto and Windus, London 1963.

M. RODINSON: *Israel and the Arabs*, Penguin, Harmondsworth 1968.

C. SYKES: *Crossroads to Israel*, Collins, London 1965.

Indonesia 1945-49

BETWEEN the first and second world wars, many of the Dutch settlers in the Netherlands Indies sought a greater degree of self-government. Among the indigenous inhabitants, nationalist sentiment strengthened, some aiming at constitutional advancement, some at a federal union with the Netherlands, some at complete independence for "Indonesia".

The official Dutch view was that the colony was not ready for self-government. The People's Council was basically only consultative. Almost all the Dutch rejected the idea of independence. There were some 300,000 Europeans and Indo-Europeans in the colony and many of them had made their permanent homes there. The Dutch had a sense of trusteeship towards the indigenous population. The economic links between the Netherlands and the colony were strong.

On 8 March 1942, the Dutch surrendered to the Japanese, who in May of the following year proclaimed the incorporation of the country into their Greater Asian Co-Prosperity Sphere. Even at this time, however, the Japanese did much which eventually assisted independence: they formed an Indonesia Volunteer Army; many of the nationalist leaders, in an alliance of convenience, worked with them in the affairs of the country. As the course of the war turned clearly against Japan, it promised independence (September 1944) and the nationalist leaders began to work out a constitution. On 14 August 1945, Japan surrendered and on the 17th, Mohammed Hatta and Sukarno proclaimed the independent Republic of Indonesia.

In the next few weeks, the Republic established control over the greater part of Java and over parts of Sumatra. On 29 September, British forces arrived to disarm the Japanese and announced that they wished the co-operation of the Republican Government in civil administration. It was also British policy to promote negotiations between the Republican Government and the Dutch. This angered the Dutch. They were beginning to rebuild their own administration and forces. Though prepared to negotiate with the Indonesian nationalists in general, they disliked the Republic because it had been instituted under the Japanese.

The Indonesian leaders at this time were continuously at odds with one another, disagreeing notably on policy towards the Dutch. Some wanted a straightforward stand on independence, by force if necessary; their armed units were much stronger than those of the British and Dutch in numbers. Others counselled negotiation. Eventually, early in the new year

51

(1946) serious discussions got under way between Sutan Sjahrir, Prime Minister of the Republic (Sukarno being President of the Republic, Hatta Vice-President) and the Lieutenant-Governor Dr J. H. van Mook, in Batavia (Djakarta).

Sjahrir's immediate aim was to get recognition of the *de facto* authority of the Republic in the two principal islands, Java and Sumatra; afterwards, more detailed issues including the shape of future relations with the Netherlands would be discussed. The opening position of the Netherlands, on the other hand, as formally stated on 10 February, was that the Netherlands Indies were to have dominion status within a Commonwealth under the Crown. Heated debates followed in the Netherlands Parliament, the outcome of which was that the Republic should be accepted as one state in an Indonesian federation under the Crown. Sjahrir, however, sought sovereignty for the Republic to be followed by an alliance with the Netherlands.

At this point, Sjahrir was temporarily overthrown yet again, and the issue became embroiled in elections in the Netherlands. Van Mook meanwhile held talks with representatives of the outer islands at Malino in the Celebes (July) from which emerged a plan for a United States of Indonesia. The idea of a federation aroused deep suspicion in the Indonesian leaders. They saw it as a device by the Dutch to mobilise the anti-Javanese sentiments and regional nationalism of the other islands so as to create a counter-balance to the Republic. However, urged on by various pressures, notably economic strain and the British warning that they would withdraw by the end of November at the latest, the two sides with British mediation reached an agreement at Linggadjati (Java) on 15 November 1946.

According to this, the Netherlands recognised the *de facto* authority of the Republic in Java and Sumatra; the two would co-operate in forming a sovereign federal United States of Indonesia of which the Republic would be a member; and they would further co-operate in creating a Netherlands–United States of Indonesia Union under the Netherlands Crown, to come into existence by 1 January 1949. Both sides would reduce their troops and the Dutch would evacuate Republican territory.

The two sides immediately differed on the interpretation of the agreement (which was not signed until 25 March 1947) and charges of bad faith multiplied. Notably, the Republic argued that, having the majority of the population, it ought to have the leading place in the federation; the Dutch argued that all the states should have equal rights. The Dutch set up a number of states; the Republic did not agree on these and accused the Dutch of acting unilaterally. The Republic sent representatives to Australia, India, the Middle East and the United States, seeking international recognition and support. The Dutch denounced this as a betrayal of co-operation.

By May, Dutch forces numbered some 100,000. In that month, unwilling to accept a drifting situation any longer, they presented "final proposals" to the Republic. An interim government and a foreign affairs council should be set up consisting of representatives of the Republic, the other Indonesian states and of the Dutch, with the latter having the deciding vote in the event of disagreement. Sjahrir felt obliged to accept these proposals but would not accept a third, that there should be a joint Directorate of Internal Security for the whole country. This he saw as a bid to take control in the territory of the Republic. Sjahrir resigned (and became the Republic's representative at the United Nations) and was succeeded by Amir Sjarifuddin, who took the same stand on the Dutch proposals. The United States intervened at this point to urge the two sides to continue to negotiate, but the deadlock on the third proposal persisted. Finally, on 21 July, the Netherlands, resuming "freedom of action to end an untenable situation", launched what came to be known as the First Dutch Police Action.

Within a few days, the Dutch took over control of the greater part of the Republic's territory, confining it principally to central Java around Jogjakarta. On 31 July, the Security Council passed a resolution calling for a cease-fire and this was given effect on 4 August. However, the Dutch continued "mopping up" operations and "frontier adjustment". On 25 August, the Security Council passed another resolution calling for an end of hostilities. A Soviet proposal that all states on the Security Council should send representatives to the area was not adopted. Instead, a Good Offices Committee of Australia, Belgium and the United States was set up. After lengthy negotiations, the two sides signed an agreement aboard the USS *Renville* on 17 January 1948, which amounted to the ending of hostilities at the existing lines of control, with a plebiscite to be held in the areas taken over from the Republic to see whether they wished to belong to the Republic or not.

In the following months, the Good Offices Committee tried to bring about co-operation between the two sides in setting up a federal government for the United States of Indonesia, but with no success. On 9 March 1948, having gone ahead with a plebiscite on its own, the Dutch announced that they intended to form an interim federal government without the Republic. In the spring and summer, dissension within the Republic intensified, culminating in an attempted Communist *coup d'état* in September.

In November, negotiations were resumed on a joint interim government but deadlock arose over the proposed right of the Dutch representative to order pacification action by Dutch troops wherever he deemed necessary. On 11 December, the Dutch informed the Committee that, negotiations having broken down, they would now set up an interim government without the Republic. In a final flurry of negotiation, the Dutch announced that they would resume hostilities against the Republic unless it forthwith accepted the principle of equality with the other states in the proposed federation. On 19 December 1948 Dutch paratroops surrounded Jogjakarta and the so-called Second Dutch Police Action began. On the 21st, the Republican government surrendered and the Dutch took control of the other towns in its territory.

Guerrilla warfare began, however, and at the United Nations opinion turned sharply and almost unanimously against the Netherlands. A resolution was quickly passed in the Security Council (22 December) condemning its action and calling for an immediate cease-fire and the release of the Republican leaders. On 28 January, a comprehensive resolution was passed calling on the Dutch to stop all military operations, release its political prisoners, and establish a federal government by 15 March. To this end, the Good Offices Committee was transformed into the UN Commission in Indonesia, with the right to initiate political action and to take decisions by majority vote. In the Good Offices Committee, Belgium had tended to share the views of the Dutch whereas Australia and the United States had taken a middle line. Now the United States exerted heavy pressure on the Dutch, including the partial suspension of Marshall Aid.

The Netherlands protested that a federal government could not be formed by March but proposed a Round Table Conference for that month in The Hague. The Republican leaders insisted that they must be released before considering the proposal. Following a further Security Council resolution of 23 March, the Dutch gave way. In April, UNCI presided over talks in Batavia (Djakarta) between the Dutch and Sukarno and Hatta, and in the following weeks, between the Republicans and the leaders of the other states. The latter were now beginning to make common cause with the Republic and a united Indonesian position was hammered out in preparation for the Round Table Conference.

With UNCI in control, the Conference met at The Hague on 23 August 1949 and finally on 2 November an agreement was signed. Sovereignty over the Netherlands Indies was to be transferred to the United States of Indonesia by 30 December. Under Article 2, Netherlands New Guinea (which together with the financial settlement between the Dutch and the Indonesians was the most contentious issue at the Conference) was to remain in charge of the Dutch Residency there pending negotiations on its future status to be held by October 1950. A Netherlands–Indonesian Union was to be formed under the titular headship of the Netherlands

Crown on the basis of absolute equality. Dutch forces would be withdrawn completely. Indonesia would respect the economic rights and concessions granted under Dutch rule and any nationalisation would include compensation, the value of the property being decided by the courts.

On 29 October, at a parallel conference at Scheveningen, representatives of the Republic and of the fifteen other states had signed an agreement on the constitution of the United States of Indonesia, which acknowledged the preponderant position of the Republic, notably in giving it a third of the seats in the Chamber of Deputies though with equal seats in the Senate. On 27 December 1949, the Netherlands formally transferred sovereignty to the new federal state.[1]

*　　*　　*

B. Dahm: *History of Indonesia in the Twentieth Century*, Pall Mall, London 1971.

J. L. Legge: *Sukarno*, Allen Lane, The Penguin Press, London 1972.

R. McVey: *Indonesia*, Human Relations Area Files Inc., New Haven, rev. ed., 1967.

L. H. Palmier: *Indonesia and the Dutch*, Oxford University Press, 1962.

A. M. Taylor: *Indonesian Independence and the United Nations*, Stevens, London 1960.

[1] For subsequent constitutional developments, see p. 83 ff.

Korea 1945-53

FOR centuries a dependency of China and subsequently a bone of contention between Russia and Japan, Korea was formally annexed by Japan in 1910. In the Cairo Declaration of 1 December 1943, Churchill, Chiang Kai-shek and Roosevelt stated that the country "in due course shall become free and independent". At the Yalta Conference in February 1945, Roosevelt and Stalin agreed that the Russians should accept the surrender of the Japanese in the north, the Americans in the south. Military representatives of the two countries reached an understanding that the line for this purpose should be the 38th parallel.

That month, the Russians arrived in the north and the following month, the Americans in the south. At the Moscow Conference of December, the foreign ministers of Britain, the Soviet Union and the United States (China adhered later) decided on a four-power trusteeship of Korea for a period of up to five years and established a Joint Commission of the Soviet Union and the United States to arrange a provisional government in consultation with "Korean democratic parties and organisations".

When the Joint Commission met in Seoul in March 1946, however, there was rapid disagreement on what should count as a "democratic party". The Soviet representatives argued that the test was acceptance of the decisions of the Moscow Conference; but the Americans, seeing that this would probably mean only the Communists since everyone else in Korea was showing vehement opposition to the trusteeship scheme, would not agree. The meeting broke up in disagreement in May.

The two sides now proceeded separately in north and south, the Russians using the Communists, the Americans the nationalist parties. A further meeting of the Joint Commission in May 1947 brought no better result; in September 1947, the United States raised the question in the United Nations General Assembly; and in January 1948, a United Nations Temporary Commission on Korea arrived in the country. Refused entry to the north, it observed the elections in the south on 10 May 1948. The National Assembly so elected adopted a constitution on 17 July, elected Dr Syngman Rhee to the presidency on the 20th and inaugurated the Republic of Korea on 15 August with its capital at Seoul. In the north, the Russians promoted the formation of a Supreme National Assembly which on 9 September proclaimed the Democratic People's Republic of Korea with its capital at Pyongyang. On 12 December, the UN General Assembly declared that the government of the Republic of Korea was the only legal government in Korea. The leading countries of the world established diplomatic relations with it except the Soviet Union which, with its allies, recognised the People's Republic.

Over the next few months, the Soviet Union and the United States withdrew their forces. Little is known of the subsequent dealings of the Soviet Government with the North Korean but general dominant influence seems certain. It maintained a very large military mission and gave considerable military aid. As to North Korean relations with the Chinese Communists, there are some indications that these were wary, even cool.

United States relations with South Korea were in some respects cordial, in others troubled. In the heated public controversy on Far Eastern affairs following "the fall of China", official statements indicated that Korea played little part in the Administration's strategic security thinking but it did sign a Mutual Defense Assistance Agreement in January 1950. The Administration persuaded a disaffected Congress to vote $160 million economic aid in the session 1949–50, but little military aid was given. At the same time, the United States was dismayed by the rapid decline in popularity of Syngman Rhee. When Rhee sought to postpone the elections of May 1950, the United States insisted that they be held. The results suggested that the population were equally discontented with the Rhee regime and the opposition politicians; 133 of the 210 seats were won by non-party candidates.

Relations between the North Korean and South Korean governments were increasingly bitter. Both were committed to unification and denounced the other as illegal. Throughout 1949, the South Koreans complained of border incidents and of a military build-up in the North and urged United States military aid and uttered occasional threatening statements. On 7 June 1950, following the elections in the South, the North Korean Government declared that all-Korean elections should be held, observed by the UN Commission, but excluding the members of the Rhee government. On the 19th, it proposed that the Assemblies of the North and South should hold a joint meeting looking to unification but again it excluded "Rhee and his treacherous gang" and again the Rhee government denounced the idea.

Despite this bitter atmosphere in Korea and the wider background of tension between the Western powers and the Soviet Union and China, the outbreak of war in Korea on 25 June was unexpected by the Western powers and still remains in some respects mysterious. What was certain to the Western powers, however, was that the North Korean army was advancing deep into the South and that far more was at stake than the future of Korea. The UN Security Council met on the 25th and, in the absence of the Soviet representative,[1] passed a resolution calling on the North Koreans to withdraw and upon all UN members to "render every assistance to the United Nations in the execution of this resolution and to refrain from giving assistance to the North Korean authorities". On the 26th, President Truman ordered United States sea and air cover and support to the South Korean forces. In a broadcast on the 27th, President Truman announced these first measures and stated the wider context in which the United States saw the matter. "The attack upon Korea makes it plain beyond all doubt that Communism has passed beyond the use of subversion to conquer independent nations and will now use armed invasion and war." Later that day, the Security Council passed a further resolution recommending that members "furnish such assistance to the Republic of Korea as may be necessary to repel the armed attack and restore international peace and security in the area". Three days later (30 June) President Truman decided to send ground troops to support the South Koreans, and to blockade the Korean coast.

Throughout July, the South Korean and United States forces retreated until only an enclave around the port of Pusan in the south-east remained. Meanwhile, however, the United States Far Eastern Commander, General Douglas C. MacArthur, poured in reinforcements. On 7 July, the Security Council established a unified command and on the following day President Truman designated MacArthur to be UN Commander. In August, a British contingent arrived and over the next few months fourteen other states contributed forces, though even then the United States and South Korea provided the bulk of the ground troops (50 per cent and 40 per cent), and the United States most of the air and sea forces. On 15 September, General MacArthur launched his counter-stroke, a simultaneous break-out from the Pusan enclave and sea-borne landing at Inchon, the port of Seoul. In the last days of the month, Seoul was retaken. On the 29th, President Syngman Rhee was re-established there and the clearing of the rest of South Korea was near completion.

At this point, the question of how to handle the underlying problem of divided Korea arose once more. The United States believed that the suppression of the North Korean forces was essential and fully justified and had already directed General MacArthur (15 September) to occupy the North, provided there was no sign of Soviet or Chinese intervention. Other UN members had some doubt whether such action would be legitimate or prudent and a few, notably India, were strongly opposed. On 1 October, General MacArthur ordered South Korean forces across the 38th parallel. On the 3rd, India transmitted a warning from China that it would not tolerate the crossing of United States forces. The United

[1] See p. 75.

States believed Chinese intervention unlikely and dismissed this and other warnings as attempts to influence the forthcoming General Assembly debate. On the 7th, the Assembly recommended with little opposition (47–5, the Soviet bloc, and 7 abstentions, Egypt, India, Lebanon, Saudi Arabia, Syria, Yemen, Yugoslavia) the taking of "all appropriate steps" towards a unified government of Korea. This was generally understood as sanctioning the occupation of the North.[2]

Two days later, MacArthur's forces began a general offensive northwards. At a meeting with President Truman on Wake Island on 15 October, MacArthur reaffirmed his belief that Chinese intervention was unlikely and could in any event be withstood. As his first units reached the Yalu river, the border with China (27 October), they clashed with Chinese units (described by China throughout the war as "volunteers"). A lull ensued in which there was some uncertainty in Washington and, under British and Indian persuasion, the Security Council invited China to send representatives (8 November). On 11 November, China accepted the invitation but stated that the Taiwan issue must be discussed first.[3] On 24 November, General MacArthur resumed his advance. On the 26th, the Chinese launched a full-scale offensive and by the end of the following month had cleared North Korea and recaptured Seoul.

The General Assembly now adopted (14 December) an Afro-Asian proposal for a three-man group to consult the opposing high commands on a basis for a cease-fire. The Chinese representatives rejected this idea, claiming as always (as did the Soviet bloc) that United Nations action in Korea was illegal, and declaring as they left New York on 20 December that China would not withdraw from Korea until the United States had done so and had ceased to protect the Nationalists on Taiwan. The three-man group was none the less set up, led by Lester Pearson of Canada, and on 15 January 1951, recommended a cease-fire, the mutual withdrawal of troops, and interim measures for the administration of Korea. China rejected these proposals in the same terms as before. The United States Administration had been sceptical of these efforts and now the anger of the American public against China could no longer be restrained. On 1 February, the Assembly adopted a United States resolution declaring that China "has itself engaged in aggression in Korea".

Against the background of mounting pressure among UN members for a cease-fire, General MacArthur decided to take action on his own account.

---

[2] The United States had shifted the scene of action to the Assembly in view of the return of the Soviet Union to the Security Council with its veto on 1 August. The high-point of United States efforts to give the Assembly security responsibility, the Uniting for Peace Resolution, whereby it could recommend action if the Council was unable, was passed on 3 November.

[3] See pp. 74–6.

On 23 March, he offered personal discussions with the opposing side to end the war and included a veiled threat to attack China if the offer was not accepted. On the 29th, China replied defiantly. MacArthur's willingness to widen the war was the latest in various points of friction between himself and President Truman who was determined that the war remain limited, and deeply alarmed the United States's allies. On 11 April, President Truman relieved him of his command, causing great domestic uproar, and appointed General Mathew Ridgway instead.

At this point the Chinese advance was brought to a halt; in May, Ridgway moved on to the offensive; in June, his troops were again across the 38th parallel at many places. On 23 June, the Soviet President of the Security Council, Dr Jacob Malik, made a broadcast suggesting a cease-fire and agreement was rapidly reached that representatives of the Chinese Volunteer Army, the North Korean army and the United Nations forces should meet at Kaesong. Their discussions began on 10 July, collapsed on 5 August amid mutual accusations of infringements of the talks zone, and were resumed on 25 October at Panmunjon.

The discussions dragged on for nearly two years. The UN negotiators succeeded comparatively quickly in confining the agenda to the war (i.e. excluding such issues as Taiwan and the withdrawal of forces from Korea). Agreement on an armistice line was more difficult. The Chinese and North Koreans argued for the 38th parallel but the UN negotiators insisted on the existing line of battle which would accord South Korea more territory on the whole and was militarily more defensible. By the end of the year, this line was agreed with a demilitarised zone two and a half miles wide along it. A cease-fire put an end to the intermittent fighting in March 1952 and by May, all points had been agreed except the question of prisoners-of-war, which proved the most difficult of all.

The Communist negotiators argued that all prisoners should be re-patriated whereas the UN negotiators insisted that they should be allowed to choose. Deadlock persisted throughout 1952. In January 1953, a Republican Administration took office in the United States, drastically anti-Communist in utterance and specifically pledged to bringing the war to a conclusion. In March, Stalin died. On 8 June, the two sides agreed that the proposed Neutral Nations Supervisory Commission, which together with the Joint Military Armistice Commission was to administer the armistice, should take temporary charge of prisoners not wishing to return home and give their home side the chance to interview them. (In the end, nearly three-quarters of the Chinese prisoners-of-war chose to go to Taiwan.) On 27 July, the armistice was at last signed.

The armistice was only an armed truce pending a settlement of the Korean question but it was clear that this would be difficult to achieve.

The two Korean governments were as hostile to each other as ever. The UN General Assembly began discussions of a conference on Korea on 17 August 1953 but by the end of the Assembly session no agreement had been reached on the composition of the conference, notably, on the participation of the Soviet Union. On 1 October 1953, the United States and South Korea signed a Mutual Defense Treaty.

At the Berlin Conference of January–February 1954 on the German question, the foreign ministers of Britain, France, the United States and the Soviet Union agreed (18 February) to call a meeting at Geneva on Korea and Indo-China.[4] The participants assembled in the last days of April but, whereas the conference on Indo-China achieved a cease-fire, the simultaneous conference on Korea, attended by all the states that had fought and the Soviet Union, did not achieve a political settlement. The Western position was that the first step towards the establishment of a united and independent Korea should be free elections for an Assembly representing the whole of Korea, supervised by the United Nations. China and North Korea insisted that the first step should be the withdrawal of all foreign troops and maintained their hostility to any form of United Nations involvement in Korea. The discussions came to an end in mid-June by mutual consent and Korea remained divided.

*   *   *

L. GOODRICH: *Korea, A Study of United States Policy in the United Nations*, Council on Foreign Relations, New York 1956.

L. GORDENKER: *The United Nations and the Peaceful Unification of Korea 1947–50*, Nijhoff, The Hague 1959.

G. PAIGE: *The Korean Decision, June 24–30 1950*, Free Press, New York 1968.

D. REES: *Korea, The Limited War*, Macmillan, London 1964.

I. STONE: *The Hidden History of the Korean War*, Monthly Review Press, New York, 2nd ed., 1969.

A. WHITING: *China Crosses the Yalu*, Macmillan, New York 1960.

[4] See pp. 62–7.

Indo-China 1945-54

OF the three ancient kingdoms of Cambodia, Laos and Annam, the first two, comparatively sparsely populated, were under Indian cultural influence, the third under Chinese. The capital of Annam was Hué, but at most periods the kingdom extended to the richer lands of the Red River delta to the north (Tongking) and the Mekong delta to the south (Cochin-China).

The French conquered Cochin-China in 1863 and made it a colony; and Cambodia in 1867, Tongking and Annam in 1883, and Laos in 1893, which they made protectorates, calling the whole French Indo-China, with a governor-general at the capital, Hanoi. French settlers started rubber plantations in the south and minerals extraction in the north.

From the beginning of the century, with the rise of Japan and the gradual increase of French-educated Annamese, respect for French culture strengthened but so also did opposition to their political and economic dominance. On the popular level, there was traditional resentment of Chinese traders and of landlords and desire for land reform. The pattern of development of opposition followed that of China. The Nationalist Party of "Vietnam" was established at Canton in 1914, the Communist Party by Nguyen Ai Quoc (Ho Chi Minh) at Hong Kong in 1930. The French suppressed the Nationalist Party after an abortive rising in 1930 but gave the Communists some respite when the Soviet Union ordered the world-wide "united front" in 1935.

Following the defeat of France by Germany in May 1940, the Vichy French governor-general signed a treaty with the Japanese (22 September) who occupied the whole of Indo-China in the course of 1941. In May 1941, Ho Chi Minh and the Communists, who had hitherto preached full-blooded Communism (collectivisation of the land and the like) with little rural success, gathered together various smaller groups into a Vietnam Independence League (Vietminh) with a programme of opposition to French and Japanese imperialism, land to the peasants, and the development of the national economy in private hands. Guerrilla warfare began and in 1944 the scattered units were drawn together into a liberation army by General Vo Guyen Giap and officers trained like him by the Chinese Communists. By early 1945, this army controlled the countryside of Tongking and was penetrating further south.

In March 1945, as the war turned against the Japanese, they dismissed the Vichy French, declared the three states independent and set up governments under the kings of Cambodia and Laos and the Emperor of Annam, Bao Dai. The Vietminh would not accept this, however, and on the surrender of Japan (August) Bao Dai abdicated, and the Vietminh proclaimed the Democratic Republic of Vietnam on 2 September and its independence on 7 September. Ho Chi Minh became president and set up his government at Hanoi, with a developing degree of control of the south also, including Saigon.

Meanwhile, the Allied powers had agreed at Potsdam in August that the Nationalist Chinese should accept the surrender of the Japanese in Indo-China north of the 16th parallel, and the British to the south, and these arrived in mid-September. The British did not recognise the Vietminh government and on 1 January 1946, the French assumed formal military control in the south, though in practice the Vietminh remained strong over much of the countryside. In the north, on the other hand, the Chinese recognised the Vietminh government and elections were held on 6 January in Tongking and Annam (and secretly in some southern areas) in which the Vietminh gained the majority in the National Assembly.

The French now negotiated an agreement with Cambodia whereby they recognised the formal independence of the kingdom, while retaining control of major affairs. In Laos, the Chinese had made a government out of an independence movement known as Lao-issarak, but when the Chinese withdrew, the French suppressed it and made the same arrangements as in Cambodia.

Ho Chi Minh also decided to negotiate with the French and a broad agreement was eventually reached at Hanoi on 6 March 1946. By this, the French recognised the Republic of Vietnam but, with Cambodia and Laos, it was to be a member of an Indo-Chinese Federation which in turn would be a member of a French Union. The Chinese withdrew in April.

French forces moved into the north, as agreed at Hanoi, but little progress was made at the further conference held at Dalat in April. The French wanted a strong federation, the Republic a weak one. Moreover, the French officials and settlers in Saigon wanted to keep the south, Cochin-China, out of the hands of the Republic. It had been agreed at Hanoi that a referendum should be held to decide this but on the day after the departure of the Vietnamese delegation led by Ho Chi Minh for further talks in France, the French High Commissioner (established in Saigon), Admiral Thierry d'Argenlieu, announced the setting up of a provisional government of Cochin-China (1 June). He then held a further constitutional conference at Dalat (1 August) to which only Cambodia, Laos and representatives of Cochin-China were invited.

In France itself at this time, the government appears to have paid only limited attention to the talks which began at Fontainbleu on 6 July and the public was preoccupied with other matters. The Vietnamese maintained a strong stand on the federation issue and at the same time resented what was being done by the French in Saigon. The talks ended in failure on 14 September. Ho Chi Minh, who may have had greater hopes of the new government of Léon Blum than his own extremists, remained behind for a while after the departure of the Vietnamese delegation. A *modus vivendi* was reached, covering economic matters and calling on both sides to end the clashes which had now begun between French and Vietminh forces.

However, on 24 November 1946 a major clash occurred when French forces sought to take control of the Haiphong customs. On 19 December, the Vietminh army launched a concerted attack on the French garrisons in Tongking and Amman. These events marked the start of eight years war.

The Vietminh in the early years used the guerrilla tactics which they had developed against the Japanese. The French concentrated on protecting the urban areas. Meanwhile, they looked about for a form of regime which would win the support of the people and the allegiance of those nationalists who were uneasy in their alliance with the Communists.

On 4 February 1947, Admiral d'Argenlieu on his own initiative declared Cochin-China a separate state and, though he was dismissed, Paris maintained this arrangement. The government was headed by Nguyen Van Xuan, formerly a general in the French army.

The French also began negotiations with the former emperor, Bao Dai, with a view to making him head of an alternative government to the Vietminh in Tongking and Annam. Bao Dai made conditions, however, notably rule over Cochin-China as well, thus preserving the unity of Vietnam; a Vietnam national army; and a degree of control over foreign relations. After eighteen months of negotiations, the French substantially conceded these points. By the Elysée Agreements of 8 March 1949, Cambodia, Laos and Vietnam became independent Associated States within the French Union. The new, alternative state of Vietnam was proclaimed on 5 July and Bao Dai became Prime Minister.

Over the following years, the Bao Dai government had only limited success. It ruled limply, it offered little to the peasants, it failed to draw together the various elements of active opposition to the Communists, notably the Catholic local defence groups of the north and the armed sects in the south, the Cao Dai and the Hoa Hao. Many nationalists were alienated by its subordination to the French but, on the other hand, many were alienated from the Vietminh by its growing links with Communist China (see below) and yet their allegiance was not won.

In October 1949, the Chinese Communists completed their conquest of mainland China. After some exchanges in which Ho Chi Minh appears to have favoured a neutral position in the conflict between the United States and the Soviet Union, Ho Chi Minh recognised Mao Tse-tung's government (December) and this was reciprocated (January) with the Soviet Union immediately following suit. Chinese assistance now increased, as did supplies of Soviet armaments through China. In the following year, the Vietnamese Communist Party was reorganised with a programme following that of China.

Meanwhile, on 7 February 1950, the United States recognised the three French-sponsored governments of Indo-China, as did Britain and others. United States financial aid to France had already included some for use in Indo-China and now the United States announced that the Government of Vietnam could expect economic and military aid in combating "internal dissension fostered from abroad".[1] This assistance increased until by 1954 the United States was financing three-quarters of what had become an enormous war effort.

Despite this, the war went badly for the French. General Jean de Lattre de Tassigny, who recognised the importance of counter-guerrilla tactics, gained some success and improved French morale but died early in 1952. His successor, General Henri-Eugène Navarre, in co-operation with United States military advisers, sought to consolidate French control in the delta areas, making drives outwards to gain prongs of rural territory. Overall, the aim was to cut the supply lines from China to Tongking and to seal off Laos, where in 1953 the successor of the Lao-issarak, the Pathet Lao, launched a campaign against the French and the Vientiane Government with Chinese and Vietnamese assistance. This involved military operations in the north where the French were most vulnerable and where the final disaster of Dien Bien Phu was to occur.

On the political front, French public opinion became increasingly aroused by the bloodshed and lack of success in the war, and in Indo-China the three Associated States began to seek complete independence from the French. On 3 July 1953, the French Government announced that the time had come to "perfect" the sovereignty of these states. This was done for Cambodia on 9 November 1953, involving notably the transfer of command of the Cambodian Army. It was done for the other two states in December 1954 after the end of the Indo-China war.

On 25 January 1954, the Foreign Ministers of Britain, France, the Soviet Union and the United States met in Berlin to negotiate on the German question and, as a by-product of this, after many soundings among the governments involved, agreed (18 February) to call a conference at Geneva to discuss the problems of Korea and Indo-China. On 13 March, the Communists began the siege of a French force in Dien Bien Phu. As

[1] US State Department, *Bulletin*, 20 February 1950, p. 291.

this critical battle developed, the question of direct American armed support became acute, but although the United States Secretary of State, John Foster Dulles, was in favour, the United States Chiefs of Staff, the Congress and important sections of American public opinion were not, and neither would America's allies agree to support such action.

In the last days of April the conference assembled at Geneva consisting of delegations from Cambodia, Laos, the two governments of Vietnam, France, China, the United States, Britain and the Soviet Union, with representatives of the latter two states acting as joint chairmen. The United States Secretary of State came to the conference initially but on 1 May handed over responsibility to the Under-Secretary, Mr Walter Bedell Smith, and left Geneva. On 7 May, Dien Bien Phu fell to General Giap's forces. On 12 June, Pierre Mendès-France formed a new French Government, stating that he would resign if he could not announce a settlement by 20 July. After long and hard negotiations, cease-fire agreements were signed on that day on behalf of the commanders of the French and Communist forces for Vietnam and Laos and on the following day for Cambodia.

The implementation of all the agreements was to be supervised by an International Commission, supplied by Canada, India and Poland, reporting to Britain and the Soviet Union as co-chairmen of the Conference. The agreements for Cambodia and Laos provided that the French and Communist forces would withdraw, except that in Laos the French would retain two bases and military training personnel. The Pathet Lao forces, pending a political settlement with the Vientiane Government, were to withdraw to the north-east provinces of the country.

The agreement for Vietnam provided that the forces of the French Union and of the People's Army of Vietnam would, within three hundred days, withdraw behind a narrow demilitarised zone along a line roughly following the 17th parallel. Pending elections to bring about the unification of the country, each side would be responsible for the administration of its zone. During the three hundred days, civilians would be assisted to move to the zone of their choice. No new forces were to be brought into either zone and neither zone would join any military alliance.

At the concluding session of the conference on 21 July, a Final Declaration, headed with the names of the delegations (except that of the United States) was read out. This included an article (7) saying that "general elections shall be held in July 1956 under the supervision of an international commission. . . . Consultations will be held on this subject between the competent representative authorities of the two zones from July 20, 1955."

The delegation representing the Bao Dai government of Vietnam made a statement at the concluding session protesting against the armistice and denying the right of the French to make it and, specifically, to give the undertaking on general elections. However, they also stated that they would not use force. Mr Bedell Smith, on behalf of the United States, made a "unilateral declaration" taking note of the agreements, undertaking to refrain from the threat or use of force to disturb them, stating that it would view any renewal of aggression in violation of the agreements with grave concern and noting its traditional support for the self-determination of peoples by free elections.[2]

* * *

V. BATOR: *Vietnam, A Diplomatic Tragedy: the Origins of United States Involvement*, Dobbs Ferry, New York 1965.

A. W. CAMERON: *Vietnam Crisis, A Documentary History*, Vol. I 1940–56, Cornell University Press, Ithaca 1971.

P. DEVILLERS: *Histoire du Vietnam de 1940 à 1952*, Editions du Seuil, Paris 1952.

B. FALL: *Street Without Joy, Insurgency in Indo-China, 1946–63*, Pall Mall, London 1963.

E. J. HAMMER: *The Struggle for Indo-China, 1940–55*, Stanford University Press, rev. ed., 1966.

J. LACOUTURE: *Ho Chi Minh*, Penguin, Harmondsworth 1968.

D. LANCASTER: *The Emancipation of French Indo-China*, Oxford University Press, 1961.

[2] For subsequent events in Vietnam see pp. 99–104; and in Laos, pp. 106–11.

Kashmir 1947–66

THE Indian Independence Act of 18 July 1947 provided for the independence of British India and for its partition into India and Pakistan. The Indian National Congress Party leaders had opposed the idea of Pakistan, seeing it as a secession from an undivided Hindu–Muslim India; but the Muslim League had insisted on the necessity of a separate Muslim state. The two states became independent on 15 August in deep mutual bitterness, intensified over the next three months by the great massacres and migrations which ensued in the divided Punjab.

The Indian Independence Act also provided for the ending of the paramountcy of the British Crown over the princely states and of its treaty relationships with them. Legally speaking, they were free to decide their own future. By the time of independence, however, most of them had agreed to accede to the Indian Union, giving up their control of communications, defence and foreign affairs. (Later, they gave up their internal autonomy also.) After some months of disorder in the small state of Junagadh, during which the Moslem Nawab acceded to Pakistan and India backed the wishes of the predominantly Hindu population, India took control of the state in November 1947. After a long period of disorder in the great state of Hyderabad, also predominantly Hindu with a Muslim ruler, India finally took control in September 1948. The remaining problem was the state of Jammu and Kashmir.

In this state, the ruler was a Hindu, Maharajah Sir Hari Singh, with a predominantly Muslim population. (There were some 3 million Muslims and some 800,000 Hindus, the latter mostly in Jammu in the south.) Though the Muslims hated their ruler, they were not all enthusiasts for Pakistan. The leading Muslim politician of Srinagar, the capital, Sheikh Abdullah, was an ally of the Congress and a friend of Jawarhalal Nehru, himself a Kashmiri Brahmin.

As independence approached, the Viceroy, Lord Louis Mountbatten, urged the Maharajah to make up his mind to accede to either India or Pakistan, consulting so far as possible the will of the people. It does not appear that Gandhi, Nehru or Sardar Vallabhbhai Patel, the Indian minister charged with negotiating with the princes, sought to influence the decision. Nor does it appear that the leaders of Pakistan sought to establish relations with the Maharajah in his dilemma. The Maharajah continued to vacillate. On 12 August, three days before independence, he merely announced that he wished to make agreements with India and

Pakistan (called in the jargon of the partition period "standstill agreements") whereby existing arrangements on communications and the like would continue. An agreement was signed with Pakistan on the 15th. The Indians made no immediate response.

In the weeks after Independence Day, the situation within Jammu-Kashmir, against the background of the events in the Punjab, became steadily more inflammable. Already in July, the Muslims of the sub-principality of Poonch in the south-west had revolted against the Maharajah in favour of accession to Pakistan. In central Kashmir, Muslim deserters from the state army had formed the Azad Kashmir Army, demanding an independent government for the state.

At the end of August, the Maharajah released Sheikh Abdullah from jail and this was interpreted by the Muslims as a move in the direction of India. Early in October, as a group of Muslims proclaimed a "provisional republican government" in the south-west, there were reports that Pathan tribesmen were moving in from Pakistan. The Government of Pakistan protested to the Kashmir Government of Hindu attacks on Muslim villages; the Kashmir Government counter-charged it with connivance at the movement of the Pathans and warned that it might call in "friendly assistance"; the Government of Pakistan replied that this would be a suppression of the will of the people of the state.

On about 20 October, a large force of Pathans crossed the western border of the state and began to advance on Srinagar. In this crisis, the Maharajah appointed Sheikh Abdullah to form an emergency government, appealed to India for assistance, and offered to accede. After deliberations with the Indian ministers, Mountbatten, now Governor-General, replied (27 October) that India would send troops to help defend the state. It accepted the accession but "it is my Government's wish that, as soon as law and order have been restored in Kashmir and its soil cleared of the invader, the question of the State's accession should be settled by a reference to the people". On the following day, a small Indian force was airlifted to Srinagar and other units followed.

Mountbatten sought to bring the governments of India and Pakistan together. However, on the 31st, Pakistan denounced the accession as based on fraud and violence. The Indians for their part were convinced that the Pakistan Government was behind the Pathan invasion.[1] Mountbatten himself talked with Mohammed Ali Jinnah, leader and now Governor-General of Pakistan, in Lahore on 1 November but inconclusively. On the 26th–

---

[1] The balance of authoritative opinion seems to be that leading members and officials of the North West Frontier Province Government assisted the invasion and that some members of the Pakistan Central Government may have known of it.

28th, Liaquat Ali Khan, Prime Minister of Pakistan, talked at length with Prime Minister Nehru in Delhi and eventually proposed that Pakistan would arrange the withdrawal of the invaders, India would withdraw the bulk of its forces, and the United Nations would be asked to hold a plebiscite. But subsequently the emotions of both sides were further inflamed by suspicions of trickery and reports of atrocities. It appears that the Pakistan authorities sought to get rid of the Pathans but it protested that it was unable to prevent volunteers entering Kashmir. These rapidly increased the Azad Kashmir Army into a force equal to the Indians.

On 1 January 1948, India appealed against Pakistan to the Security Council. After a resolution of 17 January calling for a cease-fire, another resolution of 20 January established a UN Commission for India and Pakistan (UNCIP) consisting of three, later five, members from Argentina, Belgium, Colombia, Czechoslovakia, and the United States. The Commission finally arrived in the sub-continent early in July. After negotiations, the Commission passed a resolution on 13 August 1948 incorporating a Truce Agreement according to which Pakistan troops and nationals would withdraw; the evacuated territory would be administered by the "local authorities" under the surveillance of the Commission, pending a final solution; and India would then withdraw the bulk of its forces by stages. The resolution also provided that the two sides would hold consultations looking to a plebiscite to settle the future of the state. On 1 January 1949, the cease-fire came into effect (ratified in Karachi the following 27 July) with the Indians controlling roughly the southern half of the state including the capital and the northern remaining as Azad Kashmir. A UN Military Observer Group (UNMOGIP) was stationed on the cease-fire line.

Though both sides agreed to the August resolution (endorsed by the Security Council itself on 5 January 1949) it was not implemented. In a maze of interpretation and counter-interpretation, the gist of India's argument was that it had legal responsibility for Kashmir until the people decided otherwise. If it withdrew, there was no knowing what Pakistan or its supporters in the state would do. Pakistan, for its part, was reluctant to withdraw in the absence of certainty that India would do likewise. It argued that a genuine plebiscite could not be held so long as India maintained its legal responsibility and therefore control of half the state.

In March 1950, an Australian, Sir Owen Dixon, was appointed UN mediator and his report in September advised partition along the existing cease-fire. Although at one point agreement on this seemed imminent, both sides eventually rejected it. In 1951, an American, Dr Frank Graham, took over the work and continued to negotiate with the two sides (until 1958) but without success.

Over the next few years, India took steps which confirmed the incorporation of Jammu-Kashmir (in practice, the part which India held) into the Indian Union. In February 1951, Sheikh Abdullah, the Prime Minister, announced the calling of a Constituent Assembly. This was condemned by the Security Council on 30 March as contrary to its 1949 resolution but India denied this and the work went on. In July 1952, Sheikh Abdullah and Nehru signed the Delhi Agreement which confirmed that Jammu-Kashmir was part of the Indian Union but with special rights and privileges, for example the right to an elected head of state. (Hereditary rule came to an end in October 1952; the Maharajah had left the state in 1950 and his son, appointed regent at the time, was now elected head of state.) The Sheikh's pressure for such privileges and his leanings towards autonomy, if not independence for the state, led to a rift between him and Nehru, and in 1953 he was arrested and replaced by Bakshi Ghulam Mohammed. The permanent constitution for the state came partially into force on 17 November 1956 and fully on 26 January 1957.

Pakistan sought at the United Nations to prevent these developments, proposing mutual withdrawal from Jammu-Kashmir, and the stationing of a UN force, followed by a plebiscite. On 24 January, the Security Council passed a "holding resolution", sponsored among others by Britain and the United States (the Soviet Union abstaining). A further resolution, with Britain and the United States again among the sponsores, according to which the President of the Security Council was to hold talks with the two sides, was passed in February; but their proposal that the idea of a UN force should be borne in mind, was vetoed by the Soviet Union.

Nehru was impatient with these UN resolutions. He had stated bluntly in 1956 that the idea of a plebiscite was obsolete though partition might be possible, and had argued in 1957 that the electoral victory of Bakshi Ghulam Mohammed sufficiently confirmed the desire of the Kashmiris for integration with India. Indian opinion was angered by the resolutions, especially the sponsorship by Britain and the United States. The resolutions reflected an international pattern in which Britain and the United States stood with Pakistan on this issue, their SEATO and Baghdad Pact ally since 1954, against India supported by the Soviet Union. However, a complete rupture was avoided by all parties. Britain and the United States gave economic aid to both countries. The two countries even agreed between themselves on one outstanding economic problem. After eight years of discussions under the auspices of the International Bank, India and Pakistan signed the Indus Waters Treaty on 19 September 1960.

When in October 1962 the border war between India and China broke out,[2] Britain and the United States pressed for a *rapprochement* between the two countries and in November–December there were exchanges

[2] See p. 158.

between them with a view to a meeting between Nehru and President Muhammad Ayub Khan. The exchanges were fruitless, however. India stuck to its position, formally adopted in 1958, that it was no longer bound by its plebiscite undertaking of ten years previously. The question of partition was raised, it seems, but while Pakistan wanted the Chenab Valley, India was only prepared to concede marginal adjustments to the cease-fire line. In the following year (March 1963), President Ayub visited Peking to complete, much to the anger of the Indians, a Sino-Pakistani border agreement covering Azad Kashmir. A degree of *entente* between Pakistan and China henceforth became a factor in the calculations of India, the United States and the Soviet Union, all three by now in conflict with China.

In October 1963, India announced that changes were being planned to bring the constitutional procedures of Jammu-Kashmir more closely into line with those of India as a whole. This led to a renewed wave of unrest among Muslims, jealous for the autonomy of the state, and there were also outbreaks of communal violence. Nehru, in the last months before his death (27 May 1964) continued to seek a *modus vivendi* with the state, releasing Sheikh Abdullah from prison in April.

On 4 December 1964, India announced that it was about to bring the electoral laws of the state into agreement with those of India. Exasperation at this further action, perhaps combined with such factors as the unrest in state, the weakness of India in the Sino-Indian border war of 1962 and the *entente* with China, now led to a stronger line by Pakistan. Clashes between Pakistani and Indian border guards broke out in March 1965 on the Bengal frontier. In April, further clashes occurred in the Rann of Kutch, a bleak coastal area between West Pakistan and India where the frontier had never been fully demarcated. Tension mounted and both countries moved sizeable formations to the area.

Agreements to settle the Rann of Kutch issue peacefully were reached on 30 June but tension continued to rise. Sheikh Abdullah, who had held talks in Algiers with the Chinese Prime Minister, Chou En-lai, had been re-arrested on 8 May. In Azad Kashmir, the call had gone out for freedom fighters to liberate the state. At this point, India, it seems, made the first military move, attacking Pakistani positions across the cease-fire line on 14–15 August. On 1 September, the Pakistanis mounted a counter-attack. On the 4th the Security Council called for a cease-fire and withdrawal by both sides. On the 6th, two Indian columns crossed the Pakistan frontier proper. On the 7th, the UN Secretary-General, U Thant, arrived to hold talks with the parties but on the 15th reported no progress.

Meanwhile, the United States and Britain suspended their military aid programmes with the two countries (8th). China applied pressure to India

(17th) by threatening "grave consequences" if it did not withdraw certain frontier posts in Sikkim within three days. On the same day, Alexei Kosygin, the Soviet Prime Minister, offered his services as mediator. As the diplomacy continued, the Chinese ultimatum was extended by a further three days. The Security Council again called for a cease-fire (20th). On the 22nd, India announced a cease-fire, subject to Pakistan's consent which was signified, and accepted the Soviet offer of mediation.

The UN Secretary-General now announced (23rd) the strengthening of UNMOGIP and the setting up of a further body, the UN India and Pakistan Observer Mission (UNIPOM) to observe the rest of the cease-fire line down to the Rann of Kutch. The talks between the Indian Prime Minister, Lal Bahadur Shastri, and Ayub Khan with Kosygin's mediation eventually took place in Tashkent from 3–10 January 1966. The result was the Tashkent Declaration, according to which both sides would withdraw to the 1949 cease-fire line; they would resume normal relations; the propaganda war would end; and at a future date talks on Kashmir would be held. The tension between the two countries eased greatly, the mood in India being further subdued by the death of Shastri on the day following the agreement. UNIPOM was withdrawn. The Kashmir issue remained, however. Pakistan still held that there should be a plebiscite. The state's own relations with India continued restless.

* * *

W. J. BARNDS: *India, Pakistan and the Great Powers*, Praeger, New York 1972.

C. B. BIRDWOOD: *Two Nations and Kashmir*, Hale, London 1956.

R. BRINES: *The Indo-Pakistani Conflict*, Pall Mall, London 1968.

G. W. CHOUDHURY: *Pakistan's Relations with India 1947–66*, Pall Mall, London 1968.

S. GUPTA: *Kashmir, A Study in India-Pakistan Relations*, Asia Publishing House, London 1966.

H. V. HODSON: *The Great Divide, Britain, India, Pakistan*, Hutchinson, London 1969.

J. KORBEL: *Danger in Kashmir*, Princeton University Press, 1954.

China, Taiwan and the United Nations 1949-71

IN the summer of 1949, the Chinese Communists finally won control of the mainland and, on 1 October, the Central People's Government of the People's Republic of China was formally inaugurated. The defeated Nationalist (Kuomintang) Government and forces and their leader, General Chiang Kai-shek, fled to the island of Taiwan (Formosa).[1]

These events presented the other states of the world with the twin issues of whether to recognise the Communist Government and to permit it to take over the representation of China in the United Nations where China was one of the five permanent members of the Security Council. The Soviet Union recognised the Communist Government on 2 October, followed by other Communist states, and raised the representation issue in the Security Council cursorily on 29 December. Britain gave recognition on 6 January 1950. France, another permanent member of the Security Council, did nothing, apparently waiting with an eye to the situation in Indo-China on the reaction of the United States.

The Democratic Administration in the United States had sought, despite strong pressure from the "China lobby" in Congress, to remain neutral regarding the Chinese civil war and at the present juncture it remained cautious. On the one hand, it was faced with intense popular clamour to take a strong stand against the march of Communism in the Far East as anywhere else in the world and to support the Nationalist Government. It was also faced with the seizure of American property and the mistreatment of some of its diplomatic representatives by the Communists. On the other hand, it did not fully accept the popular notion that the Communist Government was a puppet of the Soviet Union, ruling by force over a conquered country as did the puppet governments in eastern Europe. It knew or guessed at some of the elements of tension between the Soviet Union and the Chinese Communists. On balance, it merely took the line with its allies that recognition at the present time would be "premature". Moreover, when tracing the "defensive perimeter" of the United States in the Pacific in the course of a speech on 12 January, Secretary of State Acheson omitted Taiwan.

---

[1] Taiwan was surrendered by China to Japan in 1895. In the Cairo Declaration of 1 December 1943, Britain and the United States promised China that the island would be returned in the peace settlement. The Nationalists took control of the island on the defeat of the Japanese in 1945.

On 10 January, however, at the United Nations, the Soviet Union pressed the cause of Communist China, proposing that the Security Council reject the credentials of the Nationalist delegation. The United States rose to this challenge. It had previously agreed (1948) that credentials were a procedural matter (i.e. a resolution could be passed by any seven affirmative votes, there being thus no permanent member veto) and it reaffirmed this point now (12th); but it also declared that it continued to accept the Nationalist delegation's credentials and worked to defeat the Soviet proposal. In the vote on the 13th, the United States was successful. The Soviet delegation then walked out, declaring the Soviet Union would remain unrepresented until China was represented by the government that ruled there.[2]

Then followed (February) the conclusion of the negotiations for a Sino-Soviet Treaty. Some expert opinion in the United States noted the provisions that might be irksome to the Chinese but Congressional and popular pressure on the Administration to protect Taiwan as a bastion against Communism continued to mount. In February also, the UN Secretary-General, Trygve Lie, issued a memorandum to all member states arguing that a distinction should be drawn between recognition of a government by other individual governments and the question of representation in the United Nations; but this was in vain so far as United States public opinion was concerned. In the spring, international tension grew ominously and in a report of 6 June, the Secretary-General declared his belief that until the question of China's representation was settled, no progress could be made towards easing it.

On 25 June, North Korea invaded the South. In this crisis, President Truman gave in a broadcast the following picture of events and declaration of United States policy (27th): "The attack upon Korea makes it plain beyond all doubt that Communism has passed beyond the use of subversion to conquer independent nations and will now use armed invasion and war. It has defied the orders of the Security Council of the United Nations issued to preserve international peace and security. In these circumstances, the occupation of Formosa by Communist forces would be a direct threat to the security of the Pacific area and to United States forces performing their lawful and necessary functions in the area. Accordingly I have ordered the Seventh Fleet to prevent any attack on Formosa. As a corollary of this action, I am calling upon the Chinese Government on Formosa to cease all air and sea operations against the mainland. The Seventh Fleet will see that this is done. The determination of the future status of Formosa must await the restoration of security in the Pacific, a

---

[2] In the event, the Soviet Union returned to the Security Council on 1 August 1950.

peace settlement with Japan, or consideration by the United Nations."

Throughout August and September, as the fighting continued, India urged that the Security Council should at least invite Communist China to come before it to state its position. In October, the United Nations forces commanded by General Douglas MacArthur overran North Korea and in the last days of the month, as they approached the Yalu River, the first clashes occurred with Chinese Communist forces. In the brief lull which then ensued, the Security Council invited Communist China to send a delegation (8 November), but by the time it arrived, led by General Wu Hsiu-chuan, full-scale fighting had broken out and MacArthur's forces were retreating. The delegation stated, moreover, that China would not negotiate on the Korean situation until United States forces had left the country, the Seventh Fleet had been withdrawn from the Taiwan Straits and the Nationalist Chinese had been ejected from the United Nations.

From now on, United States opposition to the Communist Chinese Government was total. It made plain that if the representation issue was raised again in the Security Council, it would no longer accept that the question was procedural and would seek to use its "veto" power. In the General Assembly, it caused a resolution to be passed (14 December) according to which a representation issue which became a "subject of controversy" had to be considered "in the light of the Purposes and Principles of the Charter and the circumstances of each case"; and a further resolution (1 February 1951) according to which Communist China "has itself engaged in aggression in Korea".

In the following years, a first major event was the signature on 8 September 1951, by the United States and forty-eight other countries (not including, notably, the Communist or the Nationalist Chinese or the Soviet Union and its allies), of a peace treaty with Japan under which Japan renounced sovereignty over Taiwan. A statement on the resulting legal position was avoided. On 27 July 1953, the armistice ending the Korean War was signed, and in 1954, in addition to the eight-country South East Asia Defence Treaty (8 September), the United States signed a mutual defence treaty with the Nationalist Government on Taiwan (2 December). All this time, high tension continued between the Communist and Nationalist governments. The events of 1954 were accompanied by a crisis over the off-shore islands, Quemoy and Matsu, and there was a further crisis in 1958.[3]

At the United Nations, meanwhile, every year from 1951 to 1960, the Soviet Union proposed that China's representation be included on the General Assembly agenda and every year the United States or an ally

[3] See pp. 151–4.

proposed instead that consideration of the issue be postponed. Such resolutions were settled by a simple majority vote and this the United States was always able to secure. Over the years, however, the tactic became harder to sustain. In 1951, out of a total membership of 60, 11 favoured discussion and 37 postponement, with 4 recorded abstentions. In 1960, by which time membership had risen to 98, the figures were 34–42–22. Moreover, as the 1960s opened, the United States was faced with the prospect of yet further new states entering the United Nations who might well not accept the continual postponement of the issue.

Accordingly, in 1961, the United States and its supporters shifted their ground. They caused a simple majority motion to be passed (61–34–7) according to which the question of Chinese representation was "an important question" in terms of the UN Charter. This meant that a resolution to change China's representation required a two-thirds majority. By 1965, the state of opinion in the Assembly was such that the United States had thenceforth to promote a resolution annually confirming that the issue was "an important question". The degree of difficulty varied from year to year, affected by the current state of world politics and Assembly diplomacy and attitudes to China. In some years the margin of victory narrowed (1965, 56–49–11), in others it widened again (1968, 73–47–5).

As to the main issue, each year from 1961 onwards a resolution to change China's representation was voted upon, sponsored by the Soviet Union until its public breach with China in 1963 and from that year by Albania. The United States and its supporters were always able to prevent a two-thirds majority.

However, the voting figures moved steadily against them over the years[4] and indeed by the late 1960s, within the United States itself, an increasing number of voices began to be raised against the policy towards China. In March 1966, the Senate Foreign Relations Committee held hearings on the matter and there, as elsewhere at this time, the possibility of a "two Chinas" policy was raised, namely that mainland China and Taiwan should be two separate states, each represented in the United Nations. Both the Communists and the Nationalists condemned this idea and so accordingly did the United States Administration. None the less, the altered background of world affairs, the apparent permanence of the Communist regime, the plain evidence of the Sino-Soviet quarrel that it was no mere puppet of the Soviet Union, the deepening problem of reaching a settlement of the war in Vietnam, and the movement of world opinion as reflected at the United Nations, all suggested that change in United States policy was only a matter of time and tactics.

[4] Tables of voting figures are given by Halpern and Luard.

In 1969, the new Republican Administration, paralleling its changes in Vietnam policy, took the plunge. It made various conciliatory gestures, notably the progressive relaxation of its trade and travel embargo. At the United Nations, it continued the struggle as before but made plain that the reason was not hostility to the representation of the Communist Government but unwillingness to abandon the government and people of Taiwan.

In July 1971, the United States surprised the world by a sudden, major step, the announcement that President Nixon would visit Peking in the following year. (The date later agreed was 21–28 February 1972.) As the 1971 General Assembly session approached, there was some speculation that the United States would adopt some variant of the "two Chinas" policy. In the event, it maintained its policy, but this time it was defeated. The "important question" resolution, co-sponsored by the United States and Japan, was lost 55–59–15; the resolution for a change in representation, sponsored by Albania, was passed 76–35–17 (25 October); the Nationalist delegation immediately withdrew, and shortly afterwards a Communist delegation arrived to take its place.

* * *

A. M. Halpern (ed.): *Policies towards China, Views from Six Continents*, McGraw-Hill, New York 1965.

R. B. Russell: *The United Nations and United States Security Policy*, The Brookings Institution, Washington D.C. 1968.

A. T. Steele: *The American People and China*, McGraw-Hill, New York 1966.

US Senate, Committee on Foreign Relations: *US Policy with respect to Mainland China*, USGPO, Washington 1966.

E. Luard: "China and the United Nations", *International Affairs*, October 1971.

Tibet 1950-59

FROM the eighteenth to the early twentieth century, Tibet acknowledged the supremacy of China. On the 1911 revolution, the overthrow of the Manchu dynasty and the troubles in China, the Tibetans showed signs of wishing to change this relationship. The British in India maintained a mission in Lhasa, and after 1947 the Indian Government did likewise. In the late 1940s, the successes of the Communists in China made the Tibetans, in addition, apprehensive for their religion. They brought about the departure of the Chinese mission (1947), fearing, they said, that its members might turn Communist, and requested the assistance of India in strengthening their army, a request which was, it seems, favourably received.[1]

On 1 October 1949, the Government of the People's Republic of China was formally inaugurated and over the following months established control of the western provinces of China. India warned China of the ill effect on its international relations of any use of force to settle its relationship with Tibet. There were inconclusive exchanges between the Tibetans and the Chinese whose declared policy was to "liberate Tibet" and "consolidate the defences of China's western frontiers".

In October 1950, the Chinese entered Chamdo province (eastern Tibet) and dispersed the Tibetan army. Tibet appealed to the United Nations but without response though there was much international protest, led by India. The Dalai Lama left Lhasa for the monastery at Dunghhar on the road to India. In December he ended his minority and assumed full powers. However, the main negotiations with the Chinese were conducted by two successive delegations, dispatched under his authority, in Peking.

On 23 May 1951, Chinese and Tibetan representatives signed a seventeen-point agreement called Measures for the Peaceful Liberation of Tibet.[2] China was to control external affairs, the Tibetan army was to be absorbed into the People's Liberation Army, and a Chinese Military and Administrative Commission was to be established in Lhasa. On the other hand, Tibet had the right of "national regional autonomy under the unified leadership of the Central People's Government". "In matters related to various reforms in Tibet, there will be no compulsion on the part of the central authorities. The local government of Tibet should carry out reforms of its own accord, and, when the people raise demands for

[1] Richardson, p. 178.
[2] Ibid., Appendix 18.

reform, they shall be settled by means of consultation with the leading personnel of Tibet." There was to be freedom of religion. The status, powers and functions of the Dalai Lama were confirmed. He was to restore the Panchen Lama.[3]

The Chinese divided Tibet into three administrative areas: the bulk of the country, ruled by the Dalai Lama, and known as the area of the Local Government; the Shigatse district under the Panchen Lama; and the province of Chamdo under a Chinese military governor. In the first few years there was suspicion and friction between the Tibetans and the Chinese Communists but, on the whole, it seems, both sides were circumspect. Both the Dalai Lama and the Panchen Lama attended the First National People's Congress in Peking in July 1954 which formally adopted the constitution of the People's Republic and confirmed the regional autonomy of Tibet as an integral part of China. On the external front, India and China signed an agreement on trade and cultural relations between India and "the Tibetan region of China" (29 April 1954). The preamble to the Agreement contained the five principles which were to govern relations between India and China, called by the Indians the *panch shila*: mutual respect for each other's territorial integrity and sovereignty; mutual non-aggression; mutual non-interference in each other's internal affairs; equality and mutual benefit; peaceful co-existence.

From 1954, the pace of change in Tibet began to quicken. The Chinese launched a great road building programme. Tibetans, including monks, were conscripted for labour. Surplus grain, traditionally held as reserves, was exported to China. Large numbers of Chinese immigrants were brought into the northern and eastern parts of the country. A Preparatory Committee for the Tibetan Autonomous Region was established in 1955 and began work early in 1956, under the nominal chairmanship and vice-chairmanship of the Dalai Lama and the Panchen Lama, to plan the development of Tibet into an Autonomous Region. A secular school system was inaugurated. Pressure for other social reforms increased.

By the middle of 1956, there was widespread unrest. The Khampa, a nomadic tribe in Chamdo, had begun harassing attacks on the Chinese. The following spring, Chairman Mao Tse-tung, Prime Minister Chou En-lai and other spokesmen made a series of statements indicating that the pressure for "democratic reform" would be relaxed and promising to reduce the numbers of Chinese officials. They warned, however, that

[3] In the interwar years, as in earlier times, there had been continual conflict between the ruler, the Dalai Lama, and the other spiritual head, the Panchen Lama, in alliance with China, in which the latter had eventually been worsted and expelled from his monastery at Shigatse. In 1950, his guardians (the Panchen Lama was then a minor) had declared his willingness to co-operate with the Chinese.

insurrection would be suppressed. The tribal attacks intensified and spread and in March 1958 a "rectification campaign" was launched against them. On 5 August, Tibetan leaders in Kalimpong (India) addressed an appeal to the nations of the world, and in particular India, which had watched events with growing concern. The Dalai Lama, despite Chinese urging, would not dissociate himself from the appeal. The Indian Government sought to calm the tension.

The crisis came in March of the following year (1959). Lhasa was full of pilgrims who had gathered from all parts of the country to celebrate the Tibetan New Year. Tension was further increased by the presence outside the city of large numbers of Khampa and Golok tribesmen who had retreated there under the pressure of the Chinese campaign. The Dalai Lama had for some time been at odds with the Chinese over his refusal to allow Tibetan army units to be used against the tribesmen. Discontent inside the city exploded on the news of an invitation from the Chinese to the Dalai Lama to attend a play at their military headquarters, unaccompanied by his usual retinue (10th). Fearing for his safety, the crowds prevented the Dalai Lama from leaving the summer palace. As Chinese troops moved to disperse them, riots broke out and swelled into attacks, assisted by Tibetan military units, on the Chinese garrison. Messages passed between the Dalai Lama and the Chinese commander, General Tan Kuan-san, in which the Dalai Lama professed little sympathy with the rioters and said that he was seeking to calm the situation. The Kashag (cabinet) and Tsongdu (assembly) were in continuous session in the palace, debating rebellion or compromise or the flight of the Dalai Lama.

On the 17th, the Chinese, probably as a deliberate sign that they were prepared to force the issue, fired two shells into the palace pond. The Dalai Lama and the Kashag immediately left the city and set out to take refuge in India. It is possible that the Chinese connived at this. The Kashag's last act was to denounce the 1951 Agreement on the grounds that the Chinese had persistently violated it (subsequently in India, the Dalai Lama declared it void on the grounds that it had been made under duress) and, together with representatives of the principal monastries and many members of the Tsongdu, to declare Tibet independent.

The Chinese now shelled and seized the palace, suppressed the rioting in the city, and intensified their campaign against the tribesmen. They seem at this time to have had some 300,000 troops in the country and it appears that they brought it rapidly under control. On the 28th, they announced that the revolt was over and that the Local Government was dissolved and was to be replaced by the Preparatory Committee with the Panchen Lama as Acting Chairman. Over the following years there was sporadic guerrilla activity but not apparently on a large scale. The Chinese felt sufficiently strong to impose a "socialist transformation" of the country. Major reforms in all areas of life were decreed in 1959, efforts being concentrated on education, land reform, and public administration.

The events of March 1959 provoked much informal protest internationally but no overt governmental action. Indian public opinion was deeply stirred by the events and by the arrival of the Dalai Lama (31st) and (both before and after the March crisis) of some 12,000 Tibetan refugees. The Indian Government, while sharing public feeling and (unknown to the public) already at odds with China over the Himalayan border,[4] sought none the less to maintain good relations. It granted asylum to the Dalai Lama, but would not permit a government-in-exile, and sought to dissuade him from raising the matter at the United Nations, and hoped instead for a reconciliation between him and the Chinese.

The Chinese, for their part, seem to have tried to maintain good relations with India. Their statement of 28 March 1959 said that the Tibetan rebels had been fomented by imperialists, Chiang Kai-shek bands and foreign reactionaries and that the command centre had been over the border at Kalimpong (India); but they did not at this stage accuse India. In late April, however, the statements of the Dalai Lama and the polemics in the Indian press, and perhaps the border conflict, led to Chinese charges that "Indian expansionists" had encouraged the rebels. The ill-will between the two countries on the Tibet question prepared the ground for the still greater ill-will when the border conflict was publicly revealed in August.

As to the rest of the world, the Dalai Lama addressed an appeal to the United Nations on 9 September. Ireland and Malaysia sponsored an Assembly resolution deploring events in Tibet and calling for respect for Tibetan human rights and recognition of their distinctive religion and culture, and this was passed in mid-October. However, the resolution was mildly worded and avoided mentioning China by name.

*   *   *

Z. AHMAD: *China and Tibet 1708–1959, A Résumé of Facts*, Oxford University Press, 1960.

G. GINSBERG and M. NATHOS: *Communist China and Tibet*, Nijhoff, The Hague 1964.

INTERNATIONAL COMMISSION OF JURISTS: *The Question of Tibet and the Rule of Law*, Geneva 1959.

F. MORAES: *The Revolt in Tibet*, Macmillan, New York 1960.

G. N. PATTERSON: *Tibet in Revolt*, Faber, London 1960.

H. E. RICHARDSON: *Tibet and Its History*, Oxford University Press, 1962.

[4] See pp. 155–6.

West Irian 1950-62

WEST IRIAN (properly, West New Guinea or Irian Barat) is a country of mountains and jungle, poor in natural resources so far as is yet known, peopled by about 700,000 Papuans. The Papuans are Melanesians and hence different racially from the Indonesians (Malays). Early in the Indonesians' struggle for independence from the Dutch, some of their leaders argued that it would be unwise to take over West Irian but Sukarno insisted that Indonesia should inherit all the territories of the Netherlands East Indies and this became the nationalist policy.

During the final independence negotiations in 1949, the future of West Irian was a major issue. The Dutch saw no reason to make a further concession to Indonesia in the shape of this special territory; they felt an obligation of guardianship towards the Papuans, as did the Australians in (east) New Guinea and Papua. They also saw the area at this time as a refuge for minorities in Indonesia such as the Eurasians, though later it became clear that these people preferred to go to the Netherlands.

The United Nations Commission on Indonesia (Australia, Belgium, United States) which presided over the independence negotiations, arranged matters so that the issue came last on the agenda. The formula eventually arrived at in The Hague Agreement (signed 2 November 1949; in force 27 December) was that the Netherlands transferred "complete sovereignty over Indonesia to the United States of Indonesia" (Article I) and that the future of West New Guinea "shall be decided" by negotiations between the Netherlands and Indonesia within a year, remaining meanwhile under the "authority" of the Netherlands (Article II).

During 1950, two successive Dutch–Indonesian commissions discussed the issue but without progress. There was much mistrust between the two countries and this was maintained during the year by Indonesia's abandonment of the federal constitution announced at the time of the independence negotiations in favour of the old nationalist aim of a unitary state.[1] On West Irian, the Indonesians did not dispute that the territory had been excepted from the transfer of sovereignty, merely insisting that the Dutch were committed to handing it over within the year. The most that the Dutch were prepared to concede, however (even this causing bitter controversy in the Netherlands), was that sovereignty should be vested in the Netherlands–Indonesia Union (a structure established by the Hague Agreement) with the Dutch in administrative control.

Neither of the two sides, it seems, called upon UNCI to intervene and

[1] See p. 55.

83

it suspended its activities at the end of 1950. In 1951, the Dutch suggested informally (formally in 1952) that the issue should go to the International Court of Justice but the Indonesians refused on the grounds that it was basically political, not legal. Further talks were held in January–February 1952 but again fruitlessly. The Indonesians now disputed the interpretation that West Irian had been excepted from the transfer of sovereignty, arguing that only the *de facto* control of the territory had been left at issue. They proposed at one point that the sovereignty question should be left in abeyance and that the two countries should meanwhile set up a joint administration; but the Dutch were unreceptive, the Indonesian Government changed, and nothing came of this.

By the end of the year, President Sukarno was speaking of "unilateral action" (10 November 1952). Relations deteriorated still further as Indonesia moved to break up the Netherlands–Indonesian Union. An agreement ending most of the links was signed on 10 August 1954.

On 18 August 1954, Indonesia formally requested that the West Irian question be placed on the agenda of the forthcoming General Assembly. However, even a compromise resolution calling for renewed talks failed to muster the necessary two-thirds majority (10 December). None the less, the Dutch, apparently impressed by the movement of opinion at the United Nations and the growing standing of Indonesia among the Afro-Asian countries evidenced by the Bandung Conference of April 1955, agreed in the following year to renewed talks. The General Assembly resolution of 16 December 1955 welcomed this and the talks were held from December 1955 to February 1956.

The talks were once again fruitless. In February, Indonesia unilaterally abrogated the remaining provisions of the Netherlands–Indonesian Union and the rest of the Hague Agreement as well and, in August, Indonesia's debt to the Netherlands. Henceforth, Indonesia no longer took its stand on the Agreement but argued that West Irian had belonged to Indonesia since the Republic was first proclaimed on 17 August 1945. West Irian had been part of the ancient Javanese empire of Madjapahit. The lack of ethnic connection between the Papuans and the Indonesians merely showed that Indonesia was a multi-racial state.

In 1956 and 1957, a number of states, mostly Afro-Asian "anti-colonialist" states, introduced resolutions calling for a UN Good Offices Commission (1956) and for continued efforts by the parties to find a solution, assisted by the Secretary-General as he deemed appropriate (1957). But the Netherlands had the support, or at least the abstention, of allies and sympathisers and though the resolutions won majorities, they were not two-thirds majorities. A notable move at the time of the November 1957 debate was a joint Netherlands–Australian declaration which stressed the geographical and ethnic identity of the whole of New Guinea and their common responsibility to prepare it for independence.

After the General Assembly vote of 29 November 1957, the Indonesian Foreign Minister, Dr Subandrio, warned the Assembly that Indonesia would now have to take action on its own account. In December, Indonesia expelled all Dutch citizens (some 50,000) and nationalised Dutch business enterprises without compensation. Over the next two years, 1958–59, against a background of mounting political troubles within Indonesia, especially rebellion in Sumatra and tension between the army and the growing Communist Party, the Indonesian Government sought to unite and mobilise the whole country under its leadership in a new course of "confrontation" with the Netherlands. In October 1959, the first Indonesian guerrilla fighters were captured in West Irian. On 17 August 1960 Indonesia broke off diplomatic relations with the Netherlands.

At this stage, the Netherlands Government decided that immobility was no longer a tenable policy and struck out on a new course of its own. On 4 October 1960, the Prime Minister, Dr Joseph Luns, told the UN General Assembly that the Netherlands was willing to submit to its scrutiny and judgement and in the following year (26 September 1961) proposed that the Netherlands relinquish sovereignty over West New Guinea and transfer its administration to the United Nations. This would be followed by Papuan self-determination in favour of independence or joining Indonesia or East New Guinea. The Netherlands would continue its financial assistance to the territory in any event.

These proposals were denounced by Indonesia, arguing that the matter was not simply one of achieving decolonisation; Indonesia had rights which must be respected. In the end (27 November 1961), nine Afro-Asian states sponsored a resolution calling for further negotiations between the disputants. This was favoured by Indonesia but failed to win a two-thirds majority. Twelve other African states, the so-called Brazzaville Group,[2] sponsored a resolution calling for further negotiations but also for examination of the possibility of a period of international administration of the territory. This was favoured by the Netherlands but also failed to win a two-thirds majority.

Indonesia now intensified its campaign against the Netherlands and now, moreover, enjoyed the support of the Soviet Union and China. Since 1958 Indonesia had had economic aid relations with the Soviet Union. In January 1961, it signed a military aid agreement and another on Sukarno's visit to Moscow in June, at which time the Soviet Union also announced its support for the claim to West Irian. On 1 April China signed a friendship agreement with Indonesia, also declaring its support. With this

[2] See p. 148.

backing, President Sukarno announced the setting up of a Liberation Committee for West Irian (October) and on 19 December proclaimed a national mobilisation to liberate the territory under a People's Triple Command (Trikora).

Up to this time, the United States had been inactive on the West Irian affair. In the mid-1950s, it had been at odds with the Sukarno regime as "neutralist" and "pro-Communist" and had promised the Netherlands its assistance in the event of an Indonesian attack, but, for the rest, had stayed in the background. In 1958, the Eisenhower Administration had reassessed the situation and had sought to improve its relations with the Sukarno regime, perhaps primarily for fear of the growing strength of the Communist Party, but still saw no reason to become involved in the West Irian affair. Now, in 1961, the Kennedy Administration abandoned inactivity. It was apparently alarmed in the context of its world policies and its problems in South-East Asia, especially in Vietnam, at the prospect of a Netherlands–Indonesia war, at the unpredictable consequences within Indonesia and at the foothold offered to the Soviet Union and China.

In December 1961, as Sukarno proclaimed his national mobilisation, President Kennedy offered United States mediation. Among other diplomatic steps, he asked the British Prime Minister, Harold Macmillan, to use his influence with the Dutch and the Australians and sent his brother, Robert F. Kennedy, then United States Attorney-General, in the course of a trip to the Far East and Europe, to Djakarta and The Hague. In January (1962), the Netherlands announced that it was willing to negotiate with Indonesia without insisting on prior acceptance of the principle of Papuan self-determination. In February, Indonesia ordered a full military mobilisation. On 20 March, the Netherlands–Indonesian talks began near Washington with the American diplomat, Mr Ellsworth Bunker, as mediator.

As the negotiations proceeded, Indonesia dropped paratroops in West Irian, maintained propaganda and publicity on Eastern bloc arms shipments and announced (July) that Indonesian forces were in invasion positions. There was simultaneously some unrest in West Irian at the prospect of an Indonesian take-over. At length, on 15 August, agreement was announced, subsequently approved by the legislatures of the two countries and the UN General Assembly (21 September).

According to the agreement, the Netherlands would transfer sovereignty over West Irian to Indonesia by 1 May 1963. Meanwhile (from 1 October), the territory would be administered by a United Nations Temporary Executive Authority. Before the end of 1969, the population would make an "act of free choice" under UN supervision to decide its future.

The arrangement for the transfer of sovereignty proceeded smoothly as agreed. In July–August 1969, Representative Councils set up in the territory declared in favour of forming part of Indonesia, and the UN General Assembly acknowledged this outcome on 19 November.

* * *

B. GRANT: *Indonesia*, Melbourne University Press, 1965.

L. H. PALMIER: *Indonesia and the Dutch*, Oxford University Press, 1962.

L. H. PALMIER: *Indonesia*, Thames & Hudson, London 1965.

J. VAN DER KROEF: *The West New Guinea Dispute*, Institute of Pacific Relations, New York 1958.

A. M. TAYLOR: "Nederlands Niew Guinea becomes Irian Barat", *International Journal*, Autumn 1962.

J. VAN DER KROEF: "The West New Guinea Problem", *World Today*, November 1961.

J. VAN DER KROEF: "The West New Guinea Settlement", *Orbis*, Spring 1963.

The Anglo-Iranian Oil Company 1951-54

THE Government of Persia granted an oil concession to an Englishman, W. K. D'Arcy, in 1901; in 1909, a year after the first successful oil strike, the Anglo-Persian Oil Company was formed (renamed Anglo-Iranian in 1935); in 1914, the British Government, with an eye to naval needs, purchased a controlling interest. In 1933, a new sixty-year concession was agreed under which the Persian Government was to receive royalties at a fixed rate per ton of petroleum sold, together with participation in the Company's prosperity in good years and some protection in bad.

In July 1941, Britain and the Soviet Union occupied the south and north of the country respectively to open a route for war supplies to the Soviet Union. At the end of the war, the Russians delayed withdrawal, set up a Tudeh (i.e. Iranian Communist) government in Azerbaijan, and demanded an oil concession. The Iranian Government agreed to the formation of an Irano-Soviet company, but after it had succeeded in getting the Russians to withdraw, assisted by United States and some British pressure, the Iranian parliament repudiated this. Over the next few years, relations with the Soviet Union were bitter. The Tudeh Party was banned. Relations with Britain and the United States were fair.

In the late 1940s, the Iranian Government (in common with the governments of other oil-producing countries, notably Saudi Arabia and Venezuela) became dissatisfied with the revenue received from the operating company. It launched a Seven-Year Plan in 1949 to develop the country's economy, and after the failure to secure substantial United States aid (a sharp setback to relations with the United States) the question of oil revenues became acute. In the event, AIOC's payments in 1949–50 were disappointing. One reason was that, in spite of higher postwar profits, AIOC was forced to "peg" dividends in compliance with Britain's domestic economic policy of dividend restraint. A standing grievance was that the royalties paid to the Iranian Government were less than the sums paid to the British Government in taxation. The Company was not subject to Iranian taxation. The fact that AIOC sold oil to the British Admiralty at an undisclosed price, while offering only a small discount to Iranian consumers, was a further source of discontent. On other aspects of relations, the Company's labour welfare record was good and it admitted the need for "Iranisation" of technical and managerial staff; but it also stressed the need to maintain efficiency.

Throughout 1949, the Government and the Company held talks on the basis of the "fifty-fifty" profit-sharing principle (also under discussion in Saudi Arabia and Venezuela and agreed there in 1950–51) but unsuccessfully. A "Supplementary Agreement", concluded on 17 July, which would have increased the benefits accruing to Iran, was rejected by the Majlis (the Iranian Lower House) as inadequate eleven days later.

The Agreement was re-submitted in December 1950 and again rejected. The previous month, Dr Mohammed Mossadegh, a member of the Majlis, long opposed to foreign oil concessions, had launched a country-wide campaign for the outright nationalisation of the Company. It was an example of "colonial exploitation". Iranian oil should be owned by Iran for its benefit. Iran should achieve genuine independence. It should also follow a policy of neutrality. The way to deal with Russian pressure was to get rid of the British and give no foreigners a concession. This campaign had tumultuous popular success. It also attracted the support of many traditionalist political and religious groups who opposed the governments of recent years and disliked all foreign interests. It was also supported by the banned Tudeh Party.

On 7 March 1951, the prime minister, General Ali Razmara, who favoured a more moderate course, was assassinated by a member of the Fedayan Islam, and on the following day, the Special Oil Commission of the Majlis voted unanimously for nationalisation. On the 14th, Britain sent a note warning that the operations of AIOC could not legally be terminated "by an act of nationalisation" but on the following day the Majlis passed a single article bill to that effect and on the 20th it was passed by the Senate. On 30 April, the Shah reluctantly entrusted Dr Mossadegh with the formation of a government. That same day, the Nine Point Law implementing the nationalisation law passed the Senate, and with the Shah's signature, which could not be withheld constitutionally, came into effect on 2 May.

The Company's first reaction was to suggest arbitration in accordance with the 1933 Concession, as did the British Government in a note of 19 May, but Iran rejected this. The Company appealed (26th) to the International Court of Justice for the appointment of an arbitrator but did not proceed further in view of the British Government's application to the Court on the same day. The British Government applied on the grounds that the affair involved sanctity of contracts, but Iran denied the Court's competence, arguing that the affair was domestic. On 5 July, the Court ruled that, pending its decision on its competence, the Company should continue operations unmolested but under the supervision of a joint board on which Iran would be represented. Iran rejected this ruling and on 10 July withdrew its recognition of the compulsory jurisdiction of the Court.

The background to the diplomatic action, then already getting under way, was a considerable economic strain on both countries. Britain success-fully mobilised a boycott by the major international oil companies of purchases from the new National Iranian Oil Company, partly by warnings of legal action, mainly because they themselves were concerned about the implications of Iran's actions for other major concessions. Iran's revenue dried up by the autumn and this, together with other British economic measures, drastically reduced imports. On the other hand, Britain was faced with the prospect of having to make its own oil purchases from United States companies, that is, with dollars which it could not afford.

In the diplomacy, the attitudes of the great powers were very important. Mossadegh would not and could not appeal to the Soviet Union and Soviet policy towards the country was indecisive and subdued. He allowed scope to the Tudeh Party for massive demonstrations in his support but their major service to him was the fear created in the United States that if he fell, they might replace him.

The United States had military aid agreements with Iran and wanted it to be strong like all countries on the perimeter of the Soviet Union, and therefore desired a rapid end to the dispute. In the early stages, it pressed Britain to make concessions. Once the British had shown that they were willing to concede the principle of nationalisation (see below), it put pressure mainly on Iran since it had an interest in the observance of contracts and the principle that nationalisation must be accompanied by adequate compensation. Eventually, it lost patience with Mossadegh's style of diplomacy, and concluded, moreover, that the right response to the threat of the Tudeh Party was not assistance to him.

The diplomatic action in the dispute began with fruitless discussions between the Company and the Iranian Government (June) and contacts between the British and United States governments. In July, President Truman sent Mr Averell Harriman to Iran and this resulted in a formula which the British then accepted as a basis for negotiations. According to this, the British recognised for the purposes of these negotiations the principle of nationalisation while Iran recognised the need to negotiate over the manner of it. On 6 August, the talks began in Teheran (the British mission was led by the Lord Privy Seal, Mr Richard Stokes) but on the 22nd broke down. The British argued that it was necessary that they retain control of the technical side of operations under a joint directorate, but the Iranians denied this.

On 27 September, Iran took over the Abadan refinery and, early in October, the oil fields, expelling the British staff. Britain now appealed to the United Nations Security Council and between the 1st and 19th October, the Council debated the issue. Dr Mossadegh, who represented his country personally, denied the Council's competence on the grounds that the issue was domestic. Sir Gladwyn Jebb, the British representative, argued that the dispute clearly had international aspects and, while willing to abandon the proposal that the Council should condemn Iran, proposed that it should at least urge continued negotiations. The Soviet Union supported Iran, the United States supported Britain, and in the end the Council adjourned its debate until an advisory opinion had been given by the International Court of Justice on its competence.

Dr Mossadegh now entered a Washington hospital and held discussions with the Americans from his bed, but without result. Next, the World Bank attempted to assist a settlement. This arose out of discussions, at the suggestion of neutral diplomats, between Dr Mossadegh and the Vice-President of the Bank, Dr Robert L. Garner. In January 1952, Bank officials visited Abadan and the oilfields, and discussions then followed on a proposal by the Bank to finance the resumption of oil operations under a neutral management committee, responsible to the Bank. The discussions reached deadlock in March on the stipulation of the Bank that it must have freedom of action and the right to include British staff.

On 23 July 1952, the International Court announced its decision that it was not competent to adjudicate the dispute. Meanwhile, however, Britain had reached an understanding with the United States and on 30 August President Truman and Sir Winston Churchill (the Conservatives had replaced the Labour government in October 1951) sent a joint message to Dr Mossadegh containing three proposals. The question of compensation would be submitted to the International Court. The Iranian Government and the AIOC would negotiate arrangements for the resumption of the flow of oil to world markets. On these conditions, AIOC would move the oil stored in Iran, Britain would lift its restrictions on exports to Iran and on Iran's use of its sterling balances, and the United States would make an immediate grant of $10 million to help the Iranian Government in its economic difficulties.

Dr Mossadegh rejected these proposals in colourful terms and made counter-proposals (24 September) which Britain rejected (14 October). On 22 October, Iran broke off diplomatic relations with Britain. The following January–February (1953), Britain and the United States concerted renewed proposals: arbitration on compensation, negotiations on commercial questions, United States financial aid. However, Dr Mossadegh would only agree to arbitration on compensation for the physical assets taken over, whereas Britain and the United States held that compensation for at least some part of the remainder of the term of the 1933 concession should be included. On the commercial side, Dr Mossadegh stood on the terms of the nationalisation law according to which all operational control must be solely in Iranian hands.

However, by this time, the balance of economic strain had tilted heavily against Iran. The British had found that they could replace Iranian oil comparatively easily elsewhere, and not merely from dollar sources but increasingly from sterling area sources, notably Kuwait, which at this time increased its production enormously. Iran, on the other hand, found only the smallest gaps in the boycott of Iranian oil and, though the United States continued military aid except for one short period (January–April 1952), it steadily refused economic aid on the grounds that Iran would have adequate resources if it would compromise in the oil dispute. Dr Mossadegh may have had greater hopes of the Republican Administration which took office in January 1953 and which weighed carefully the danger that the Tudeh Party might come to power in Iran. However, it concluded against support for the Mossadegh government and in June, President Eisenhower rejected a personal appeal from Dr Mossadegh for help on the same grounds as his predecessor.

By this time, the meteoric rise of Dr Mossadegh within Iran had reached its zenith. There had long been some opposition to his policy on the oil issue. There was growing discontent with the economic situation and resentment at the methods by which he remained in power. In August 1952, after a sharp conflict with the Shah, he had persuaded the Majlis to grant him what amounted to dictatorial powers for six months, extended in January 1953 for a further year, and this began the break-up of his National Front coalition. Moreover, many of his former supporters feared that he was falling under left-wing influences. A prolonged struggle ensued, culminating in the Shah's dismissal of Dr Mossadegh on 15 August 1953 in favour of General Fazlollah Zahedi. Dr Mossadegh resisted but royalist units installed General Zahedi on the 19th. Dr Mossadegh surrendered himself on the 20th, and was subsequently tried for treason and imprisoned for three years and then retired from public life.

General Zahedi immediately requested United States economic aid, indicating that he was prepared to reach a settlement of the oil dispute. Aid was granted and discussions got under way, diplomatic relations between Britain and Iran being re-established on 5 December. Iran remained sensitive on sovereignty and opposed to the restoration of the position of the British as operators; but the British were in any case amenable to the internationalisation of operations and the complex negotiations went smoothly.

On 5 August 1954, an agreement was concluded. A consortium had been formed of AIOC (40 per cent share), five United States oil companies (40 per cent), Royal Dutch Shell (14 per cent), Compagnie Française des Pétroles (6 per cent). Through two operating companies, which would include Iranians on their boards, this consortium would extract, refine and market the oil from an allotted area on behalf of the National Iranian Oil Company, sharing the profits on a fifty-fifty basis. Simultaneously agreement was reached that Iran would pay £25 million compensation to AIOC over ten years.

*   *   *

L. ELWELL-SUTTON: *Persian Oil, A Study in Power Politics*, Laurence and Wishart, London 1955.

N. S. FATEMI: *Oil Diplomacy*, Whittier Books Inc., New York 1954.

A. W. FORD: *The Anglo-Iranian Oil Dispute of 1951–2*, University of California Press, Berkeley 1954.

S. H. LONGRIGG: *Oil in the Middle East*, Oxford University Press, 3rd ed., 1968.

J. MARLOW: *Iran, A Short Political Guide*, Pall Mall Press, London 1963.

R. BULLARD: "Behind the Oil Dispute in Iran", *Foreign Affairs*, April 1953.

B. SHWADRAN: "The Anglo-Iranian Oil Dispute", *Middle Eastern Affairs*, June–July 1954.

Guatemala 1951-54

A REVOLUTION in Guatemalan politics occurred in 1944 with the ending of the dictatorship of President Jorge Ubico. His immediate successor, General Federico Ponce, was ousted after a few months by a revolutionary junta consisting of Francisco Javier Arana, Jacobo Arbenz and Jorge Toriello which ruled until the proposed free elections. These were duly held the following year and Juan José Arévalo won an overwhelming victory.

Describing his policy as one of "Spiritual Socialism", Arévalo was expected to initiate radical changes. By the time his term of office ended, some changes had been made, especially in the fields of education and labour reform. His original popularity had waned, however, and there was considerable dissatisfaction with the slow progress of the revolution.

In the Presidential Elections of 1950, Jacobo Arbenz received a large majority, and took office on 15 March 1951. Arbenz had established himself as the new "revolutionary" candidate and had the support of the outgoing government and the labour unions and was acceptable to the Army.

Although dedicated to continuing the Revolution of 1944, Arbenz had announced no detailed plan of action. Given his background as an army officer and landowner, many expected his government to follow a centrist line. The first months were relatively uneventful. By the beginning of 1952, however, the Government seemed to be taking a more radical line. The crucial issue was the announcement in May 1952 of an Agrarian Reform Bill.

This measure was intended to alter the very uneven distribution of land, to change the relationship between landlord and peasant, and to introduce new methods of cultivation, and so increase production. The main provision was that the uncultivated portions of estates of over 225 acres were liable to be appropriated and redistributed. Compensation was to be paid, determined by the tax assessment value of the land, in the form of 3 per cent government bonds, to be amortised in twenty-five years. Ownership of the appropriated land was to be vested in the State, which would lease it to peasants in the form of smallholdings or through co-operatives.

The bill, which was approved by an overwhelming majority in Congress and enacted on 17 June, was strongly opposed by the large landowners. They objected to the State being given title to the appropriated land; they argued that the peasants, mainly Indians, had little knowledge of cultivation; and they alleged that the Act was Communist inspired.

Criticism was particularly strong from the largest single landowner, the United Fruit Company of Boston, USA. In February 1953, some 225,000 acres of its land on the Pacific Coast were appropriated and distributed in smallholdings. In August, another 174,000 acres of its land, this time on the Caribbean coast, were claimed, although the Government delayed putting this into effect. The UFC did not question the necessity of land reform in principle, but argued that the actions taken discriminated against foreign companies in that the vast majority of the land appropriated belonged to these companies. In any case, the successful growing of bananas, one of the UFC's chief activities, entailed leaving land idle for some time; such land could not genuinely be regarded as "uncultivated". Moreover, in their view, the compensation offered was grossly insufficient. In August 1953, the United States Government took up the UFC's case and protested to Guatemala.

The UFC and the two other major foreign enterprises in Guatemala, the International Railroads of Central America (in which the UFC had important holdings) and the Empresa Electrica (a subsidiary of the American & Foreign Power Company) had privileges and immunities which were the result of long-term concessions. The Government mobilised popular resentment against their dominant position in the country's economy. Strikes broke out in which the Government seems to have been implicated.

Against this background, a second issue developed: Communism. The Communist Party in Guatemala can trace its origins to 1947. Throughout most of Arévalo's presidency it worked underground, but in 1952 the Arbenz government gave it full political rights under the title of the Guatemalan Labour Party. The Party claimed to have 532 members but there seem to have been rather more, about four thousand being the usual estimate. Few Communists held high government office and Arbenz himself was not a Communist. On the other hand, the Party was strongly placed in the organisation of the labour movement and it now extended its influence to rural areas by providing many of the personnel for the administration of the land reform. The Party also made ground with nationalists by accusing "foreign Imperialists" and "reactionary land-lords" of being the root cause of all Guatemala's ills.

Much of the domestic opposition to Arbenz which became apparent in the course of 1953 was motivated by a wish to reverse what many saw as a rapidly developing Communist take-over of the country. The deterioration of the economic situation which resulted from the land reform and consequent fall in agricultural output and from the Arbenz government's rejection of United States capital, was another grievance, but the issue of Communism appears to have been crucial. From 1944 to 1953, the Catholic hierarchy had maintained a neutral attitude to the successive revolutionary governments. Now, on 10 April 1954, the Archbishop of Guatemala issued a Pastoral Letter condemning Communist infiltration of the Government.

The fear of Communism seems also to have been a major motive in the invasion of the country led by Colonel Castillo Armas which occurred shortly afterwards. During 1953 and 1954, Armas had been forming an "Army of Liberation" in the neighbouring Republics of Honduras and Nicaragua. His supporters included businessmen, landowners and other conservative defenders of the pre-1944 regime who had tried to overthrow Arévalo, but these were in a minority. His closest supporters were liberal reformers who claimed to represent the true spirit of the 1944 revolution. Armas himself had been the Commander of the Escuela Politecnica during Arévalo's Presidency until the murder in 1949 of Arana, then Chief of Staff. Arana had seemed the most likely person to succeed Arévalo and Arbenz was alleged to have been involved in the assassination. In November 1950, Armas led an abortive *coup d'état* against the Government, was imprisoned, but escaped in 1951.

The international aspect of the dispute centred around United States fears that "international Communism" was establishing a bridgehead in the Caribbean. When John Foster Dulles took office as Secretary of State in 1953, he compared conditions in Latin America with those prevailing in China in the mid 1930s when the Communist movement was becoming established there and stressed that "the time to deal with revolutionary activities of this sort is in their early stages".

At the Tenth Inter-American Conference at Caracas in March 1954, the United States promoted a resolution declaring that "the domination or control of the political institutions of any American State by the Inter-national Communist Movement . . . would constitute a threat to the sovereignty and political independence of the American States". The majority of Latin American governments were torn between, on the one hand, opposition to Communism and economic need of the United States and, on the other, resistance to United States interference in the internal affairs of any of their number. In the end, the United States succeeded in getting the resolution passed with only one adverse vote (Guatemala) and two abstentions (Argentina, Mexico).

The United States maintained economic pressure on the Arbenz government and gave financial and technical assistance to Armas's forces in Honduras and Nicaragua. Guatemala accused these two countries of planning aggression; they counter-charged subversion. Simultaneously, the discontent within Guatemala was rising. This internal and external opposition was sharply intensified by the arrival at the Guatemalan port of Puerto Barrios in May 1954 of a ship carrying, it was estimated, some

2,000 tons of Czechoslovakian arms. The Arbenz government justified this purchase by the refusal of Western states to sell arms. The United States signed Military Assistance Pacts with Nicaragua on 23 April and with Honduras on 20 May. Internally, the arrival of the arms brought to a head the issue of arming the peasants in a civilian militia. This led to a breach between the Arbenz government and the Army. The Government, feeling increasingly insecure, relied more and more on terror to maintain support. This was particularly associated with the local peasant unions and was often the result of the excesses of local leaders not fully under the Government's control.

On 18 June 1954, Armas's force, numbering a few hundred, began its invasion of Guatemala. On landing, its numbers rose to about two thousand; even so it was not as strong as the Guatemalan Army. On 19 June, Guatemala asked the United Nations Security Council to deal with violations of Guatemala's sovereignty by Honduras and Nicaragua. The Council met on 20 June, representatives from Guatemala, Honduras and Nicaragua taking part in the discussions. After a bitter debate, a Brazilian–Colombian resolution was introduced referring the complaint to the Organization of American States for urgent consideration. This was supported by ten Council members but vetoed by the Soviet Union. The Council then passed unanimously a resolution calling for the termination of all action likely to cause bloodshed.

On 22 June, Guatemala again called on the Security Council to use its authority to halt the actions of Honduras and Nicaragua. It refused to accept a sub-committee of the Inter-American Peace Committee until the resolution of the Security Council had been fully carried out. On 25 June, the Security Council, by five to four with two abstentions, refused to endorse the Guatemalan complaint. The matter then reverted to the IAPC and Guatemala accepted the Investigation Sub-Committee. By the time this arrived in Guatemala, however, the Arbenz government had fallen.

The fighting in Guatemala which followed Armas's invasion quickly reached a stalemate and the conflict was settled by political action in Guatemala City. The population at large seems to have been indifferent to the Government's fate; they did not rise in its defence but neither did they rush to support Armas. The main decisions were taken by army leaders. The decisive factor seems to have been the Army's refusal to arm the peasant and worker organisations. On 27 June, Arbenz resigned and this appears to have been at the request of a group of army officers.

Arbenz resigned in favour of Colonel Carlos Enrique Diaz but Armas refused to accept him because of his close friendship with Arbenz. On 29 June, a new Junta was formed under Colonel Elfego Monzón, a known anti-Communist, and it was announced that he would hold talks with Armas at San Salvador. The United States Ambassador to Guatemala, John Peurifoy, had been active in the events in Guatemala City and now joined in the talks together with the Ambassador to El Salvador and the President of El Salvador, Oscar Osorio.

Agreement was announced on 2 July. A military junta was to rule with Monzón as temporary President but was to elect a permanent President after no more than fifteen days. The insurgent government which had been established at Chiquimula was to be dissolved and the Liberation Army incorporated into the regular army.

On 8 July, the Junta elected Armas President. In August, as a result of army pressure, the Liberation Army was dissolved and not incorporated into regular units. In October, Armas was elected President by the people, the voters being given no other candidate. As regards land reform, Arbenz's Act was repealed but the Government divided two government-owned estates among the peasants and appealed to other landowners to do likewise. The UFC gave 100,000 acres for redistribution.

* * *

R. N. ADAMS: *Crucifixion by Power*, University of Texas Press, Austin 1970.

R. M. SCHNEIDER: *Communism in Guatemala 1944–1954*, Frederick A. Praeger, New York 1959.

J. GILLIN and K. H. SILVERT: "Ambiguities in Guatemala", *Foreign Affairs*, April 1956.

F. B. PIKE: "Guatemala and Communism", *Review of Politics*, April 1955.

P. B. TAYLOR: "The Guatemalan Affair, A Critique of United States Foreign Policy", *American Political Science Review*, September 1956.

Vietnam 1954-69

AFTER nearly eight years of fighting, France signed a cease-fire agreement at Geneva on 20 July 1954 and completed the transfer of sovereignty to Vietnam on 29 December 1954.[1] There were at this time two rival governments in the country: in the North, the Government of the Democratic Republic of Vietnam, first proclaimed in September 1945, which the French had fought to suppress; in the South, the Government of the Emperor Bao Dai, which the French had sponsored. Both governments were committed to achieving the unity of the country.

In the South, the strongest governmental figure was Ngo Dinh Diem, chief minister since 16 June 1954. He faced an extremely difficult situation. Since the 1930s, he had played a leading part in the independence movement against the French; on the other hand, he was a Catholic (only some 2 million of the population of 13 million were Catholics, the rest following Taoism, Buddhism and Confucianism) and came from an old ruling-class family. In the country, much of the rice-land was uncultivated, communications were in disrepair, and the army (still commanded by the French until April 1956) was in disarray. Saigon was inundated with refugees from the North (an estimated 800,000 moved from North to South during 1954–55) and the administration was largely controlled by gangsters known as the Binh Xuyen. In the South as a whole, religious-political sects, notably the Cao Dai and the Hoa Hao, were seizing control wherever they could. There were strong grounds for believing that the Government of the South could not survive.

In the event, Ngo Dinh Diem outdid his opponents. In the course of 1955, he broke the Binh Xuyen and curbed the power of the sects. On 23 October 1955, he held a referendum in which the choice lay between the Emperor Bao Dai and himself and in which he was credited with 98 per cent of the votes. On the 26th, the Republic of Vietnam was proclaimed with himself as president.

In mastering the situation in South Vietnam, President Diem was greatly helped by the United States. Like the President himself, the United States disapproved of the Geneva agreement as a partial victory for the Communists and was determined that they should make no further advance. In the last critical months of the Indo-China war, it had developed the view that the situation in the whole of South-East Asia was in danger of slipping under the pressure of the Soviet Union and China, and (the

[1] See pp. 65–7.

so-called "domino theory") that if the South Vietnamese or any other friendly government was allowed to fall to the Communists, the others might topple one by one. In the months following the Geneva agreement, the Eisenhower Administration took the basic decision to assist the South Vietnamese Government economically and to help it to build up its forces for internal security. On 8 September 1954, it led Australia, Britain, France, New Zealand, Pakistan, the Philippines and Thailand in the signature of the South-East Asia Collective Defence Treaty. The "free territory under the jurisdiction of the state of Vietnam" together with Cambodia and Laos were designated in a protocol as coming under the provisions of the Treaty.

The Final Declaration of the Geneva Conference had affirmed (Article 7) the unity of Vietnam and had envisaged the holding of general elections in July 1956. However, the South Vietnam Government had protested against the proceedings at Geneva and now proved to have no intention of holding elections jointly with the North. It took the view that even if such elections could be organised, they would not genuinely be free in the North. The Government of North Vietnam, for its part, continually proclaimed its desire throughout 1955–56 for country-wide elections, but, for the rest, concentrated like the Government of the South on consolidating its position and building up its strength.

Although the wartime destruction had been still greater in the North than in the South, the problem was less to the extent that there was no one to challenge the authority of the Dang Lao Dong (the Workers' Party, i.e. the Communists) and President Ho Chi Minh. Progress was made in economic reconstruction but at the same time great effort was devoted to the "socialist transformation" of society. Mines, factories and local industries were nationalised or taxed out of existence; landlords were removed and agricultural holdings collectivised. These measures, especially the last, roused much popular resentment. Many executions and "suicides" were reported and in November 1956, there was open rebellion in Nghe An province. This was suppressed but the pace of collectivisation was eased.

At this time the Government of North Vietnam appears to have depended heavily on the assistance of the Soviet Union and China. In the following years it appears to have sought to reduce this dependence, as indicated by the fact that the share of foreign aid in its budget seems to have fallen from 65·3 per cent in 1955 to 19·9 per cent in 1962.[2] When the quarrel between the Soviet Union and China developed in the late 1950s, it appears to have sought to avoid identification with either side.

From 1956 onwards discontent with the rule of President Diem grew in the South. His manner of ruling, arbitrary arrests, censorship, sup-

[2] Fall, p. 177.

pression of dissent, were resented. Some economic progress was made but this was largely confined to the towns. In the countryside, a token land reform was implemented but little more. The Communists were able to make use of this discontent. Following the Geneva agreement, the Dan Lao Dong in the South had been ordered by the leadership in Hanoi to conceal their arms and refrain from militant action. In 1957, they became active again. They showed sympathy with the grievances and needs of the peasants while avoiding elaboration of long-term socialist aims and, at the same time, developed a selective technique of terror. By killing or torturing village headmen, officials, teachers or any other leaders, they were able to assert covert or overt control over chosen areas. By the end of 1959, such incidents had become frequent and now, apparently, with the endorsement of Hanoi. The Communists drew together "a loose, disparate collection of dissident groups, often with nothing more in common than hostility for the Diem government, into a tightly-knit movement",[3] known militarily as the Vietcong and politically as the National Liberation Front (officially proclaimed, 20 December 1960). Southern Communists trained in the North began to return to the South as supply carriers and as fighters. By the end of 1960, the South Vietnamese Government was faced with full-scale insurgency, with the Communists in control of parts of the Mekong delta, the coastal provinces north-east of Saigon, and the highlands of central Vietnam.

Over the next three years, the new United States Administration of President John F. Kennedy, simultaneously facing a deteriorating situation in Laos,[4] increased United States support for the South Vietnamese military effort. From 1954, United States aid had mostly been directed to building up the South Vietnamese army. The Military Assistance Advisory Group from the French period had been retained and expanded. Now, in 1961, the United States sent combat advisers to accompany South Vietnamese troops and combat support units. By October 1963, United States military personnel in South Vietnam numbered some 16,000.

Despite this assistance, the South Vietnamese Government continued to lose control of the countryside to the Communists. The policy adopted in 1962 of seeking to concentrate the peasants in "strategic hamlets" appears to have made little security contribution to counterbalance the resentment aroused. The rule of President Diem and the influence of his brothers and sister-in-law, Ngo Dinh Can, Ngo Dinh Nhu and Madame Nhu, were increasingly feared and hated. In November 1960 and again in February 1962, groups of officers attempted *coups d'état*. In May 1963, Buddhist demonstrations against the regime began in Hué and spread to

[3] Pike, p. 111.
[4] See pp. 108–9.

Saigon and were met with harsh repression. Finally, on 1 November, a group of officers led by General Duong Van Minh mounted a successful *coup*, with the knowledge of the United States. President Diem was killed.

The military junta so established had no concerted political-military programme and was riven with factional discord. In the course of the following year (1964) the United States Administration, now headed by President Lyndon Johnson, concluded that the United States must take stronger action to demonstrate its determination, to stiffen the South Vietnamese Government, and to influence the policy of the North Vietnamese both towards South Vietnam and Laos. In February, it launched an increased programme of South Vietnamese commando attacks on the North and in March began to consider United States air attacks, warning the North Vietnamese of this privately in June.

On 2 August, following commando attacks in the Gulf of Tongking, North Vietnamese torpedo boats fired on two United States destroyers. The Administration promoted a resolution in Congress, passed almost unanimously on 7 August, which approved and supported the determination of the President "to take all necessary measures to repel any armed attack against the forces of the United States and to prevent further aggression" and declared that the United States "is . . . prepared, as the President determines, to take all necessary steps, including the use of armed force, to assist any member or protocol state of the Southeast Asia Collective Defense Treaty requesting assistance in defense of its freedom". United States aircraft immediately made retaliatory strikes in the Gulf of Tongking. In October, they began attacks on the "Ho Chi Minh" supply trails from North to South in Laos. In November, President Johnson won the presidential election. In March 1965, bombing of the North began.

In April 1965, President Johnson decided to send United States troops to Vietnam. Commanded by General William Westmoreland, who adopted an aggressive "search and destroy" strategy, their numbers increased from some 180,000 at the end of 1965 to 550,000 in 1968. In the last months of 1965, North Vietnamese army units entered the South to support the Vietcong.

From April 1965 onwards, President Johnson stated the readiness of the United States to engage in peace talks unconditionally. In reply, the North Vietnamese and the National Liberation Front made four demands: the United States must end the bombing and withdraw its troops; Vietnam must be neutralised as in the Geneva agreement; the NLF's programme for South Vietnam must be accepted; and the country must be reunified peacefully. The United States made pauses in its bombing from 8–12 May 1965, 24 December 1965–31 January 1966, 8–12 February 1967. Many peacemakers were active internationally, notably Canada, the Vatican, the UN Secretary-General, U Thant, the British Prime Minister, Harold Wilson, in talks with the Soviet Prime Minister, Alexei Kosygin, at the time of the February 1967 bombing pause. None of these efforts was successful, however.

In 1967, the North Vietnamese and the NLF reformulated their demands, calling for a United States withdrawal and a coalition government in the South including the NLF. In January 1968, they declared their readiness for talks if the United States would halt its bombing but the United States hesitated to do this without some corresponding concession by them. In the final days of January 1968, the Vietcong–North Vietnamese forces, hitherto fighting for the countryside, launched the great Tet (Lunar New Year) offensive against the towns of South Vietnam.

At this point, the Johnson Administration lost confidence in its policy. It was influenced in this by the dissension within the United States, which had grown rapidly over the past year, and by the unpopularity of its policy in the world at large. Only local states, Australia, Malaysia, New Zealand, the Philippines, South Korea, Thailand, showed considerable sympathy and support. In February, General Westmoreland was recalled and on 31 March, President Johnson announced that the bombing of the North would be reduced, repeated the offer of peace talks, and stated that he would not stand for re-election as President in November.

On 3 April, President Johnson announced that the North Vietnamese Government had agreed to talks but the two sides then haggled for a month over the venue. The talks began on 10 May in Paris but made no progress, the North Vietnamese insisting on a complete end to United States bombing, the United States requiring a decrease in Vietcong action first. In October, the North Vietnamese appear to have made some concession on this point and on the 31st, President Johnson announced that all bombing of the North would end and that the NLF would be admitted to the talks together with the South Vietnamese Government.

The South Vietnamese Government disliked this implied recognition of the standing of the NLF and the following months were spent in discussions of the shape of the conference table, the point being whether the NLF had independent status or not. Eventually an ambiguous seating arrangement was arrived at and in May 1969, the new United States Administration of President Richard Nixon, inaugurated that January, unveiled major proposals: the bulk of non-local forces would withdraw from South Vietnam over a twelve-month period; a cease-fire between the Vietcong and the South Vietnamese would be arranged by an international commission; prisoners of war would be exchanged; the Geneva agreement would be reinstated; country-wide elections would be held. Both the North and South Vietnamese raised many objections to these proposals, and the talks dragged on without progress.

Meanwhile, the new Republican Administration, pressed by United States public opinion and assisted by the considerable gains from the political and military efforts of recent years, had developed a new policy: the "Vietnamisation" of the war. After the period of chaos following the overthrow of President Diem, South Vietnam had been ruled with an improved degree of concord and confidence by a succession of military leaders until finally, on 1 April 1967, a new constitution had been adopted and, in September–October elections for the presidency and the two chambers had been held, in which two of the military leaders, General Nguyen Van Thieu and Air Vice-Marshal Nguyen Cao Ky, became President and Vice-President respectively. They henceforth appointed governments with a high civilian membership and these appear to have made progress in stabilising the administration and winning standing in the countryside with such measures as local elections, land reform and various social programmes. In the North, President Ho Chi Minh died on 3 September 1969.

On 8 June 1969, President Nixon announced that he would order the withdrawal of 25,000 United States troops and that he intended to make further withdrawals by stages subject to three factors: progress in the ability of the South Vietnamese army to take over the conduct of the war; the level of Vietcong–North Vietnamese military action; and progress in the Paris peace talks. Despite the anxieties of the South Vietnamese and the lack of fulfilment of the third criterion, President Nixon felt sufficiently confident of the other factors and convinced of the necessity of unburdening the United States, to announce further withdrawals over the course of the year. By April 1970, some 120,000 United States troops had left.

*			*			*

J. Buttinger: *Vietnam, A Political History*, André Deutsch, London 1969.

A. W. Cameron: *The Viet-Nam Crisis, A Documentary History, Vol. I, 1940–56*, Cornell University Press, Ithaca 1971.

D. Duncanson: *Government and Revolution in Vietnam*, Oxford University Press, 1968.

B. Fall: *The Two Vietnams*, Praeger, London, rev. ed., 1964.

D. HALBERSTAM: *The Making of a Quagmire*, Bodley Head, London 1965.

P. HONEY: *Vietnam, Genesis of a Tragedy*, Ernest Benn, London 1968.

D. PIKE: *Viet-Cong*, Massachusetts Institute of Technology Press, Cambridge 1968.

NEIL SHEEHAN and others: *The Pentagon Papers*, New York Times (and Quadrangle Books, Chicago, and Bantam Books, New York) 1971.

R. THOMPSON: *No Exit from Vietnam*, Chatto and Windus, London 1969.

Laos 1954-62

THE kingdom of Laos, a mountainous country of about 100,000 square miles, had a population in the 1950s of some 2 million, about half Lao (i.e. belonging to the Thai group of peoples) and the rest various mountain tribes. A French protectorate from 1893, the kingdom was proclaimed an independent sovereign state within the French Union on 19 July 1949 and became fully independent on 29 December 1954 after the Geneva armistice ending the Indo-China war.[1]

By the Laos armistice agreement between the French and the Pathet Lao rebels and their North Vietnamese allies, signed at Geneva on 20 July 1954, the French and the North Vietnamese were to withdraw from the country, except that the French might retain two bases and military training personnel, and no new foreign forces were to be brought in. The Pathet Lao were to withdraw to the north-eastern provinces of Phong Saly, bordering on China, and Sam Neua, bordering on North Vietnam, pending a political settlement with the Government at Vientiane.

In the following years, the King (Sisavang Vong, succeeded in 1959 by Savong Vatthana) at the royal capital Luang Prabang played on the whole only a secondary role in the political affairs of the country. The two principal leaders of the country were members of a younger branch of the royal house, Prince Souvanna Phouma and his half-brother Prince Souphannouvong. They had been associated in the Lao-issarak movement in 1945 which had vainly sought to prevent the return of the French. Subsequently Souvanna Phouma had taken the course of peaceful pressure on the French and was now (1954) prime minister, whereas Souphannouvong had become head of the Pathet Lao rebels.

In line with the Geneva agreement, Souvanna Phouma believed that the best future for the country lay in reconciliation with the Pathet Lao and neutrality internationally. From 1954 to 1957, during most of which time he continued as prime minister, he sought a settlement with the Pathet Lao. At first, the Pathet Lao concentrated on strengthening their grip on the two north-eastern provinces but in 1956 negotiations got under way and finally, in November 1957, an agreement was reached. The Pathet Lao undertook to disband with the exception of two battalions, one near Luang Prabang and the other on the Plain of Jars, in the heart of the country, which were to integrate with the Royal Laotian Army. Their political party, the Neo Lao Hak Sat, was recognised. They accepted royal authority

[1] See pp. 62–6.

106

over the two provinces while retaining most of the senior administrative posts. Prince Souphannouvong and another Pathet Lao colleague were given posts in the Vientiane government.

The two sides also agreed that special elections should be held for 21 seats in the National Assembly. When these were held the following May (1958), the NLHS won 9 and sympathisers 4.

This striking success for the NLHS was the last straw for those Lao politicians such as the Sananikone family who had long feared that Souvanna Phouma was going too far in his efforts to conciliate the Pathet Lao. It was also the last straw for the United States. The United States had disliked the Indo-China armistices as too favourable to the Communists; it had placed Laos, Cambodia and South Vietnam under the protection of the South-East Asia Collective Defence Treaty (8 September 1954); and it had poured in military and economic aid. Now (June 1958) the United States Central Intelligence Agency promoted the formation of the Committee for the Defence of National Interests, a political movement of those who believed that the Pathet Lao were first and foremost Communists, that conciliation of Communists was a delusion and that they would not be content until they controlled the country. In July, the United States suspended its economic aid, Souvanna Phouma was voted down in the National Assembly, and Phoui Sananikone became prime minister with CDNI support.

Over the following months, relations between the new Government and the Pathet Lao steadily worsened. Phoui Sananikone showed his determination to curb the power of the Pathet Lao in their two provinces. Internationally, he believed in neutrality but choice or circumstances caused him to veer some points from the course set under Souvanna Phouma. Insurgency had begun again in South Vietnam. Phoui Sananikone recognised its Government along with the Nationalist Government on Taiwan. North Vietnam, as 1959 opened, was moving towards assistance to the insurgents and sought to make sure of the use of the trails through Laos ("the Ho Chi Minh trail"). Clashes occurred, whereupon Phoui Sananikone secured emergency powers for a year from the National Assembly (January 1959) and denounced North Vietnam and the Pathet Lao as their agents. In May, he issued an ultimatum to the two Pathet Lao battalions outside the north-eastern provinces. One of them replied by decamping with its equipment to the Pathet Lao sanctuary. Phoui Sananikone responded by arresting Prince Souphannouvong and fifteen of his colleagues.

Amid the high tension and rumours of impending North Vietnamese invasion which followed, Phoui Sananikone appealed to the United States for further military aid. United States military technicians arrived, disguised as civilians in deference to the Geneva armistice. In September, Phoui Sananikone appealed for a United Nations force and on 15 September a UN investigation team arrived which reported (4 November) strong evidence that the Pathet Lao were receiving assistance from North Vietnam but for the rest, inconclusively. Tension subsided somewhat. In mid-November, the UN Secretary-General, Dag Hammarskjöld, visited Vientiane and, it seems, advised Phoui Sananikone to revert to a policy of reconciliation with the Pathet Lao and greater neutrality.

Along these lines, Phoui Sananikone now decided to reorganise his government, dropping the CDNI ministers, including General Phoumi Nosavan, its leader. The General responded on 31 December by a *coup d'état*. The United States hesitated to endorse this drastic action and, internationally, France was opposed and so were Britain and still more strongly the Soviet Union which, interest apart, had standing as co-chairmen of the 1954 Geneva conference. A temporary, non-partisan government was appointed by common consent pending the elections of April 1960. The announced result of these was an overwhelming victory for the CDNI. However, at this point, Prince Souphannouvong and his colleagues escaped from imprisonment to rejoin the Pathet Lao, and scarcely had General Phoumi installed a government to his liking, when Captain Konglae mounted a *coup d'état* which re-established Prince Souvanna Phouma in Vientiane (9 August).

This re-establishment of the old pattern in Laos was short-lived, however. Over the next few weeks, Prince Souvanna Phouma sought to conciliate the Pathet Lao on the one side and General Phoumi and the United States on the other, but the latter gradually came together in common opposition to him. In December, General Phoumi set up a rival government under Prince Boun Oum at Savannakhet and launched a successful attack on Vientiane. Prince Souvanna Phouma took refuge in Cambodia, Konglae joined forces with the Pathet Lao and, at the end of the month, war between the Government and the Pathet Lao began.

The Pathet Lao immediately proved more than a match for General Phoumi's forces and by the end of January (1961) had seized control of the Plain of Jars. They were stiffened by North Vietnamese troops and were receiving most of their armaments from the Soviet Union. The Soviet Union, which continued to recognise Prince Souvanna Phouma, had already called (15 September) for the reconvening of the 1954 Geneva Conference. In mid-December it had endorsed an Indian proposal for the re-activation of the International Control Commission (Canada, India, Poland) which had been set up to supervise the 1954 agreements and had adjourned *sine die* just before Souvanna Phouma fell in July 1958. Britain, the other co-chairman, though recognising the Boun Oum government, had been responsive, but the United States was suspicious. On 31 December, it had taken the first steps to activate the South-East Asia Treaty Organization. Against a background of ever-increasing insurgency in South Vietnam and the proclamation there of the National Liberation Front,[2] it passed the Laos situation to the new Kennedy Administration as its most acute crisis.

The Kennedy Administration immediately adopted a different line of approach. On 22 January it called for a cease-fire supervised by the ICC and on 25 January, President Kennedy stated, in his first news conference, that the United States goal for Laos was "an independent country not dominated by either side". He soon made plain that this meant that the United States would settle for Prince Souvanna Phouma and his policies.

Over the next few weeks, however, the Pathet Lao continued to advance and by the end of March were threatening both Luang Prabang and Vientiane. The stated position of the Communist powers was that a conference must begin before a cease-fire. It seems that among the Communist powers, the Soviet Union was the most restrained, China and North Vietnam the boldest. As the international diplomacy continued, the United States took various steps to influence Communist deliberations.

At Key West on 26 March, President Kennedy secured the British Prime Minister's support for intervention if necessary, and the other SEATO powers (except France) followed suit at their meeting on 27th–28th. On 4 April, the Soviet Union suggested a cease-fire after a conference had been agreed though before it opened. On 18 April, fearing that the Bay of Pigs fiasco in Cuba[3] would suggest United States weakness, President Kennedy ordered the United States military advisers in Laos into uniform. On 24 April, Britain and the Soviet Union were able to announce the re-activation of the ICC to supervise a cease-fire and the calling of a new Geneva Conference.

The ICC confirmed on 10 May that there was a general cease-fire and the Conference opened on the 16th attended by the nine participants of 1954 (Britain, France, the Soviet Union, the United States, Communist China, Cambodia, Laos[4] and North and South Vietnam) and by Burma, India, Thailand, Canada and Poland. Negotiations went slowly, however, and threatened to break down over United States protests at the continual violations of the cease-fire. At his meeting with Chairman Krushchev at Vienna on 3–4 June, President Kennedy secured a statement in the *communiqué* that both sides wanted a neutral Laos and would work for a

[2] See pp. 100–1.
[3] See pp. 177–8.
[4] i.e. delegations from Prince Souvanna Phouma and Prince Souphannouvong. Prince Boun Oum refused to send one. Phoui Sananikone joined the Conference later as the representative of the Vientiane political parties.

genuine cease-fire. Gradually, over the next few weeks, the intermittent fighting died down. But meanwhile the United States had run into trouble with its own side. Prince Boun Oum, with General Phoumi Nosavan behind him, would not accept the new United States line of policy. Thailand, with its close links with Laotian politics, was also deeply apprehensive.

For the next twelve months, the three Laotian princes, Souvanna Phouma, Souphannouvong and the evasive Boun Oum, engaged in continuous intricate diplomacy, meeting occasionally in colourful conclave under the bemused eye of the Geneva powers. Prince Souvanna Phouma was determined that the power of General Phoumi must be reduced. The problem for the United States was to help reduce it but not so drastically as to give encouragement to the Communists. Meanwhile, though the international crisis had diminished, the Geneva Conference remained stalled.

At length, in May 1962, the Communists (it seems) precipitated a new crisis. They suddenly attacked and on 6 May seized Nam Tha in north Laos. Thailand, in particular, feared a new general offensive to seize Laos. On the 12th, the United States ordered its Seventh Fleet to the Gulf of Siam and on the 13th announced the despatch of troops to Thailand. In the event, there were no general hostilities. The blow at Nam Tha greatly weakened the position of General Phoumi. On 12 June, Prince Souvanna Phouma was able to announce that he had reached agreement with Prince Souphannouvong and Prince Boun Oum on a provisional government representing all sides, with himself as premier and Prince Souphannouvong and General Phoumi as vice-premiers.

This success meant that at last a joint Laotian delegation could be sent to take part in the Geneva Conference. On 23 July, a Declaration and Protocol on the Neutrality of Laos was signed. All foreign military personnel were to leave the country within seventy-five days. The ICC would supervise this. The signatories would respect the neutrality of Laos. The Laotian Government repudiated the protection of the South-East Asia Treaty Organization.

Over the following years, Laos remained in a troubled state. Prince Souvanna Phouma continued to preside over an uneasy coalition of neutralists, anti-Communists and Pathet Lao. The anti-Communists maintained their feud against the Pathet Lao. The Pathet Lao, dominating the mountain areas, assisted the North Vietnamese in the use of the trails to South Vietnam. Many neutralists, including Konglae and his troops, became disillusioned with the Pathet Lao and, in the outburst of fighting on the Plain of Jars in 1964, fought against them. On the whole, however, even at the height of the war in South Vietnam in the late 1960s, the outside powers remained content with the neutrality of Laos and countered each other's infringements as covertly as possible without seeking to provoke a major international crisis.

*   *   *

A. J. DOMMEN: *Conflict in Laos*, Praeger, New York, rev. ed., 1971.

B. FALL: *Anatomy of a Crisis*, Doubleday, Garden City 1969.

R. HILSMAN: *To Move a Nation*, Dell, New York 1964.

P. F. LANGER and J. J. ZASLOFF: *North Vietnam and the Pathet Lao*, Rand Corporation, Cambridge (Mass.) 1970.

G. A. MODELSKI (ed.): *International Conference on the Settlement of the Laotian Question*, University Press, Canberra 1962.

H. TOYE: *Laos*, Oxford University Press, 1968.

Muscat and Oman 1954-59

IN the large but for the most part sparsely populated sultanate of Muscat and Oman, Oman proper is the district lying to the south of Jabal Akhdhar. In 1913, the tribesmen of Oman, long disaffected with the hereditary Sultan who ruled from the largely Indian and African populated trading town of Muscat on the coast, revolted against him and elected an Imam to rule over them. In 1919, negotiations for an agreement began. In 1920, the Imam was murdered and the Sultan made the Agreement (sometimes called Treaty) of Sib with the sheikhs.

This agreement has never been published but unofficial versions appeared in the press during the 1957 crisis. From these and from the circumstances of 1920, it seems clear that the agreement could not be described as an international treaty. It neither stated nor denied the ultimate sovereignty of the Sultan. It granted a vaguely defined autonomy. In practice, the Sultan left the Imam's successor to rule the area without interference. The Omani tribesmen, in return, ceased to attack the coastal towns. For the next thirty years, relations remained relatively peaceful.

In May 1954, Ghalib bin Ali became Imam and immediately began to quarrel with the Sultan. Religious feeling played some part in this but not, it seems, the main one. The fervour of the imamate movement seems to have waned in the preceding years. Moreover, there was some doubt whether Ghalib had been elected in strict accordance with Ibadhiya doctrine. There was no general coalescence of the tribes behind him as there had been in 1913; only some leaders and their followers joined in. The driving force in the affair seems from the first to have been the Imam's brother, Talib bin Ali.

The Imam began by complaining that the concession granted in 1937 by the Sultan, Said bin Taimur (who had succeeded, 1932) to Petroleum Development (Oman) Ltd., a subsidiary of the Iraq Petroleum Company, was a violation of the Sib Agreement. The Company had recently started serious prospecting though so far without success. He went on to claim that the Agreement had acknowledged the independence of Oman. He applied for membership of the Arab League on the grounds that Oman was a sovereign state governed according to Islamic Law. Consideration of this application was postponed by the League for further study. He began to issue his own passports. Most serious of all for the Sultan, he developed relations with Saudi Arabia and with Egypt.

Egypt, at this time, under Colonel Gamal Abdel Nasser, had embarked on a drive for leadership of the Arab world and was especially hostile to any government influenced, as was the Sultan of Muscat and Oman, by the "imperialist" power, Britain. In 1955, an Imamate of Oman Office was opened in Cairo and propaganda support for the Omani rebels and, it seems, the smuggling of arms to them began.

Saudi Arabia was also at odds generally with Britain's Middle East policy, notably its sponsorship of the Baghdad Pact, but in addition it had a specific concern. In 1949, it had claimed a portion of Abu Dhabi and had declared that the Buraimi Oasis, six of the villages of which were ruled by the Sheikh of Abu Dhabi and two by the Sultan of Muscat and Oman, belonged to other sheikhs. In 1952, it claimed Buraimi and established a military post in the area.

Britain had no formal defence obligation to Abu Dhabi or Muscat and Oman but its friendship and external assistance was understood, as signified most recently in the case of the sultanate in a Treaty of Friendship, Commerce and Navigation of 20 December 1951. Arbitration proceedings began at Geneva in 1954 but the hearings, which opened in September 1955, immediately broke down. The British Government thereupon advised the two rulers to make a display of force against the Saudi post with the support of the British-raised and officered Trucial Oman Scouts. This they did in October, forcing the Saudis to withdraw, and established their own posts at the Oasis.

The Sultan also took this opportunity to overawe the rebels in Oman. In December 1955, his troops entered Nazwah, the Imam's headquarters town. There was no resistance; Ghalib and his brother fled. The sheikhs re-affirmed their loyalty. Ghalib was allowed to return to live in a remote village.

Talib, however, remained in Dammam (Saudi Arabia). In the course of 1956, he recruited and trained an Omani Liberation Army with the help of Saudi Arabia. Saudi Arabian and, it seems, Egyptian money assisted the resurgence of the movement inside Oman. The leaders of both the traditional coalitions into which the tribes were divided, Sheikh Salih bin Isa, leader of the Hinawi coalition, and Sheikh Suleiman bin Hamyar, leader of the Ghafaris, played a part in the movement.

At the beginning of 1957, propaganda from the Imamate Office in Cairo, accusing the Sultan and the British of occupying an independent Arab country, increased and members of Talib's Liberation Army began to return surreptitiously to Oman through the port of Dubai on the Trucial Coast. After a minor incident of fighting in April, Talib himself returned and the Imam reasserted his claim to independence. By July, several centres in Oman had declared their support for him. The Sultan, believing that he could not deal with the situation unaided, in that month formally appealed to Britain for assistance.

Britain at this time was only just beginning to recover from the depths of unpopularity among Arab nationalists plumbed in the Suez crisis of the previous year. A better understanding had been reached with the United States, but British action in the Middle East was still a sensitive matter there and world-wide and at home. On the other hand, the external support for the Omani rebels was clear and Britain's moral obligation to the Sultanate was well known on all sides in the region. The British feared that if they did not support the Sultan, the credibility of their promises to the Persian Gulf states, faced with their formidable neighbour, Saudi Arabia, and the spreading influence of Egypt, would be severely shaken. They decided to respond.

In July, accordingly, the Sultan's army launched an attack on the rebels with the aid of British air support and a British force of five hundred men. Throughout the Middle East, there was an outcry against British "oil imperialism" led by Egypt. Egypt and its allies called for a meeting of the Security Council to consider "the armed aggression" by Britain against "the independent sovereignty and territorial integrity of the Imamate of Oman". However, nothing came of this. Within Oman, resistance was slight, the fighting little and the casualties low. On 14 August, the Sultan announced that the rebellion was over. He had already declared that in view of the Imam's violations, the Sib Agreement was no longer valid and there were now no negotiations or formal terms. The Imam, Talib and Suleiman fled to the mountain, Jabal Akhdhar, which Suleiman controlled.

Over the next two years, the rebel leaders continued their activity and there were incidents from time to time. In November 1959, the Sultan determined to dislodge them from their mountain stronghold. Again British assistance was requested and the operation, with the support of two hundred men of the British Special Air Service, was a success. By January 1960, the rebels had capitulated. The Imam, Talib and Suleiman fled into exile. In the following years, propaganda from Egypt continued, there were occasional incidents in Oman, a special envoy of the UN Secretary-General investigated some of the problems of the area (1963) and a General Assembly Special Committee declared that the Oman issue was still a serious international problem. In fact, however, regional and world politics had moved on and the issue had died away.

*   *   *

D. Hopwood: *The Arabian Peninsula*, George Allen and Unwin, London 1972.

J. B. Kelly: *Sultanate and Imamate in Oman*, Chatham House Memorandum, Oxford University Press, 1959.

J. Morris: *Sultan in Oman*, Faber, London 1957.

R. G. Landen: *Oman since 1856*, Princeton University Press, 1967.

W. Thesiger: *Arabian Sands*, Longmans, London 1959.

Cyprus 1955-1968

THE population of Cyprus in the mid-1950s numbered some 500,000, about four-fifths Greek and a fifth Turkish. In 1878, Turkey had ceded the island for administrative purposes to Britain which formally annexed it in 1914, making it a Crown Colony (1925), ruled by a governor and executive council.

From the beginning of the nineteenth century, a movement of opinion developed among the Greek-Cypriots for union with Greece, *enosis*. Muted during the Second World War and the Greek civil war, it strengthened rapidly in the late 1940s, endorsed by the Greek Orthodox hierarchy, led from 1950 by Archbishop Mikhail Makarios, and supported with increasing vehemence by the people and government of Greece.

The British opposed *enosis*. From the beginning, Cyprus had formed part of their strategic line to the Middle and Far East. After the Anglo-Egyptian Treaty of 1954, it became their General Headquarters for the Middle East. Moreover, they argued, any move towards *enosis* would set the two Cypriot communities at each other's throats, and disrupt relations between Greece and Turkey, their NATO allies. On all these grounds, it was best to maintain the existing position.

In the spring of 1955, however, as the Greek-Cypriot demonstrations of recent years continued, the first attacks on British government buildings and residences began, carried out by EOKA (the National Organisation of Cyprus Fighters) led by Colonel Giorgios Grivas. Moreover, the climate of international opinion, including United States opinion, nowadays favoured self-determination. The Greek Government had raised the issue at the United Nations General Assembly in 1954 and, if nothing were done, might make better headway in 1955. Accordingly, Britain now sought to bring Greece and Turkey together in an understanding that the interests of all three allies would be best served by maintaining the existing status of the island, while at the same time introducing greater internal self-government there. After preliminary discussions which seemed moderately promising, they convened a conference in London on 29 August. However, the Greek Government finally adhered to its insistence on self-determination whereas the Turkish Government remained opposed. The conference ended without agreement on 6 September.

The Greeks had long taken the view (and the United States and others were inclined to it) that the British exaggerated the feelings of the Turks in order to justify retaining Cyprus; if *enosis* were swiftly and firmly conceded, the Turks would accept it; Britain's delaying tactics were fomenting Turkish feeling. The British declared this wishful thinking. However this may be, public opinion in Turkey had now become vocal and there were riots against the Greek community in Izmir. On the island, the Turkish Cypriots continued to make known their opposition to *enosis* but, for the rest, kept quiet. EOKA terrorism increased.

On 25 September 1955, General Sir John Harding was appointed Governor and a state of emergency was proclaimed (27 November). Over the next few months, in addition to the drive to suppress EOKA, he held discussions with Archbishop Makarios, as leader of the Greek-Cypriot community, and international diplomacy also continued. Little progress was made. It seems that the Archbishop was not deeply interested in measures of self-government until a promise of self-determination had been made; and the most that the British Government would concede on this was that, "It is not their position that the principle of self-determination can never be applicable to Cyprus" (20 October). It also seemed to the British that the Archbishop's attitude and statements confirmed the rigidity of the Greek Government. Eventually, the British decided that their policy would have a better chance of success if he were out of the way. On 9 March 1956, citing his association with EOKA, they deported him to the Seychelles.

Throughout 1956, the struggle with EOKA intensified and meanwhile the British appointed Lord Radcliffe to draw up proposals on self-government under British sovereignty. These were made public on 19 December and provided complete autonomy, subject to Britain's retention of responsibility for defence, external affairs and internal security, while at the same time seeking to balance and protect the interests of both the communities. Turkey accepted these proposals with some reservations. The Greek Government and the Greek Cypriots rejected them, continuing to insist on self-determination.

Then followed a development in Turkish policy. On the publication of the proposals, the British Government, recalling its recognition that self-determination was a future possibility, added that "the exercise of self-determination in such a mixed population must include partition among the eventual options".[1] The Turkish Government henceforth adopted this view publicly. In the course of the next year (1957), the British showed signs of considering abandoning their sovereignty over Cyprus, provided only that they could retain a base there. This was now important to them in terms not only of the Middle East but of strategic nuclear deterrence. Turkey henceforth urged the partition of the island. It did so, apparently, less because it desired this solution than as a way of warning Greece to abandon *enosis*.

[1] House of Commons, 19 December 1956.

In March 1957, the Secretary-General of NATO, Lord Ismay, offered mediation. Britain accepted this, as did Turkey in principle, but Greece and the Greek Cypriots rejected it. In December, Sir Hugh Foot became Governor, sought to promote discussions between the Greek and Turkish communities, and recommended the return of Archbishop Makarios as indispensable to progress. The British Government rejected this but permitted him to move to Athens, and here in the spring of 1958 and also in Ankara, the British Foreign Secretary, Selwyn Lloyd, and Sir Hugh Foot held renewed inter-governmental discussions.

On 19 June 1958, the British Government announced a new plan. The island would be ruled for seven years by a Council consisting of the governor, representatives of the Greek and Turkish governments, and Greek and Turkish Cypriot ministers; each community would have its separate house of representatives. The Turkish Government accepted the plan after slight modifications. The Greek Government rejected it on the grounds that it postponed self-determination and gave Turkey standing in the government of the island and thus in all probability a veto on eventual *enosis*.

At this point, nonetheless, a way out of the *impasse* began to appear. By the autumn of 1958, Archbishop Makarios had begun to indicate privately to the Greek Government that he would be willing to settle for the independence of the island. The Greek Government was ready to reach the same conclusion. Britain had achieved the understanding and support of the United States and other NATO allies and they redoubled their pressure for a settlement in the light of the crisis in relations with the Soviet Union over Berlin (November).[2] The United Nations General Assembly could not be brought to endorse *enosis* (a Greek resolution failed for the fifth consecutive year on 5 December) but might well support independence. British public opinion had become increasingly impatient of the Cyprus problem and hostile to the Greeks as a result of the activities of EOKA. The British Government had stated its determination to implement its plan and if deadlock persisted, might simply withdraw with unforeseeable consequences.

Diplomacy ensued along usual channels, at the United Nations and within NATO; at Christmas, EOKA announced a truce and Britain declared willingness to grant independence, subject to base rights; and on 5 February 1959, the Greek and Turkish Prime Ministers, Constantinos Karamanlis and Adnan Menderes, met in Zürich, whither they summoned Archbishop Makarios and Dr Fazil Kutchuk, leader of the Turkish Cypriots. The scene then shifted to London where on 19 February 1959, the London Agreement was signed.

[2] See pp. 168ff.

The Agreement comprised three treaties and a constitution. The Treaty of Establishment declared Cyprus a sovereign republic save for two base areas retained under British sovereignty. The Treaty of Alliance between Cyprus, Greece and Turkey included provision for 950 Greek troops and 650 Turkish troops to be stationed on the island (to train the Cyprus army). The Treaty of Guarantee signed by Britain, Cyprus, Greece and Turkey gave the three outside states the right to act singly or collectively to maintain the status of the island (i.e. to prevent either *enosis* or partition).

Under the constitution, there was to be a Greek Cypriot president and a Turkish Cypriot vice-president, each with a veto power. They were to be elected separately by the respective communities and so were the members of the House of Representatives. The Council of Ministers, the House of Representatives, the civil service and the police were to be 70 per cent Greek Cypriot, 30 per cent Turkish; and the army, limited to 2,000 men, 60 per cent–40 per cent. There were also to be separate assemblies for communal affairs and separate municipal governments in the five principal towns.

The British withdrew and the Agreement came into effect on 16 August 1960, by which time Archbishop Makarios had been elected president and Dr Kutchuk vice-president (December 1959). Cyprus was admitted to the Commonwealth in March 1961.

Friction between the two communities soon developed. Archbishop Makarios had objected to certain features of the London Agreement at the time it was made but had been told by the British that he must accept it as it stood or accept responsibility for the breakdown of negotiations. He was irked by the Treaty of Guarantee, considering it an infringement of Cypriot sovereignty. He considered the separate powers given to the Turkish community made the constitution unworkable. In December 1961, a peak of friction was reached when the Turkish Cypriot members of the House of Representatives vetoed new income tax laws and another in December 1962 when the Greeks opposed the continuance of separate municipal governments. Overall by this time, central and local government were paralysed and both sides were building up armed strength.

Finally, on 30 November 1963, Archbishop Makarios, in a memorandum to Dr Kutchuk, proposed thirteen amendments to the constitution. The drift of these was towards a unitary state with guarantees for the Turkish minority. The Turkish Cypriots, on the other hand, believed that they must have the full rights as a separate community given to them by the London Agreement. On 16 December, the Turkish Government declared the proposals unacceptable. On the 22nd, shooting started when a Greek police patrol insisted on searching a Turkish car. Accumulated tension erupted and fighting spread quickly.

Archbishop Makarios and Dr Kutchuk both appealed for a truce, but in vain. On 24 December, the Turkish community appealed to Turkey for assistance, which replied that if the fighting continued it would intervene under the terms of the Treaty of Guarantee. The British persuaded Archbishop Makarios to allow them to form the British, Turkish and Greek units on the island into a temporary peace-keeping force (26th) and a tense truce ensued. On 1 January (1964), Archbishop Makarios announced that he intended to abrogate the London Agreement but, under British persuasion, relaxed this to "desired to abrogate" and consented to discussions in London between the heads of the Greek and Turkish Cypriot communal assemblies, Glafcos Clerides and Rauf Denktash. These took place in mid-January, with a UN observer present, but both sides stuck to their positions, the Greeks arguing for the ending of the Treaty of Guarantee and reform of the constitution, the Turks insisting on the London Agreement.

With the support of the United States, Britain now proposed a NATO peace-keeping force and a mediator from a North Atlantic (though non-NATO) country. Archbishop Makarios, on the other hand, in line with Greek and Greek Cypriot policy in earlier years, wished to draw in the United Nations. As fighting developed in Limassol and Turkey again threatened to intervene, Britain finally consented to take the matter to the Security Council (15 February 1964). On 4 March, the Council unanimously adopted a resolution sponsored by the non-permanent members recommending the establishment of a UN force and the appointment of a mediator. The mandate of the United Nations Force in Cyprus was for three months (later continually extended in three- or six-month instalments) to "prevent a recurrence of the fighting" and "contribute to the maintenance and restoration of law and order".

In July–August, the UN mediator, Sakari Tuomioja of Finland, held talks in Geneva with Greek and Turkish representatives. He died on 9 September before announcing any results but it seems that little progress was made. One set of proposals under discussion were those concurrently worked out by President Lyndon Johnson's special mediator, former Secretary of State, Dean Acheson, in talks in Athens and Ankara. He appears to have made some progress on a plan for association between Cyprus and Greece with Turkish enclaves. However, Archbishop Makarios denounced the plan and nothing came of it. In the years following the independence of the island, Greek Government sympathy with the policies of Archbishop Makarios had declined but they still felt obliged to maintain their support for him.

Meanwhile, large-scale fighting in Cyprus had so far been avoided but both communities were now running their own affairs and continued to build up their armed strength. The Greek Government had sent Colonel Grivas back to the island (primarily for liaison with Archbishop Makarios and, it seems, as a counter-weight to him), and he took command of the Greek Cypriot forces. There was compulsory conscription in the communities and a secret inflow of arms and soldiers from Greece and Turkey (by 1967 there were an estimated 8,000 Greek and 1,500 Turkish national troops on the island). There was considerable migration, a blockade of Turkish communities, and where mixed communities still persisted, recurrent violence.

On 6 August 1964, heavy fighting broke out at Kokkina. On the 7th, Turkey appealed to the Security Council and sent aircraft to fire warning shots. On the 8th, the aircraft attacked the Greek Cypriot forces. Archbishop Makarios appealed to the Security Council and on the 9th, it adopted a British–United States resolution calling for an immediate cease-fire. Turkey complied. The fighting between the communities subsided.

Representatives of the Greek and Turkish Cypriots met on the 15th for discussions with Galo Plaza Lasso of Ecuador, the UN Secretary-General's Special Representative since May and mediator from September. In his report of the following spring (30 March 1965), the mediator advised that the London Agreement, *enosis*, partition, or federation were all in one way or another impracticable. The best course was for the two communities on the island to continue discussions until they (rather than outside governments) arrived at a workable solution to their problems. Both the Greek Government and Archbishop Makarios responded favourably to this report but the Turkish Government and community were opposed. They recognised by this time that the 1960 constitution was unworkable and favoured some form of federation; but above all they stood by the Treaty of Guarantee and Turkey's right to intervene on behalf of the Turkish community. Galo Plaza finally resigned in December 1965.

In May 1966 the UN Secretary-General, U Thant, raised the idea of suspending the London Agreement and substituting a guarantee by the Security Council of the independence of Cyprus and the security of the Turkish Cypriot community. However, this idea came to nothing in face of general opposition, especially strong from Greece. In renewed Graeco-Turkish talks that month, no progress was made.

Following the *coup d'état* in Greece in April 1967, there was much speculation that the new military regime might favour a rapid settlement. However, the Graeco-Turkish talks ended fruitlessly in September; in October, the Greek military regime made pronouncements favouring *enosis*; and in November, Greek Cypriot forces launched an attack, beginning with the Turkish Cypriot post at Aiyos Theodoros, and a new international crisis erupted. On the 24th, President Cevdet Sunay informed various governments that "Turkey is determined to settle the Cyprus problem once and for all". Massive Turkish military intervention and Greek counter-intervention seemed in prospect.

The Security Council met on the 24th and intense diplomacy ensued along these and other channels. The United States appointed Mr Cyrus Vance to act as intermediary between the Greek and Turkish governments. On the island, the UN force was able to interpose between the conflicting forces and Turkey's minimum demand proved to be the withdrawal of all illegal troops, the departure of Colonel Grivas and the disbandment of the Greek Cypriot National Guard. On the 29th, the Greek Government agreed to these terms, and, after some demur as regards the National Guard, Archbishop Makarios did likewise.

In the following months, international tension eased and relations between the communities on the island improved. By 15 January 1968, some 7,000 Greek national troops had been withdrawn. The United Nations Force remained in position. On 7 March, the Cyprus Government announced a set of pacification measures and dealings between the communities began to be resumed. On 3 June, Glafcos Clerides and Rauf Denktash, representing the two communities, began discussions in Beirut on the form which the constitution and administration of Cyprus should take.

*　　*　　*

C. FOLEY: *Legacy of Strife, Cyprus from Rebellion to Civil War*, Penguin Books, Harmondsworth 1964.

L. B. MILLER: *Cyprus, The Law and Politics of Civil Strife*, Center for International Affairs, Harvard University, Cambridge 1968.

J. A. STEGENGA: *The United Nations Force in Cyprus*, Ohio State University Press, Columbus 1968.

R. STEPHENS: *Cyprus, A Place of Arms*, Pall Mall, London 1966.

S. G. XYDIS: *Cyprus, Conflict and Conciliation, 1954–58*, Ohio State University Press, Columbus 1967.

The Suez Canal 1956

AFTER fifteen years of planning and digging led by the Frenchman, Ferdinand de Lesseps, the Suez Canal was opened in 1869. The Compagnie Universelle du Canal Maritime de Suez, which held a ninety-nine year concession from that date from the Egyptian and Turkish authorities, was an Egyptian company but its headquarters were in Paris and most of its capital was subscribed by the French public. The British Government bought the Khedive of Egypt's shares in 1875. In 1888, the leading European powers signed the Constantinople Convention according to which the Canal was to be open to the shipping of all countries whether in peace or war.

Egypt at this time was a province of the Ottoman empire, but from 1882 the British governed the country under the nominal authority of the Khedive and the still more nominal authority of the Porte. With the development of nationalist feeling after the First World War, the protectorate was ended and the country was proclaimed a monarchy, though Britain reserved to itself the defence of the country and of the Canal in particular (1922). The next major step was the Anglo-Egyptian Treaty of 26 August 1936 which converted the relationship into a defence alliance and under which Britain could maintain 10,000 troops in the Canal Zone, evacuating the rest of the country. The Treaty provided for revision in twenty years.

In the Second World War, Egypt and the Canal bulked larger than ever in British strategy and this survived into the postwar world with the decline of the Empire and the growth of the Commonwealth, the conflict with the Soviet Union and the troubles in the Far East. Commercially, about a third of the tonnage of shipping passing through the Canal was British; about a quarter of Britain's imports came that way (1956); the shipment of Middle East oil was of ever-increasing importance.

In Egypt, on the other hand, nationalist feeling continually strengthened, intensified by events in Palestine and the humiliation in the war against Israel (1948–49), and there were growing demands for the ending of the Anglo-Egyptian condominium of the Sudan (established in 1899) and the departure of the British from the Canal Zone. On 8 October 1951, the Egyptian Government abrogated the 1936 Treaty but the British reinforced their troops. Incidents in the Canal Zone multiplied.

On 26 July 1952, a Committee of Free Officers, headed by Major-General Mohammed Neguib, overthrew the monarchy and proclaimed a

123

new era in Egypt's history. In the first two years, relations with Britain gradually improved. On 12 February 1953, the two countries reached agreement on the Sudan and on 19 October 1954 (Colonel Gamal Abdel Nasser having replaced General Neguib in April) they signed a new agreement on the Canal. This ended the 1936 Treaty and provided for the withdrawal of British troops from the Canal Zone and for the maintenance of the British military base by British civilian contractors. The British had the right to send troops back to the Zone if Egypt or any Arab League state or Turkey were attacked by an outside power. (This envisaged the Soviet Union and excluded Israel.) The sovereignty of Egypt over the base area was confirmed and, in recording Egypt's acceptance of the 1888 Constantinople Convention, the two countries recognised the Canal as "an integral part of Egypt".

At the beginning of 1955, relations between the two countries worsened once more. Britain and Turkey were seeking to organise a general defensive alliance in the Middle East. President Nasser seized the leadership of popular Arab opposition to the plan in the name of Arab freedom from external domination and unity against Israel. He denounced the Turkey–Iraq Treaty signed at Baghdad on 24 February 1955; he denounced still more vehemently Britain's adherence to the pact on 4 April; and he worked passionately to prevent the adherence of further Arab countries, notably Jordan.

This quarrel went hand-in-hand with a worsening of Egypt's relations with Israel. On the grounds that it was still legally at war with Israel and as part of the Arab economic boycott (the first measures of which began in 1945), Egypt continued to deny the use of the Canal to Israel. Now, in addition, the tense military armistice was being increasingly breached. Border raids from Egypt were countered from 1953 onwards by punitive attacks from Israel. These *fedayeen* raids increased in intensity at the beginning of 1955. A heavy Israeli counter-attack in the Gaza Strip coincided with the formation of the Baghdad Pact (February 1955). Simultaneously, Egypt's relations with France were worsening. The French believed that Egypt was giving heavy assistance to the rebels in Algeria. Military co-operation between the French and the Israelis began to grow.

There were still wider developments in Egypt's foreign relations in 1955. In April, Colonel Nasser, whose diplomatic horizons had hitherto been mainly confined to the West, took part in the Bandung Conference, consorting with China and India and other "non-aligned states" which had begun to open relations with the East. In August, Egypt made a trade agreement with China and on 27 September 1955, announced an arms supply agreement with Czechoslovakia. With increasing urgency in view of the mounting tension with Israel, Egypt had pressed Britain and the United States for armaments but they had made conditions in the name of Middle East peace. Now, to their deep dismay, Egyptian cotton was to be bartered for Soviet bloc arms.

The United States, in the past two years, while approving the Baghdad Pact, had sought to avoid alienating Saudi Arabia and to improve its relations with Egypt, hitherto clouded by its support for the survival of Israel. To the annoyance of the British Prime Minister, Anthony Eden, the United States Secretary of State, John Foster Dulles, decided against American membership of the Pact. The United States now decided to join Britain in a move designed to improve relations with Egypt and to check the growth of relations between Egypt and the Soviet Union. The Soviet Union having shown some interest, the United States announced on 16 December 1955 that it would contribute $56 million to the first stage of the Egyptian regime's greatest and proudest project, the new Aswan Dam. Britain was to contribute $14 million. Anglo-American participation fulfilled one of the World Bank's conditions for providing the bulk of the foreign funds, $200 million.

Egypt, however, had not yet reached agreement on terms and conditions with the three Western lenders and in the early months of 1956 continued its discussions with the Soviet Union also. The United States Congress was already restive on aiding "neutralist" states and in May United States opinion was further irritated by Egypt's recognition of the Communist government of China. The dismissal of Lt.-General John Glubb from command of the Arab Legion by King Hussein of Jordan in March was seen by some important sections of the British Government and public as a further blow in Egypt's campaign against Britain. All three Western lenders were doubtful whether the Egyptian regime, committed to heavy armaments expenditure, would in the event provide its share of the funds for the Dam and would fulfil the other commercial conditions. Egypt withheld an undertaking not to seek to draw in the Soviet Union.

On 19 July 1956, Secretary of State Dulles cut short the negotiations by telling the Egyptian ambassador that the United States would not participate. On the 21st, the Soviet Union stated that it was not committed to the project. On the 26th, the anniversary of the 1952 revolution, Colonel Nasser announced a decree nationalising the Suez Canal Company. The shareholders would be compensated at current share prices. The future profits of the Company would be used for the Aswan Dam.

The international uproar caused by this action was enormous. The British and French governments were not certain of the illegality of the nationalisation decree. They believed none the less that Egypt's action was to be seen and would be seen as the seizure by Egypt of a great international waterway in defiance of their power. If they allowed this to pass unchallenged, an aggressive state would be left in control of Britain's lifeline and would have scored a dazzling victory in its drive for supremacy in the Arab world by methods reminiscent of the Axis dictators. On a more technical level, Colonel Nasser's announcement raised fears that he would sacrifice the necessary investment in the development of the Canal to his project at Aswan.

The British and French governments immediately began consultations. They discovered that they could not mount a military operation forthwith and, moreover, Secretary Dulles, who arrived in London on 1 August, while not denying that force might ultimately be necessary, stressed that every effort should first be made to mobilise international opinion in favour of an international regime for the Canal. Accordingly, the three of them decided to call an international conference, and on 16 August, representatives of twenty-two states with a close interest in the Canal met in London. Egypt refused to attend. The Soviet Union, India, Indonesia and Ceylon argued for an international advisory body but the eighteen others proposed on 23 August that, under Egypt's sovereignty, an international body should control the Canal. They deputed a committee of Australia, Ethiopia, Iran, Sweden and the United States, headed by the Prime Minister of Australia, Robert Menzies, to put their proposals to Colonel Nasser, and this they did in Cairo from 3–9 September.

The British and the French meanwhile made troop movements, but President Eisenhower said in the course of a news conference (31 August): "We are committed to a peaceful settlement of this dispute, nothing else." Mr Menzies, like Britain and France in their argumentation throughout the dispute, placed the emphasis on the need to detach the Canal from politics but Colonel Nasser, now as throughout, made little of this concept. He rejected the London proposals, merely requesting discussions on technical and commercial issues between Egypt's new Suez Canal Authority and interested states.

At this stage, the parliamentary opposition in Britain and a large section of public opinion, many of whom suspected that Britain and France were moving towards the use of force, urged their government to lay the matter before the United Nations. The British and French governments were willing but the United States would not agree to the basis which they laid down, namely, absolute adherence to the spirit of the London proposals and retention of freedom of action.

Instead, Secretary Dulles proposed that the users of the Canal should form an association which would manage the movement of their traffic through the Canal, employ the pilots and collect the dues. The British Government, and still more the French, were reluctant to accept this plan;

they already had Colonel Nasser under some pressure in as much as they were organising the withholding of dues from Egypt's new Suez Canal Authority and the pilots had been withdrawn so that (they believed) Egypt would prove incapable of operating the Canal; any further elaboration would simply muddle the situation. However, on 11 September, the two governments decided to agree and on the 19th a second conference met in London to discuss the plan. The Suez Canal Users Association of fifteen states was established on 1 October.

The ambiguity of the United States, however, on the withholding of dues from Egypt by the Association, strengthened Britain and France in their fears that SCUA was a sidetrack. On 23 September, they appealed on their own to the UN Security Council. After long discussions, the Egyptian Foreign Minister, Dr Mohammed Fawzi, agreed to six principles, adopted unanimously by the Council on 13 October. These provided "free and open transit through the Canal without discrimination"; "the sovereignty of Egypt should be respected"; "the operation of the Canal should be insulated from the politics of any country"; "the manner of fixing tolls and charges should be decided by agreement between Egypt and the users"; "a fair proportion of the dues should be allotted to development" (of the Canal); "in case of disputes, unresolved affairs between the Suez Canal Company and the Egyptian Government should be settled by arbitration". A second part of the resolution stated that the London proposals conformed to these principles and called on Egypt to put forward its proposals; but this part of the resolution was vetoed by the Soviet Union.

Various states sought to bring the disputants together for further negotiations at Geneva at the end of the month. However, in the Middle East, at this time, border raids and political tension between Israel and its neighbours were reaching crisis point. Immediately after the UN proceedings, Israel and France entered into discussions with Britain on the Anglo-French response to an attack by Israel on Egypt, and an understanding was reached.

On 29 October, Israel invaded Sinai. On the 30th, Britain and France, invoking the need to protect the Canal, called on Egypt and Israel to cease fire and to withdraw ten miles from the Canal and on Egypt to permit the temporary stationing of Anglo-French forces along it. In the event of non-compliance within twelve hours, their forces would intervene to secure compliance. Egypt rejected this ultimatum. On the 31st, British planes began bombing raids and on 5 November, Anglo-French troops seized Port Said and advanced down the Canal. Israel completed the conquest of Sinai.

The action of the three countries raised a storm of opposition internationally and a deep division of opinion within Britain. On 30 October, the United States introduced a resolution in the Security Council calling on Israel to withdraw and on other states (i.e. Britain and France) to refrain from force. Britain and France vetoed this resolution. Next, the United States moved a resolution in the General Assembly calling for an immediate cease-fire and withdrawal, passed on 2 November by 64–5 (Australia, Britain, France, Israel, New Zealand). As a further pressure it refused co-operation with Britain against the heavy movement out of sterling. The Soviet Union, deeply engaged in the simultaneous crisis in Hungary,[1] also sponsored condemnatory resolutions. The only mitigation of United States hostility was a warning response to the more flamboyant threats and proposals of the Soviet leaders.

In the debate on 2 November, the Canadian Minister for External Affairs, Lester Pearson, arguing that calls for a cease-fire and withdrawal were not enough, proposed the creation of a United Nations force to police the border between Egypt and Israel. On the 3rd, Britain and France assented to this idea in principle. On the 5th, the day of the Anglo-French landing, the General Assembly established the United Nations Emergency Force, to be recruited from countries other than permanent members of the Security Council. At midnight on the 6th, the British and French halted their advance twenty-five miles south of Port Said and ceased fire.

Over the next few weeks, the British and French withdrew step by step with the build-up of UNEF. The first officers of UNEF arrived in Egypt on 10 November; the last British and French units left on 22 December. Israel made more complex demands and, while evacuating Sinai, held on to the Gaza Strip and to positions commanding the Gulf of Aqaba. At length, United States pressure was successful and Israel withdrew from these places also (9 March 1957).

Meanwhile, in Britain, illness forced Prime Minister Anthony Eden to break off work for three weeks from 23 November followed by his resignation on 9 January 1957. In Egypt, the Egyptian authorities had sunk block-ships in the Canal at the start of the Anglo-French-Israeli attack and refused to have it cleared until the last British and French troops had left. It was then cleared under the auspices of the United Nations, at Egypt's request, and reopened for traffic on 9 April.

On 24 April, Egypt made a declaration to the UN Secretary-General whereby in accordance with the Constantinople Convention and the six principles of 13 October 1956, it would maintain free and uninterrupted navigation of the Canal for all nations. It did so as regards Israel until February 1959.

[1] See p. 131ff.

The World Bank acted as intermediary between Egypt's Suez Canal Authority and the Compagnie Universelle and finally an agreement between them was signed on 13 July 1958. Egypt was to pay compensation for the assets taken over in Egypt of £E28·3 million (£28·9 million) over five years. Thereafter the company took to other lines of business as the Suez Finance Company.

* * *

M. DAYAN: *Diary of the Suez Campaign*, Weidenfeld and Nicolson, London 1966.

A. JAMES: *The Politics of Peace-Keeping*, Chatto and Windus, London 1969.

T. ROBERTSON: *Crisis, The Inside Story of the Suez Conspiracy*, Hutchinson, London 1965.

H. THOMAS: *The Suez Affair*, revised edition, Penguin Books, Harmondsworth 1970.

D. WATT: *Documents on the Suez Crisis*, Royal Institute of International Affairs, London 1957.

Hungary 1956

BETWEEN 1945 and 1948, Hungary, controlled by the Soviet Union, was progressively given a Soviet-type regime. After the death of Stalin on 5 March 1953, Imre Nagy became Prime Minister (July), although Matyas Rakosi, "Hungary's Stalin", remained First Secretary of the Communist Party. Nagy condemned past policies in his first speech to Parliament and promised major reforms. A New Course was to be followed similar to that announced by Georgi Malenkov in the Soviet Union. This meant, notably, greater emphasis on the production of consumer goods and a slowing down in the compulsory collectivisation of agriculture.

This programme was not in the event carried out since Nagy was at no time in full control of either Party or Government. In February 1955, in the Soviet Union, Malenkov resigned and was succeeded as Chairman of the Council of Ministers by Nicolai Bulganin on the proposal of Nikita Krushchev, the First Secretary of the Party, who subsequently achieved primacy. In April, Nagy was dismissed, being succeeded by the relatively unknown Andras Hegedüs. Rakosi was once more in control and Stalinist economic policies were restored. Some relaxation continued, however, notably the rehabilitation of political prisoners, victims of the various purges of 1945–51.

The reversal of Nagy's policies and his expulsion from the Party at the end of 1955 provoked considerable resentment among Party members. Opposition to Rakosi and his policies gradually grew among writers and journalists and technical-administrative people through the media of the Writers' Association and the *Literary Gazette*, and a society called the Petöfi Circle. The strongest criticism came from the rehabilitated political prisoners. Such criticism was emboldened by the continued "thaw" in the Soviet Union. Despite the overthrow of Malenkov, there was no return to Stalinism and Soviet foreign policy continued a relaxation of tensions, notably, the beginnings of a rapprochement with the rebel against Stalin, Tito of Yugoslavia.

Outside the Hungarian Communist Party, there was widespread popular hatred of the Communist regime. The foundations of this were laid in the immediate postwar years but it was not apparently until after the enforced merger of the Social Democrats with the Communist Party in February 1948 and the establishment of a one-party state under Rakosi that discontent rapidly increased. Vigorous steps were taken to change Hungary into a socialist state on the Soviet model, sacrificing national individuality.

Terror and the "cadre-card" system became the methods of Party control. The peasants resented attempts at collectivisation and the industrial workers came to hate the "production norms".

However, though there was deep discontent, the general mood appears to have been one of despair and apathy. Even the criticism of the regime which began within the Party in the mid-1950s did little to rouse the industrial workers and peasants; it seems they were sceptical of the idea of genuine reforms within the communist system. They apparently saw little hope and took little action until the events of October 1956.

The ferment within the Party was heightened in 1956 and the eventual popular rising was touched off by events outside the country. Krushchev's attack on Stalin at the 20th Party Congress of the Soviet Union in February 1956 had powerful repercussions in the Hungarian Party. The attack on the "personality cult" could equally be applied to Rakosi. On 18 July, Rakosi was made to resign. This may have been due partly to a Soviet desire to make a gesture to his enemy, Tito of Yugoslavia. Rakosi's successor, Erno Gerö, was a known Stalinist and Hegedüs remained Premier. Discontent within the Party, far from being allayed, was increased. It was further stimulated by the continued success of Yugoslavia's brand of socialism, by Soviet friendliness towards Yugoslavia and by the new course in the Chinese Communist Party with its principle "let every flower bloom and every bird sing".

The revolt at Posnan in Poland at the end of June intensified the atmosphere throughout Eastern Europe. However, it was the events in Poland following the opening on 19 October 1956 of the 8th Session of the Central Committee of the Polish Communist Party that led to the crystallisation of the situation within Hungary. The Poles, in defiance of a Russian delegation of Krushchev, Laza Kaganovich, Anastas Mikoyan and Molotov and reports of Russian troop movements, refused to countenance Russian interference in their Party's internal affairs. Wladyslaw Gomulka was appointed First Secretary and, in a resolution of 21 October, a policy of liberalisation was adopted. Gomulka did, however, stress the continued dominant position of the Party in Polish politics and reaffirm his country's loyalty to the Warsaw Treaty Organisation. On the 23rd, Krushchev accepted the situation and the Russian troops returned to their garrisons.

Inspired by the Polish example, Budapest students organised a number of meetings on 22 October to discuss the situation in Hungary. Various demands were voiced, including the withdrawal of Russian troops from the country, free and secret elections, and the re-emergence of other political parties alongside the Communists. The following afternoon, demonstrations in various parts of the city by students and others led in the evening to a mass demonstration in the parliament square. At 8 p.m., Gerö, who had been away in Yugoslavia in the preceding days, made a radio broadcast reaffirming an uncompromising Stalinist line, and when some of the demonstrators sought to enter the Hungarian Radio building to make a counter-broadcast, security police fired on them.

Bitter street fighting between the populace and the security police now engulfed Budapest. To appease opinion, Nagy was hastily made Prime Minister. Gerö appealed to the Russians for aid but when Mikoyan and Mikhail Suslov came to Budapest, Gerö was forced to resign and withdrew to the Soviet Union with Hegedüs. Janos Kadar was made First Secretary and Nagy formed a Cabinet. On the 28th, Nagy announced that a cease-fire between government and the rebels had been reached. The Soviet Union had agreed that Russian troops (inactive during the fighting) would be withdrawn from Budapest.

Meanwhile, the insurrection had spread beyond the capital in a spontaneous, unorganised way. In the countryside it was a more root-and-branch attack on Communism. Little resistance was encountered; the Communists "simply melted away",[1] Russian military units stood passively by.

In the next few days, the Nagy government proved unable to master the situation. The events of 23–28 October had unleashed the latent anti-Communism throughout Hungary and the Government was swept along on it. "The Hungarians were swayed by the feeling that their country had a natural right to independence and neutrality and did not stop to think of the consequences."[2] Nagy was unable to follow Gomulka's course of playing off the people and Russia, winning restraint from each with the threat of the other. He tried to do this but failed.

The majority of the insurgents refused to surrender their arms in deference to the Nagy government. Instead, the various revolutionary committees set up throughout the country remained in being and voiced increasing demands. On 30 October, the Government announced that the one-party system was to be abolished. This immediately led to the formation or reconstruction of a large number of non-Communist parties. The Communist Party itself, discredited and humiliated, was rapidly disintegrating. Many of the emerging parties refused to co-operate with Nagy so long as the Communists retained a majority in the Cabinet. The Catholic Church, led by Cardinal Mindszenty, adopted a similar attitude. On 3 November, Nagy reconstructed his Cabinet. It became mainly non-Communist.

Nagy also announced (1 November) that Hungary would leave the

[1] Zinner, p. 261.
[2] Fejtö, p. 235.

Warsaw Treaty Organisation. This step seems to have been first demanded by the insurgents at Gyor on 28 October. It was quickly taken up by the emerging political parties. By the time Nagy made his announcement, it was being demanded throughout the country.

When Mikoyan and Suslov made a series of visits to Budapest in the last days of October the Soviet Union was to all appearances still willing to work with Nagy. This now changed. On 2 November, the Nagy government protested to the Russians about Red Army reinforcements entering the country since, it seems, the 29th. Negotiations between the Government and the Russians followed but, on the night of 3–4 November, the Hungarian negotiator, Defence Minister Pal Malater, was arrested and early on the morning of 4 November, Nagy announced that Russian troops had begun an attack on Budapest "with the obvious intention of overthrowing the lawful and democratic government". From eastern Hungary, it was announced that a "Hungarian Revolutionary Worker-Peasant Government" had been formed under Janos Kadar and that it had appealed for Russian assistance. With overwhelming military superiority, the Russian forces crushed Hungarian resistance completely in the next few days. On 9 November, the Kadar government was installed in Budapest.

The outside world at this time was in uproar over the British, French and Israeli invasion of Egypt which began on 29–30 October.[3] This was currently the major concern at the United Nations. On 1 November, the Nagy government requested "that the question of Hungary's neutrality and the defence of this neutrality by the four Great Powers" be placed on the General Assembly agenda. On 4 November, a Security Council resolution condemning the Soviet Union's military intervention was vetoed by it. The matter was immediately referred to an emergency General Assembly meeting and a United States sponsored resolution calling on the Russians to halt their action and withdraw their forces was passed. This resolution also called on the parties to let observers, appointed by the Secretary-General, enter the country and investigate the situation and upon member states to make available food, medicine and other supplies for Hungary. Further United Nations pressure took the form of continued debate and the formation of a Special Committee on Hungary. The Kadar government was unwilling to co-operate, however, and by 26 November was openly denouncing United Nations activity as "unwarranted interference" in Hungary's domestic affairs.

Strikes, demonstrations and acts of violence occurred in Hungary throughout November and December but the Government, backed by Russian military forces, was able to impose order by means of martial

[3] See p. 127ff.

law and mass arrests. Not until March 1958 did the Russians begin to withdraw some of their troops.

The situation in Hungary did not revert in every respect to that before October 1956. The dominance of the Communist Party was restored and in March 1957 Hungary's allegiance to the Warsaw Treaty Organisation was reaffirmed. On the other hand, Kadar, who had spent most of the Rakosi period in prison, had a reputation for being an anti-Stalinist and his government announced a number of reforms, especially in the economic field. There was to be no return to forced collectivisation. Foreign trade agreements were, in future, to be based on mutual advantage. The interim Three Year Plan, announced in 1957, placed greater emphasis on raising living standards. This was assisted in the next few years by economic aid, mainly from the Soviet Union but also from other Eastern European countries.

*　　*　　*

P. Ignotus: *Hungary*, Ernest Benn, London 1972.

F. Fejtö: *Behind the Rape of Hungary*, David McKay, New York 1957.

P. Kecskemeti: *The Unexpected Revolution*, Stanford University Press, 1961.

M. Molnar: *Budapest 1956*, Allen and Unwin, London 1972.

F. A. Vali: *Rift and Revolution in Hungary*, Harvard University Press, Cambridge 1961.

P. Zinner: *Revolution in Hungary*, Columbia University Press, New York 1962.

Lebanon and Jordan 1956-58

IN common with the rest of the Middle East, the politics of Lebanon and Jordan were in turmoil throughout the 1950s. A crisis was reached simultaneously in Iraq, Lebanon and Jordan in the summer of 1958, leading to United States and British military intervention in Lebanon and Jordan.

In Lebanon, which together with Syria achieved effective independence of the French in the course of 1944, politics were personal, oligarchic and sectarian. The oligarchy was commonly known as "the forty families". The majority of the one-and-a-quarter-million population in the 1940s were Christians (Maronite, Greek Orthodox, Greek Catholic and others), though it was generally believed in the 1950s that the Muslims (Sunni and Shia) were approaching equality.

In 1943, as the take-over from the French approached, the Maronite President, Bishara al-Khuri, reached informal understandings with the Sunni Muslim Prime Minister, Riad al-Solh, known as the National Convention. The President was always to be a Maronite, the Prime Minister a Sunni Muslim, the Speaker of the Chamber of Deputies (the only chamber) a Shia Muslim and the Deputy Speaker a Greek Orthodox, while the Greek Catholics and another sizeable sect, the Druzes, were to be represented in the Cabinet. Seats in the Chamber were to be allotted proportionately to the sects (this was subsequently made part of the electoral law) and similar agreements were reached regarding the army and the civil service.

More broadly, it was understood that the Christians would not imperil the independence of Lebanon by seeking protection agreements with the European powers. The Muslims, for their part, would respect the religious and cultural links of the Christians with the West and would not seek to merge the country with its predominantly Muslim neighbours.

In the late 1940s and early 1950s, in keeping with the character of the country and these understandings, Lebanon shared the hostility of other Arab states towards Israel but in practice was the least belligerent and intransigent in its policy. It showed clear sympathy with the Western powers in their conflict with the Soviet Union but avoided any commitment.

In the summer of 1952, a political coalition formed against President Bishara al-Khuri in the name of modernising the political system; on 18 September, following a general strike, he resigned; on 23 September, the Chamber elected to the presidency one of the leaders of the coalition, a Maronite, Camille Chamoun.

135

In the next few years, there was little change in the political system; the coalition broke up; cabinet followed cabinet in the usual way. However, at this time, in Lebanon as throughout the Middle East, the effects of the revolution of 26 July 1952 in Egypt began to make themselves felt. Following the accession to power in Egypt of Gamal Abdel Nasser in April 1954, the outbreak of his quarrel with Iraq and Britain, and the launching of his campaign for Arab unity, Lebanese opinion was riven apart, largely between Christians and Muslims, though as always with sectarian and personal cross-currents.

Christians on the whole sympathised with the formation of the Baghdad Pact, signed by Turkey and Iraq on 24 February 1955 and joined by Britain, Iran and Pakistan in the following months. The Pact promised economic and military assistance to Middle East members; it responded to fears of the Soviet Union and Communism; membership for Lebanon would counterbalance the possible pretensions of its neighbour, Syria. To Muslims, on the other hand, many of whom now looked for leadership to Egypt and Syria, the Pact was anathema, dividing the Arabs and their front against Israel and buttressing the position of the "British imperialists" in the Middle East.

In the event, President Chamoun avoided the Pact and the counter-alliance which Egypt was seeking to organise but passionate suspicions were aroused and these were doubled the following year when, on the Anglo-French invasion of Egypt (October 1956) the President did not break off diplomatic relations with the two states. The President justified this as necessary to helping negotiate an Anglo-French cease-fire but the move still further divided opinion, the Christians generally approving, the Muslims bitterly opposed.

The Anglo-French debacle and the links between Egypt and the Soviet Union convinced the United States that it must take some new action to deter Soviet penetration into the Middle East. On 5 January 1957, President Eisenhower made a policy statement, immediately named "The Eisenhower Doctrine", requesting Congress to authorise economic and military assistance to Middle East states and the use of United States forces "to secure and protect the territorial integrity and political independence of such nations requesting such aid against overt armed aggression from any nation controlled by international communism". (Aggression was to cover both "direct and indirect".) After controversy over whether the Doctrine was a realistic assessment and response to the situation, Congress passed a Middle East Resolution in these terms in March.

The Iraqi and Lebanese governments were alone in the Middle East in voicing approval of the Doctrine. When the Lebanese Government made a formal statement of acceptance on 16 March, President Nasser deplored this as a "deviationist and unfriendly act". Middle East popular opinion generally saw the Doctrine as an obscure but doubtless sinister move, perhaps portending a United States effort to succeed to the position of the British under the same transparent disguise of defence against the Soviet Union. President Chamoun argued that acceptance of the Doctrine was not an alliance and did not involve alignment for or against any Arab state; but Muslim leaders denounced the move as a breach of Arab solidarity and a threat to the National Convention.

As the elections of May 1957 approached, an added element of passion was the widespread suspicion that the President was planning a renewal of his term of office when it expired in fifteen months time (September 1958). This would require a constitutional amendment and this in turn would need a two-thirds majority of the deputies in the new Chamber. To the accompaniment of charges of corruption and trickery, customary at the country's elections, the result of the voting was a victory for President Chamoun. Several leading politicians were unseated, notably Kamal Jumblat, the Druze leader, opposed to Chamoun since the break-up of the 1952 coalition, and Abdullah al-Yafi and Saeb Salam who had broken with him over the Suez affair.

From now on Nasserist street demonstrations and counter-demonstrations and clashes were frequent. The merger of Egypt and Syria in the United Arab Republic on 1 February 1958 further excited the situation, raising the hopes of the Nasserists and deepening the fears of those who stood for Lebanese independence. On 7 May 1958, the editor of the Nasserist, pro-Communist *Al-Telegraf*, Nassib al-Matni, a Maronite, was murdered, and with accusations of complicity against Chamoun, vigorously denied, fighting erupted. There was apparently no central plan. Chamoun's opponents raised rebellion wherever local conditions were favourable. Saeb Salam took control of the Muslim quarter of Beirut; Kamal Jumblat, of the Druze populated Shuf mountain area; the local oligarchs, of Tripoli; and groups of Nasserist sympathies, of most of the border areas with Syria. They proclaimed a new political alliance, the United National Front, appealing to all opponents of Chamoun. Predominantly Muslim and Nasserist, it contained many shades of opinion and also included some Christians and had the approval of the Maronite Patriarch, long at odds with Chamoun.

The fighting was mostly between the rebels and Maronite and other Lebanese-independence volunteers. The army, under General Fuad Chehab, stood aloof. The Government, for its part, laid emphasis on external factors in the crisis. On 13 May, it notified Britain, France and the United States that it would request military assistance against external aggression if necessary and soon began to complain publicly of Syrian assistance to the rebels. On 27 May, President Chamoun announced that he would not seek a further term of office in the autumn but this did not appease the situation. The rebels demanded his immediate resignation. On 6 June, having raised the matter to little effect at the Arab League, the Lebanese Government complained before the Security Council of massive intervention by the United Arab Republic. The Council established a United Nations Observer Group in Lebanon (7th) and this reported on 4 July that it found no evidence to substantiate the Lebanese charge. Western commentators pointed out that UNOGIL was only a hundred strong and was denied access to long stretches of rebel-held frontier. The Lebanese Government continued to complain of Syrian infiltration. It began urgent discussions with the United States Government.

This was the situation when on 14 July, Western policy and anti-Nasserist forces in the Middle East were dealt a shattering blow by the revolution in Iraq. Faisal II and, a few days later, Prime Minister Nuri es-Said were killed and a republic was proclaimed under General Abdul Karim Qassim. With first the union of Syria and Egypt and now the revolution in Iraq, it seemed to Western opinion that the whole Middle East situation was collapsing in favour of the ambitions of Egypt and perhaps of the Soviet Union. On the 15th, President Eisenhower announced that in response to an urgent request from President Chamoun, United States troops would land in Lebanon "to protect American lives and by their presence there to encourage the Lebanese Government in defence of Lebanese sovereignty and integrity".

Two days later, Britain announced the same response to the same request from the Kingdom of Jordan, a country similarly riven in the past few years by the contending forces in the Middle East.

The future of Jordan was already in doubt at the time of the coronation of King Hussein at the age of seventeen on 2 May 1953. Since the ending of the British mandate on 22 March 1946, Jordan had been in a treaty alliance relationship with Britain (a revised treaty was signed on 15 March 1948) and was to become increasingly reliant from 1954 on British budgetary assistance. These links with Britain were coming under mounting attack from Arab nationalist opinion.

Jordan's only certain friend in the Middle East was Iraq. Faisal II was Hussein's cousin. To the south, the ruling house of Saudi Arabia had a long-standing feud with the two Hashemite kings. To the west was Israel, presenting the continual possibility that Jordan would be swept into a renewed Arab war and, since the war of 1948, cutting off Jordan from access to its traditional seaports.

The possibility of a new war with Israel was outstripped in significance by the serious consequences of the last. The Arab Legion had over-run the territory on the west bank of the Jordan during the 1948 war and on 1 December 1949, Hussein's grandfather, Abdullah, had formally annexed it, so adding some 400,000 Palestinians to the population. In addition, about the same number of refugees from Palestine moved into Jordan, mostly dependent henceforth on the support of United Nations agencies. The Palestinians not merely outnumbered the Jordanian tribesmen two to one, but despised their customs and had less loyalty to the Hashemites and a deeper hatred of Israel. They became a continual, powerful source of agitation for constitutional change and the adoption of Arab nationalist policies.

In the first months of his reign, the King attempted co-operation with the reformers. In January 1954, however, all political parties were dissolved and arrangements made for licensing new ones. In June, Parliament was dissolved and a number of newspapers suspended. The reformist government was replaced by a traditionalist government which in August received special powers by the promulgation of defence regulations. The elections in November resulted in a large majority for the Government but were accompanied by rioting in which the Arab Legion had to intervene.

Simultaneously, external pressures intensified. Border incidents between Israel and its neighbours were increasing and Egypt, now under President Nasser, launched its massive campaign for Arab solidarity, unity and modernisation which included mounting criticisms of the "reactionary, royalist regimes" of Iraq and Jordan.

Then in the new year, 1955, came the affair of the Baghdad Pact. After an initial negative reaction, it became clear that King Hussein wished to follow Iraq's lead, and towards the end of the year British, Turkish and Iraqi efforts to persuade him to take the plunge and Egyptian efforts to dissuade him became acute. In December, his government indicated that Jordan was considering joining. Serious rioting followed, the Prime Minister resigned, and a new government declared that Jordan would not join.

The King temporarily silenced his opponents when on 1 March 1956, he dismissed the British commander of the Arab Legion, Lt.-General John Glubb. In the summer, the passions aroused by the Suez crisis pulled Jordan strongly in the direction of Egypt. The elections of October 1956 resulted in a left-wing coalition cabinet (including one Communist) under Suleiman Nabulsi. On 25 October, in view of the growing crisis with Israel, Jordan signed an agreement with Egypt and Saudi Arabia, placing their armies under Egyptian command in the event of war. Following the Anglo-French-Israeli invasion of Egypt, the three Arab countries and Syria signed in Cairo (19 January 1957) an Arab Solidarity Agreement under which Egypt and Saudi Arabia agreed to contribute £5 million annually and Syria half that figure to replace British budgetary assistance. On 1 March, the Anglo-Jordanian treaty and the British subvention were formally ended.

At this point, co-operation between King Hussein and his cabinet collapsed, and correspondingly the accord with Egypt. The King and the traditionalists had become increasingly fearful that the Nasserist, pan-Arabist, reforming enthusiasm would end in the extinction of the monarchy and of Jordan's independence. A particular issue was the licence given to the Communists. The Cabinet rejected the King's remonstrances on their small but growing activity. Whereas the King approved of the Eisenhower Doctrine, the Cabinet followed Egypt in condemning it. On 3 April, the Cabinet announced that it intended to establish diplomatic relations with the Soviet Union and to recognise the Communist Government of China.

Matters came to a head a few days later. On the 7th, armoured cars encircled Amman, an obscure movement subsequently explained by the King's supporters as the beginning of a *coup d'état* by the Chief of Staff, General Ali Abu Nuwar, and by the King's opponents as a move by him against Prime Minister Nabulsi. On the 10th, the King dismissed Nabulsi. On the 14th, the King was warned of trouble at the military camp at Zerqa and, hastening there, faced down the dissidents. In the following days, there were continuous riots in Amman and rumours of troop movements in Syria. On the 24th, the King appointed a personally chosen cabinet which proclaimed the abolition of political parties, the suspension of parliament and the imposition of martial law. Simultaneously, the United States expressed its concern for the integrity of Jordan and signified this by moving its Sixth Fleet to the eastern Mediterranean and granting budgetary support to the new Jordanian Government.

By the beginning of 1958, King Hussein had re-established much domestic authority but propaganda attacks from Egypt and Syria continued unceasingly. As in Lebanon, the announcement on 1 February of the formation of the United Arab Republic by Egypt and Syria aroused extreme emotion. On the 14th, as a counter-measure, Jordan joined Iraq in an Arab Union, whereby each retained its sovereignty but with a federal superstructure. Then, on 14 July, came the revolution in Iraq, the withdrawal of Iraq from the Union, the isolation of Jordan and, like Lebanon, the request (16th) to Britain and the United States for military assistance against a *coup d'état* and invasion by the United Arab Republic.

As 10,000 United States marines began to land on the beaches outside Beirut and 2,000 British airborne troops at Masraq airport, the two countries reported their action to the United Nations; the United States introduced a resolution in the Security Council proposing the replacement of its forces by a UN force; and Jordan complained to the Council of United Arab Republic intervention in its internal affairs.

The Soviet Union denounced the American and British action, declared that their immediate withdrawal was the only action necessary, and vetoed the proposal for a UN force in Lebanon. Chairman Krushchev sent letters to President Eisenhower, President de Gaulle and Prime Minister Macmillan (19th) proposing that they meet to consider the Middle East crisis; but the Western powers were unresponsive, arguing that any such meeting should take place within the Security Council framework, and the proposal lapsed.

Over the next few weeks, the attitudes of Israel played some part in the unfolding of the crisis, especially as regards Jordan. When on 20 July, Jordan broke off diplomatic relations with the United Arab Republic, Syria closed its border to commerce with Jordan and, at about the same time, Iraq halted oil supplies. The United States immediately sought to arrange an airlift of essential supplies from Saudi Arabia but its government refused permission. Israel, on the other hand, had made only a formal protest at the overflying of the British troops, and now permitted supply overflying by the United States. There was also much speculation that if Syria and Iraq, whether in competition or collusion, should dismember Jordan, Israel would take the opportunity to strengthen its position by seizing the West Bank.

By the end of the month, the crisis had at least not deepened and there were even some signs of general restraint. In Lebanon, on 31 July, the Chamber of Deputies agreed by a large majority on General Chehab as Chamoun's successor. At an emergency session of the UN General Assembly on 7 August, the Arab states joined together to sponsor a resolution reaffirming the pledge given in Article 8 of the Arab League Agreement to "respect the systems of government established in the other member states and regard them as the exclusive concern of those states".

Throughout August and the first weeks of September, there was continued fighting in Lebanon and tension and unrest in Jordan but on a diminishing scale. The new regime in Iraq had quickly stabilised the situation there and, though it had withdrawn from the Arab Union with Jordan and from the Baghdad Pact, showed no signs of bellicosity or of subservience to Egypt. UN Secretary-General Hammarskjöld's tour of Amman, Cairo, Baghdad and Beirut gave further indications that the general mood had turned conciliatory. In Lebanon, on 23 September, Chamoun's term of office ended and General Chehab succeeded. A sharp crisis followed because the first government appointed contained only rebels and neutrals. Their opponents organised a widespread strike and for a while renewed fighting seemed likely. However, on 14 October, a new cabinet was announced in which the posts were evenly divided between the two sides and from then on the tension subsided.

The United States troops left Lebanon in the third week of October. On 16 November, Lebanon withdrew its complaint against the United Arab Republic and on the 19th UNOGIL left. The bulk of the British troops left Jordan in the first days of November. Simultaneously, communication was resumed between Egypt and Jordan though formal diplomatic relations were not re-established until August of the following year.

*   *   *

A. H. ABIDI: *Jordan, A Political Study 1948–57*, Asia Publishing House, London 1965.

M. S. AGWANI: *The Lebanese Crisis of 1958, A Documentary Study*, Asia Publishing House, London 1965.

F. I. QUBAIN: *Crisis in Lebanon*, The Middle East Institute, Washington 1961.

B. SHWADRAN: *Jordan, A State of Tension*, Council for Middle Eastern Affairs Press, New York 1959.

Algeria – Morocco 1958-70

THE French and Spanish protectorates over Morocco, established in 1912, came to an end on 2 March and 7 April 1956 respectively. Over the next two years, feeling gradually grew within the country for "the restoration of our Sahara", that is, a large area of the north-western Sahara included by the French in Algeria, and Spanish Sahara and the French colony, Mauritania. The people of these territories, Moroccans claimed, had been carved off from Morocco in the past under arrangements made solely to suit the European powers which should now be superseded.

The first person to arouse the Moroccan public on the issue was Allal el Fassi, head of Istiqlal, the main political party. He had expounded the idea of "Greater Morocco" since 1948 and did so again in the last months of the protectorates and increasingly after independence. El Fassi took no part in the final negotiations with the French and was thus somewhat overshadowed by the other Istiqlal leaders, and it has been speculated that the issue was helpful to his standing.[1]

In the course of 1956–57, there were continual incidents in the region between remnants of the Moroccan National Liberation Army, calling themselves the Army of the Liberation of the Sahara, and French and Spanish troops. The Moroccan Government described these irregulars as uncontrolled bands. In November 1957, a major incident occurred, an attack by a large band on Ifni, the Spanish enclave in Morocco, and in the following January the French and the Spaniards began a successful joint offensive against them in the region. This aroused much resentment in Morocco.

At this point, the Moroccan Government made the Sahara claim official state policy. It had been adopted by the Istiqlal party congress of August 1956 but was now taken up actively by the party leaders and endorsed by King Mohammed V in speeches on a tour of the south (25–26 February 1958).

The party and the Sultan were facing serious internal problems at this time. The party had become increasingly disunited and the leaders were in rivalry for popular support. There was also growing discontent with the party and the Sultan among the small farmers of the Berber regions of the Rif, the Middle Atlas and southern and eastern Morocco, who felt that Rabat was neglecting their interests and who resented the fact that govern-

[1] de la Serre (cited below, p. 150), p. 320.

143

ment officials were drawn from Istiqlal and thus likely to be Arabs, rather than from the local Berber tribes. Dissidence reached such a pitch in the course of 1958 that the army moved into these regions at the beginning of the following year. The smaller political parties decided in 1959–60 to oppose the "Greater Morocco" claim and accused Istiqlal of using it to distract attention from their incompetence in internal affairs.

The area in dispute with Algeria[2] was that bounded in the east by the Zousfana-Souara and in the west by the Mauritanian border, the principal centres being Colomb-Béchar, Tabelbala and Tindouf. There is fair evidence that in the mid-nineteenth century, the French acknowledged that a least the eastern part of this remote area belonged to the Moroccan empire though the degree of allegiance of the tribes to the Sultan is obscure.[3] After the French had penetrated to the area at the end of the century and after they had made Morocco a protectorate, their authorities in Morocco and Algeria disagreed continuously on where the border lay. Successive administrative arrangements were made and it seems gradually to have been accepted by the French that the Colomb-Béchar district was part of Algeria; but it was not until 1953 that Paris finally settled on the existing line favouring Algeria for the rest of the border and the French authorities in Morocco accepted it. At that date, the independence movement in Morocco was coming to a head and there were high estimates of the mineral wealth of the area, notably of the hard coal, iron, copper and manganese around Colomb-Béchar, the iron south-east of Tindouf and of the possibility of oil and natural gas.

In the months after Morocco's claim was made official in February 1958, there were incidents between Moroccan and French forces, but on 23 May the two sides made a standstill agreement without prejudice to their claims. By this time, the independence struggle in Algeria which had begun in 1954 was at its height. The Moroccans appear to have made no attempt to reach a settlement with the French but, on the contrary, acknowledged the rebel government, the Gouvernement Provisoire de la République Algérienne (formed in June 1958), as the rightful body with which to decide the issue. Contacts with the GPRA eventually resulted in a secret agreement of 6 July 1961 between Hassan II (who had succeeded his father on 26 February) and Ferhat Abbas, president of the GPRA, whereby the problem of the border "arbitrarily imposed by the French" was to be settled by means of a joint Algerian–Moroccan commission as soon as Algeria was independent.[4]

---

[2] For the dispute with Mauritania, see pp. 147–50.
[3] Trout, pp. 23–5.
[4] The text was published by the Moroccans on 22 October 1963. For the principal passages, see Méric, p. 744.

When Algeria became independent on 3 July 1962, the Moroccans sent a delegation to Algiers, and simultaneously, for reasons which are unknown, moved auxiliaries into various posts in the disputed area and accepted the allegiance of the tribes of Tindouf. In October, the Algerians were able to force their withdrawal. In March 1963, Hassan II visited Algiers but without apparent result. There was now mounting public ill-feeling between the two countries. This included expressions of ideological hostility, republicanism and socialism versus monarchy.

In September 1963, fighting broke out along the whole length of the disputed border, heaviest in the south where the Moroccans took and held Hassi Beida. It is not clear which side first moved troops. The Algerians widened the scope of the fighting a little by occupying territory just to the north of the disputed area, around Ich and Figuig.

Publicised partisan intervention by outside states favoured Algeria; the Soviet Union gave diplomatic support, Egypt sent token troops and equipment, Cuba offered a consignment of tanks. The Foreign Ministers of the two countries met in Morocco on 5 October, and in the next fortnight offers of pacificatory intervention abounded. On the 12th, President Bourguiba of Tunisia, appealing to sentiments of Maghrib unity, called for a cease-fire and for a meeting of the two heads of state with himself at Bizerta. On the 16th, the Syrian Prime Minister offered to mediate and on the 17th President Nkrumah of Ghana did likewise. An Iraqi mission held talks with both governments, and on the 19th, the Arab League Council called for a cease-fire, and on the following day passed an Egyptian motion calling upon both sides to withdraw their forces to positions held before the fighting began, and setting up a mediation committee. The Moroccans rejected this because it involved the evacuation of territory they claimed as theirs and probably also because Egypt favoured Algeria.

On 19 October, Emperor Haile Selassie of Ethiopia, acting on behalf of the Organisation of African Unity, visited Morocco and offered mediation. At first he was unsuccessful but at length, with the assistance of President Keita of Mali, a meeting was arranged between Hassan II and Ahmed Ben Bella (who had become President of Algeria on 15 September) at the capital of Mali, Bamako. This took place together with the mediators on 29–30 October and resulted in an agreement for a cease-fire, a withdrawal of troops from the area of conflict, and for the determination and supervision of a demilitarised zone by a Commission of Observers drawn from Ethiopia and Mali.

The cease-fire duly came into effect and on the following 20 February it was announced that arrangements (unpublished) for the demilitarised zone had been made. The Bamako Agreement also provided for the setting up by the OAU of an Arbitration Committee and accordingly, on 18

November (1963), the Foreign Ministers of the OAU, meeting in Addis Ababa, appointed representatives of Ethiopia, Ivory Coast, Mali, Nigeria, Senegal, Sudan and Tanganyika. This was accepted by both parties to the dispute.

Beginning its work in December, the Arbitration Committee met periodically until 1967 but without announcing any conclusion. Algeria made plain from the time of the 1963 fighting that it insisted on the borders which it had inherited from France. In this it had the support of the doctrine held by most African states and formally adopted by the OAU (July 1964) of the acceptance of the colonial borders throughout the continent. Morocco, for its part, did not withdraw its claim and yet it proved willing to mend its relations with Algeria. At the Arab Summit Conference of January 1964, called to consider the Jordan waters problem, Hassan II, Ben Bella and President Nasser of Egypt had a series of private talks which helped to lessen discord. On 2 February, the two countries announced the resumption of diplomatic relations. Then followed, on the 20th, the demilitarised zone agreement and on 12 May, a joint statement committing the two countries to peaceful procedures only in their dispute and declaring the resumption of normal relations.

Little was heard of the dispute in the next few years. At the end of the 1960s, Algeria, Morocco and Mauritania began a general *rapprochement*. The Algerian – Moroccan Treaty of Solidarity and Co-operation of 15 January 1969 made no explicit reference to the dispute but dedicated the two countries to the principles of non-violence, co-operation and the strengthening of the links of the Maghrib. In May 1970, King Hassan and President Houari Boumedienne met at Tlemsen in western Algeria, and in addition to stating general principles of co-operation, said that demarcation of the frontier would begin and that a joint company to work the Tindouf iron ore would be formed.

* * *

N. Barbour (ed.): *A Survey of North-West Africa* (*The Maghrib*), Oxford University Press, London, 2nd ed., 1962.

F. E. Trout: *Morocco's Saharan Frontiers*, Droz Publishers, Geneva 1969.

E. Méric: "Le Conflit algero-marocain", *Revue Française de Science Politique*, August 1965.

A. S. Reyner: "Morocco's International Boundaries", *Journal of Modern African Studies*, September 1963.

P. B. Wild: "The OAU and the Algerian-Moroccan Border Conflict", *International Organization*, Winter 1966.

W. Zartmann: "The Sahara, Bridge or Barrier", *International Conciliation*, January 1963.

Mauritania – Morocco 1958-70

UNDER the *Loi-Cadre* of 23 July 1956, the French colony of Mauritania became an Overseas Territory with considerable internal autonomy. However, that spring, Morocco achieved independence from France (March) and Spain (April) and over the next two years sentiment gradually gathered within the country for "the restoration of our Sahara", including Mauritania. This claim was made state policy by King Mohammed V in late February 1958.[1]

Rulers of Morocco had exercised influence among the tribes of Mauritania from the eleventh century onwards and sometimes, it seems, their suzerainty had been acknowledged. Effective control was rare and by the time the French began to penetrate into the area in the mid-nineteenth century it had long been unexercised. Nonetheless, Morocco had inherited from the past "an imperial outlook and air which it at no time entirely lost".[2] Moroccans believed that allegiance once given, religious as much as political, could never rightly be abandoned. Moreover, in the entire region, borders were in some places ill-defined and were for the most part seen by Moroccans as arrangements made solely by the European powers in the days of their domination. The borders between Morocco, Spanish Sahara and Mauritania, they pointed out, cut through the life of the area. The inhabitants of Mauritania were mostly of similar descent to the Moroccans, that is, Arab and Berber (about 500,000), the exception being the negroid people in the south (about 50,000). The growing interest in the 1950s in the economic potential of the Sahara centred in the case of Mauritania on the iron ore at Fort Gouraud and the copper at Akjoujt.

As sentiment gathered in Morocco in 1956–57, Moroccan irregulars[3] skirmished with the French and Spanish and found allies among Mauritanian tribes disaffected with their government. This disaffection died down, however, at the end of 1957. When the King of Morocco made the Saharan claim official in February 1958, a number of leading Mauritanians took refuge in Rabat and pledged allegiance to him. For the rest, sympathy in Mauritania with the Moroccan cause seems to have been confined to dislike of the border by merchants in the north and disregard of it by the nomads.

From 1958 to 1961, the dispute became increasingly heated. In 1958,

[1] See p. 143.
[2] Barbour, p. 209.
[3] See p. 143.

147

Moroccan propaganda began to call on the Mauritanians to rise in favour of Morocco. In that year also, the Societé Anonyme des Mines de Fer de Mauritanie (Miferma), a consortium with French governmental and private capital and smaller British, German and Italian participation, began large-scale exploitation of the iron ore at Fort Gouraud, and with the support of the French Government applied for a World Bank loan. The Moroccan Government protested to the World Bank but the loan was eventually granted (March 1960, $66 million). Against Moroccan protests to the French Government, a new constitution for Mauritania was declared on 5 October 1958, leading on 28 November to the proclamation of the Islamic Republic of Mauritania as a member state of the French Community, with full internal autonomy.

In June 1960, Mauritania requested complete independence and at the end of July, France announced that it agreed in principle to this. Intensifying previous diplomatic activity, Morocco took its case to the Arab League Foreign Ministers meeting at Chtara in Lebanon in August. Here a resolution was passed urging the return of Mauritania "to the mother country". Tunisia was absent from this meeting and made clear its opposition to Morocco's claim. Later Tunisia announced that it would recognise Mauritania, a decision which led to the recall of the Moroccan ambassador.

On 28 November 1960, Mauritania became fully independent. Tension between the two countries was now acute. On 8 November, Mauritania had accused Morocco of fomenting internal disorder and of responsibility for the murder of the Mayor of Atar. There is no evidence available, however, that either side considered full-scale war and perhaps little likelihood of it in terms of practicalities and of the wider international situation of the two countries.

Morocco brought "the problem of Mauritania" before the United Nations First (Political) Committee that autumn but no agreement was reached. Later the UN Assembly discussed the dispute but again no progress was made. The Moroccans were able, however, to use the Assembly and other UN organs as forums in which to attack the status of Mauritania.

Meanwhile, Mauritania had applied for UN membership and this request came before the Security Council on 3 December, jointly sponsored by France and Tunisia. It was vetoed by the Soviet Union, partly it seems to assist its relations with Morocco and partly because Mongolia's application had been rejected.

By this date, a division of the newly independent states of Africa into two groupings was becoming apparent. In the same month, December 1960, twelve former French colonies including Mauritania met at Brazzaville to discuss an association for closer political and economic co-operation. This "Brazzaville Group" became firm supporters of Mauritania's position. The following January (1961), Mohammed V invited a number of states to a conference at Casablanca to consider the crisis in the Congo. Out of this, the "Casablanca Group" emerged, Egypt, Ghana, the former French colonies Guinea and Mali, and Morocco. This group, with the exception of Ghana, declared opposition to Mauritania's independent existence and the conference passed a resolution condemning "colonialist intrigues aimed at dividing the territories of the African states in order to weaken them" and more specifically, the French action in setting up "the puppet state of Mauritania".

In the next few years, however, this support for Morocco's claim crumbled. Mauritania was admitted soon after independence to associate membership of the International Labour Organisation, the World Health Organisation, and the UN Economic Commission for Africa. In June 1961, it signed an agreement with France specifying full co-operation in foreign and economic policies, defence and currency matters, France agreeing to train the Mauritanian army and to provide "technical personnel". In the autumn, Mauritania was admitted to the UN. When the Security Council considered its application (October), a compromise had been reached among the members whereby the United States and Nationalist China would not veto Mongolia and the Soviet Union would not veto Mauritania.

Morocco bitterly resented the Soviet action and continued to protest against Mauritania's membership of the United Nations and its organs but without success. This same year (1961), the Arab League dropped the Moroccan case, the main reason apparently being Egypt's wish to bring Tunisia back into the organisation. In May 1963, having established itself with its neighbours except Morocco, Mauritania was accepted as a member at the constituent meeting of the Organisation of African Unity. Relations with Mali had been very tense, particularly in 1962 when Mauritania accused it of training subversive agents, but by 1963 relations had improved to such an extent that a treaty was signed concerning their common frontier. In that year Mauritania also sent a goodwill mission to the UAR which promised technical assistance and in 1964 recognised Mauritania and made a commercial and economic agreement with it. Later in 1964, the Soviet Union and Yugoslavia opened diplomatic relations with Mauritania.

The Istiqlal ministers resigned from the Moroccan Government in January 1963 and King Hassan II, who had succeeded his father in February 1961, seems to have been on the point of abandoning the claim. However, there was strong popular protest. Senegal attempted mediation in 1963 and 1964 and Tunisia in 1964 but without success.

It was not until 1968 that signs of an end to the dispute appeared. Late that year, Morocco abolished its Ministry of Mauritanian Affairs. In the following year, it composed its simultaneous dispute with Algeria to the extent of a Treaty of Solidarity and Co-operation.[4] As host country to the Islamic "summit conference" (Rabat, 22–24 September 1969) it invited Mauritania to take part, and during this, with President Houari Boumedienne of Algeria as intermediary, King Hassan held discussions with President Moktar Ould Daddah of Mauritania. At a press conference on 26 September, the King announced that he had decided to renounce his reservations about recognising Mauritania "in the interests of the Moroccan people, of regional inter-state relations in that part of Africa bordering on the Atlantic and the Mediterranean, and of relations within the Islamic Community". This was followed on 8 June 1970 by a Treaty of Solidarity, Good Neighbourliness and Co-operation. The accompanying communique said that the two countries would co-operate to hasten the liberation of Spanish Sahara on the basis of self-determination.

*   *   *

N. BARBOUR (ed.): *A Survey of North West Africa* (*The Maghrib*), Oxford University Press, 2nd edition, 1962.

I. W. ZARTMANN: *Problems of New Power: Morocco*, New York, Atherton Press, 1964.

D. E. ASHFORD: "The Irredentist Appeal in Morocco and Mauritania", *Western Political Quarterly*, December 1962.

F. DE LA SERRE: "Les revendications marocaines sur la Mauritanie", *Revue Française de Science Politique*, April 1966.

H. Pick: "Independent Mauritania", *The World Today*, April 1961.

[4] See p. 146.

Quemoy and Matsu 1958

WHEN the Chinese Nationalists fled from the Communists to Taiwan (with its adjacent group of islands, Penghu or the Pescadores) in the autumn of 1949, they retained control of various groups of islands lying just off the coast of mainland China, a hundred miles away, notably, Quemoy, off Hsia-men (Amoy), and Matsu, off Fu-chou.

On the outbreak of the Korean War, President Truman announced (27 June 1950) that the United States would protect Taiwan and, as a corollary, that it would prevent Nationalist attacks on the mainland.[1] When the Republicans took office, President Eisenhower removed this corollary, telling Congress (2 February 1953) that the Seventh Fleet would no longer be employed to shield Communist China. This implied threat to the Chinese Communists, popularly known as "unleashing Chiang Kai-shek", was apparently part of the Administration's drive to end the deadlock in the Korean armistice negotiations.[2] It was accompanied by an exchange of notes between the United States and the Nationalists according to which the Nationalists would not attack the mainland without United States consent; but this was not made public at the time.

Then followed the Korean armistice (June 1953), the climax and end of the Indo-China War (Geneva, July 1954) and the efforts of the United States to create a security network in the Far East, notably the Manila Conference which established the South-East Asia Treaty Organisation (8 September 1954). The Manila Conference was accompanied by re-doubled threats between the Communists and the Nationalists and the bombardment of Quemoy and the counter-bombardment of Hsia-men and a period of general high tension over Taiwan which persisted until the following April. On 2 December 1954, the United States and Taiwan signed a mutual defence treaty, approved by the US Senate on 9 February 1955 and followed, for the Senate's reassurance, by a public exchange of notes with the Nationalists according to which military action outside the immediate area of Taiwan and the Pescadores (i.e. an attack on the mainland) would be a matter of joint agreement.

During the discussions of the Treaty, the position regarding the off-shore islands of Quemoy and Matsu was generally considered unclear and the Administration sought to give itself the necessary scope by promoting a Congressional resolution of 24 January which authorised the President

[1] See pp. 57–8.
[2] See pp. 60.

151

to use United States forces to protect Taiwan and the Pescadores, "this authority to include the securing and protecting of such related positions and territories of that area now in friendly hands and the taking of such other measures as he judges to be required or appropriate in assuring the defence of Formosa (Taiwan) and the Pescadores".

Over the following years, the Nationalists built up their forces on the off-shore islands to about a hundred thousand men, roughly a third of their total strength. Though the defensive aspect of this was plain, they also continually repeated their picture of the future according to which, when the time was ripe, their forces would invade the mainland, giving the signal for a general uprising against the Communists. The Communists, for their part, frequently described the build-up as provocative, built up their own forces on the mainland opposite and maintained their position that one day they would liberate Taiwan.

At length, on 23 August 1958, after three weeks of increasing tension and shooting, a crisis erupted when the Communists started a full-scale bombardment of Quemoy. It is sometimes said that the motives for this may have extended beyond the Taiwan situation to the general development of relations between China, the Soviet Union and the United States. Communist China's entry into the United Nations would shortly be considered yet again in the UN General Assembly. From 31 July to 3 August, Chairman Krushchev of the Soviet Union visited Peking. Concurrently, there was a crisis in the Middle East over Iraq, Lebanon and Jordan[3] and a new Berlin crisis opened in November.[4] However, the connection between these various events remains a matter of speculation.

In the United States and still more among its allies, there was from the first some uncertainty about the right response to the Communist action. The United States had no treaty commitment to defend the off-shore islands. The broad statement contained in the Congressional resolution of January 1955 seemed to cover the islands only in so far as their defence was necessary to the defence of Taiwan. Was their defence necessary in these terms; in particular, was the Communist attack a prelude to an attack on Taiwan?

In the last days of August and throughout September, the United States Administration tended to a stark view, though with some caution in action. In his first statements, Secretary of State John Foster Dulles depicted the Communist bombardment as a threat to peace "in the region" and this was endorsed by President Eisenhower in a press statement of 27 August. On the 28th, the Communists called on the Nationalists on Quemoy to surrender. A landing seemed imminent. Alternatively the island might fall

[3] See pp. 135–42.
[4] See p. 168ff.

simply to bombardment and the blockade of supplies. The United States began to concentrate an enormous naval force in the Taiwan Straits with behind it, as always, the strategic nuclear arsenal; but United States ships escorting Nationalist supply ships stopped short at China's territorial waters. On 4 September, Secretary Dulles issued a statement that the United States would not hesitate to use force if Taiwan were threatened; but he did not include any explicit undertaking to defend the off-shore islands as President Chiang Kai-shek urged and he stressed United States willingness to discuss a cease-fire.

On 6 September, the Communist Prime Minister, Chou En-lai, repeated the Communist determination "to liberate Taiwan" but said that China was willing to hold ambassadorial discussions. Such discussions between the United States and China had originally begun with a British intermediary at the end of the Indo-China conference at Geneva in 1954, concerning at that time the release of seventy-six Americans held captive in China since 1949. The discussions had languished in 1957 and had seemed likely to end when the United States proposed representatives of a lower rank. However, on 28 July 1958 (that is, shortly before the full-scale crisis over Quemoy and Matsu), the United States had proposed talks in Warsaw at the ambassadorial level. It was this proposal that Premier Chou En-lai now accepted.

On 7 September, the Soviet Union publicised a letter to the United States warning that it would consider a United States attack on China as an attack on itself. On the 11th, President Eisenhower made a broadcast stating that the United States would not retreat before aggression, that an assault on the off-shore islands would lead to a situation envisaged in the Congressional resolution of January 1955 but stressing that the United States welcomed discussions. The ambassadorial discussions began on 15 September, though without any substantive progress, the United States seeking a cease-fire, Communist China wishing to discuss "the liberation of Taiwan". On the 19th, Chairman Krushchev sent a further public letter to the United States containing a generalised attack on United States policy, a letter which the United States Administration returned unanswered.

Meanwhile, to the Administration's dismay, the principal allies of the United States showed that in their view the defence of the off-shore islands was not worth the risk of a major war. Within the United States itself, public alarm was growing; on 29 September, the Senate Foreign Relations Committee expressed its doubts to the President. Meanwhile also, in the Taiwan Straits, the blockade of Quemoy had been broken, the Nationalist air force, equipped with United States Sidewinder air-to-air missiles, was proving a match for the Communists in the battle for air supremacy, and any prospect of a Communist landing on Quemoy seemed to have waned.

Against this background, on 30 September, Secretary Dulles relaxed his line of policy. He commented that the Nationalists had been "rather foolish" to place so many troops on the off-shore islands; that they need not be kept there if a dependable cease-fire could be achieved; and that the return of the Nationalists to mainland China was "highly hypothetical". On 2 October, President Chiang Kai-shek made an indignant rejoinder. On the 6th, the Communists suspended their bombardment. On the 20th, as Secretary Dulles arrived in Taiwan for discussions with President Chiang, the Communists resumed their bombardment for forty-eight hours. On the 25th, they announced that they would confine the bombardment to alternate days (the odd days) of the month. On the 27th, President Chiang and Secretary Dulles produced their communique.

In this communique, the United States reaffirmed its support for the Nationalists as the true representatives of the Chinese people. The Nationalist Government reaffirmed its sacred mission to restore freedom to them. But this, the communique added, was a matter of "minds and hearts" and "not the use of force".

Thereupon, over the following months, the Nationalists reduced their forces on the off-shore islands, and the United States Navy ceased to escort Nationalist supply ships, and at the end of the year, the Communist bombardment finally stopped.

*   *   *

ROYAL INSTITUTE OF INTERNATIONAL AFFAIRS: *Survey of International Affairs 1956–58*, Oxford University Press, 1962.

D. D. EISENHOWER: *The White House Years, Vol. 2, Waging Peace, 1956–61*, Heinemann, London 1963.

R. MACFARQUHAR (ed.): *Sino-American Relations 1949–71*, David and Charles, Newton Abbot 1972.

R. STEBBINS: *The United States in World Affairs, 1958*, Harper and Bros., New York 1959.

K. T. YOUNG: *Negotiating with the Chinese Communists, The United States Experience 1953–67*, McGraw Hill, New York 1968.

The China-India Border 1958-62

IN the years after Indian independence (1947) and the establishment of the People's Republic of China (1949) relations between the two countries were friendly. China's enforcement of control over Tibet (1950) caused a period of ill-feeling but this was smoothed over and on 29 April 1954, the two countries signed a trade and cultural agreement relating to Tibet, the preamble of which contained the doctrine of Panchsheel or the Five Principles of Peaceful Coexistence, principles which the two proclaimed in their own relations and advocated to the rest of the world.[1]

In gaining control of Tibet the Chinese had, it seems, made use of an old track from Yarkand (in Sinkiang) to Taklakot (western Tibet, on the Nepal frontier) across Aksai Chin, and in the spring of 1956 they began to convert this into a road, finishing the work in the autumn of 1957. So remote was the region that the Indians apparently knew nothing of this until a year later. When they did learn of it, they protested in a note (18 October 1958) that the road went through "indisputably Indian territory" and inquired about the fate of an Indian reconnaissance patrol. The Chinese replied that the patrol had intruded into Chinese territory and had been ejected.

In the much controverted history of this border, the scanty evidence relating to the period before 1865 is particularly conflictory and obscure. In 1865, W. H. Johnson of the Survey of India explored the area and suggested the line of the Kuen Lun range and this became standard in British atlases, thus ascribing the Aksai Chin tract to India. In the 1890s, the Chinese gave indications that they considered the tract theirs, whereupon in 1899, the British proposed a line (the Macartney-MacDonald line) which roughly halved it, but the Chinese made no reply. In the twentieth century, British and subsequently Indian atlases and maps customarily showed Aksai Chin as part of India.

Further east along the Himalayan border, in the so-called middle sector, other small areas (around the Shipki pass, Jadhang and Barahoti) were in dispute between India and China in the mid-1950s but the other great area lay beyond Nepal, Sikkim and Bhutan at the other end of the Himalayas. Two months before their protest on Aksai Chin, the Indians sent a note (21 August 1958) to the Chinese urging them to revise their maps of this area. On a visit to China in October 1954, the Indian Prime Minister, Jawarhalal Nehru, had raised the fact with the Chinese Prime Minister,

[1] See p. 80.

155

Chou En-lai, that Chinese maps showed the eastern border as lying only some twenty miles north of the Brahmaputra river. This had been the border of British India in the late nineteenth century but from 1914, following negotiations with the Chinese and the Tibetans, the British had adopted a line some seventy miles further north (the McMahon line) enclosing the tribal country subsequently known as the North-East Frontier Agency. The Chinese, however, did not sign the documents of the 1914 conference. Chou En-lai in 1954 had merely remarked that China's maps were old and that there had not yet been time for revision. Now, in October 1958 the Chinese explained that this meant that there had not yet been time to survey the area and embark on consultations with India.

In December 1958, Nehru and Chou En-lai engaged in a still amicable correspondence. Nehru said that he was puzzled by the talk of surveys and consultations; the tracts of territory concerned in both east and west were unmistakeably India's. Chou En-lai, on the other hand, put the view that the border between India and China had never been delimited; hence there were map discrepancies and occasional disputes and hence there was need for surveys and consultations; meanwhile, the two countries should maintain the existing position. (This meant, it should be noticed, that China would maintain its position in Aksai Chin.) In the bitter dispute which developed in the following years, neither side budged from these basic standpoints.

In March 1959, relations between the two countries became envenomed by the crisis in Tibet and the flight of the Dalai Lama to India.[2] On 25 August, there was a border incident at Longju in the east, resulting in part, it seems, from discrepancies on where the McMahon line ran at that point but blamed by each side on the policy of the other. The incident was made public in India and so simultaneously was the situation in Aksai Chin, hitherto known only to the governments. Indian public opinion was outraged by China's "aggression"; by its propaganda demands for the "liberation" of Sikkim and Bhutan; by its "cartographic aggression" (a letter of 8 September 1959 from Chou En-lai to Nehru indicated that China could claim some 50,000 square miles of "Indian" territory); and finally by another major incident, at the Kongka Pass in Aksai Chin, on 28 October. There was much warlike talk in India which Nehru sought to ridicule while at the same time asserting that India would not yield to China's claims.

On 7 November 1959, Chou En-lai proposed that both sides should withdraw their troops twenty kilometres from the McMahon line and the

[2] See p. 81.

line of existing control in the west so as to avoid incidents and that there should be a meeting between Nehru and himself. Nehru rejected this, declaring that there could be no negotiations while the Chinese remained on Indian soil. The following February, he invited Chou En-lai to Delhi but insisted that there was no question of negotiation. The meeting took place from 19–25 April 1960 and it seems that Chou En-lai proposed that China would drop its claim in the east if India would drop its claim to Aksai Chin. In the Indian view, this amounted to getting the fruits of one crime by offering to abandon another. The two sides agreed only on meetings of experts to collate all the evidence on where the border lay. At the beginning of 1961, the experts produced two contradictory reports.

As regards the world at large, India had the sympathy of the great majority of states. Since 1957, the United States had abated its hostility to India's "neutralism" and had begun large-scale economic aid. India feared that the Soviet Union, with which it had also developed strong economic aid relations, would take China's part, but in the event the Soviet Union remained broadly neutral throughout. The reason for this became clearer when the quarrel between the Soviet Union and China became public knowledge.

In the south Asian region, China had some successes. In October 1960, it completed negotiations for a border treaty with Burma, accepting the McMahon line in that area. It also reached amicable border agreements with Afghanistan and Nepal. In May 1962, China and Pakistan announced border talks, the stretch in question lying in Kashmir. This infuriated India in view of its claim to Kashmir but the Sino-Pakistani *rapprochement* developed rapidly from this time. Their eventual border treaty (March 1963) adopted roughly the Macartney-MacDonald proposal of 1899.

Meanwhile, from 1960 to 1962, there was deadlock between India and China on the diplomatic level. Militarily, on the other hand, the Indian Government in 1960 set about the task of building up the organisation needed to support the army in these remote border regions. At length, in November 1961, it apparently decided on a "forward policy"; the army was to set up posts in Aksai Chin, dominating the Chinese posts and making their position tactically untenable, while avoiding outright clashes.[3] The following spring (1962), as the patrols manoeuvred and counter-manoeuvred, there was a flurry of notes of protest from the two sides and again when shooting occurred in July. It was now India that proposed discussions but on the basis that China must withdraw from Aksai Chin first, though use of the road was conceded. In September, in the east,

[3] Maxwell, 221.

Chinese troops were observed taking up positions on the Thag La ridge which in the Indian view lay on their side of the McMahon line. The army was ordered to eject them. Shooting between posts first occurred on the 20th. On 3 October, China proposed a new meeting of prime ministers but India refused.

On 20 October, the Chinese launched a full-scale attack on both the western and eastern sectors. The Indian posts in Aksai Chin were immediately engulfed and destroyed. In the east, the Indian army was thrown back. The Government of India declared a state of national emergency (26th). Nehru momentarily requested United States armed intervention, subsequently reduced to United States and British military aid. This rapidly began. On 24 October and again on 4 November, in notes to India, China repeated its proposals of 7 November 1959. India, in reply, proposed talks, conditional on the withdrawal of the Chinese troops to their positions at the beginning of September. While the Commonwealth mostly supported India, the Soviet Union and Nationalist China were non-committal and so, to the consternation of India, were the ' non-aligned'' countries. By the 19th, the Chinese had taken the Se La pass and Bomdi La and, in the extreme east, Walong, and were approaching the limits of the area they claimed, with the Brahmaputra valley and the Assam plains apparently open before them.

To the general amazement of the world, on 21 November, the Chinese halted their advance. They announced that they would observe a unilateral cease-fire along the entire length of the boundary, and that from 1 December, Chinese forces would withdraw twenty kilometers behind the line of actual control of 7 November 1959. They called upon India to do the same.

The Indian popular reaction was one of furious indignation. The Indian governmental reaction was to ask for clarifications. None the less, they observed the cease-fire. On 1 December, the Chinese began their withdrawal which they soon completed. Various "non-aligned" countries had meanwhile adopted the role of peacemakers and on the 12th, six of them, meeting at Colombo (Burma, Cambodia, Ceylon, Egypt, Ghana, Indonesia), proposed that the McMahon line should be the cease-fire line in the east, while in the west the Chinese should withdraw twenty kilometers behind the line of actual control, with Indian civilian administrators being admitted alongside the Chinese to the demilitarised strip thus created. The Chinese eventually baulked at the proposal as regards the west (January) and it lapsed. In the following years, the dispute lay dormant, the Chinese, as announced, simply retaining Aksai Chin and observing the McMahon line.

*   *   *

A. LAMB: *The China–India Border, The Origins of the Disputed Boundaries*, Oxford University Press, 1964.

N. MAXWELL: *India's China War*, Jonathan Cape, London 1970.

G. N. PATTERSON: *Peking versus Delhi*, Faber and Faber, London 1963.

W. VAN EEKELEN: *Indian Foreign Policy and the Border Dispute with China*, Nijhoff, The Hague 1964.

F. WATSON: *The Frontiers of China*, Chatto and Windus, London 1966.

ANON.: "Peking and Delhi", *The Times Literary Supplement*, 2 January 1964.

The Chinese in Indonesia 1959-60

In most of the countries of South-East Asia in the mid-twentieth century, the Chinese were only a small fraction of the population. The main exceptions were Malaya, about one-third Chinese, and the island of Singapore, about three-quarters. In all the countries, none the less, they were in certain respects very important and prominent. Though they were to be found in all occupations, they provided a high proportion of the small businessmen, especially shopkeepers, produce-middlemen and moneylenders. Next to the Europeans, they also provided most of the large-scale enterprise. Gathered mostly in communities in the cities and towns, they were physically different and, especially in the Malay countries, culturally separate with their own language, newspapers, schools and temples and with little intermarriage with the other peoples.

To the age-old suspicions and animosities thus aroused, the coming of independence in South-East Asia added new and powerful elements. Having suffered under the Japanese, the Chinese generally welcomed the return of the Europeans and in any case (leaving aside Singapore) played little part in the movements which achieved independence. Aloof from the popular passion of the time, their own unpopularity was deepened.

In other ways, too, the nationalism which had expelled the Europeans now looked askance at them. Political independence must be completed by economic independence and this required, along with economic development, that nationals take the place of Europeans and Chinese in business enterprise. The European administrations in their time had discriminated in some respects against the Chinese in an effort to encourage the advance of the other inhabitants. The South-East Asian governments now discriminated against them mildly or markedly in business also.

A further element in the situation was the relationship of the Chinese with China. Legally, Chinese governments had always claimed that the overseas Chinese remained Chinese by virtue of their ancestry whatever the country in which they were born. Culturally, developments in China affected their feelings and opinions. Neither of these aspects mattered much to the European administrations in the time of China's weakness and the civil war between the Nationalists and the Communists. When, however, in 1949, the Communists consolidated their control of the mainland, the relationship immediately became a sensitive matter. Both the Communist government and the Nationalist government on Taiwan had to be considered as patrons and protectors of the overseas Chinese. Both, though especially the weaker party, Taiwan, sought their favour by propaganda and other blandishments. The overseas Chinese on the whole carefully kept their own counsel and no one knew what they thought. They were thus always liable to the suspicion that they were a secret subversive instrument of the Communists or the Nationalists; and they were always liable to have the unpopularity of Taiwan or Peking of the local Communists visited upon them.

All these problems of the Chinese were most acute in the case of Indonesia, the most troubled of the newly independent countries of South-East Asia. The Chinese there numbered some two million, 2–3 per cent of the population. When independence was finally achieved in 1949, the Indonesian Government inherited from the Dutch the legal view that those born in Indonesia were Indonesian citizens. It announced that they would automatically be considered such unless within two years they formally rejected this citizenship in favour of another. At the same time, legal citizenship made little difference to the incidence of discrimination. To encourage non-Chinese in business, they were given preference in import and export licences over Chinese, whether citizen or alien. A regulation requiring Chinese concerns to take Indonesians into partnership affected all of Chinese ancestry.

The Peking and Taiwan governments disliked these policies but in a restrained manner; for in competition with one another they were interested in the goodwill not only of the overseas Chinese but of the Indonesian and other South-East Asian governments. At length, in 1954, as the Peking government set out on a major campaign to strengthen goodwill in Asia, endorsing "non-alignment" in the East–West conflict with particular reference to current United States sponsorship of the South-East Asia Treaty Organisation, it announced that it was willing to reassess its attitude on the citizenship of the overseas Chinese. A proportion of the Chinese in Indonesia, conceivably even a majority, welcomed the change. They believed that their future lay in assimilation into the Indonesian nation, not perhaps culturally or only gradually in that respect, but certainly in the feelings and duties of citizenship. That year, with the approval of the Peking government and of President Sukarno, a Chinese organisation was formed known as Baperki with this as its professed objective. In the spring of 1955, during the Bandung Conference of "non-aligned" states, a Sino-Indonesian treaty was signed (22 April) relating to those "who hold simultaneously the nationality" of China and Indonesia. They were to choose whether to be Indonesian citizens or Chinese citizens. The Chinese citizens would respect Indonesian laws and customs; Indonesia would protect their rights and interests according to its laws.

The promising atmosphere of 1955 did not last long. The Sino-Indonesian treaty was not ratified or implemented for reasons which appear to have lain primarily in the growing turmoil in Indonesia. The Indonesian leaders, the factions in Parliament, the Communist Party, the Muslim groups, the armed forces, were in ever-increasing conflict. The small-scale rebellions in West Java and Kalimantan (Borneo) dragged on and were compounded in 1957 by rebellions in the outer islands and above all, in February 1958, by the setting up in Sumatra of an alternative government in protest against the rule of Sukarno in general and the growing standing of the Communist Party in particular. The economy made little progress and in some respects deteriorated. The food supply position of Java, always difficult, worsened markedly. Inflation increased sharply.

The outcome of these troubles was to be the establishment in the winter of 1959–60 of a regime of "guided democracy" under President Sukarno, holding a tense balance between the Communist Party and the armed forces. Meanwhile, it was not a time for progress in the assimilation of the Chinese; on the contrary, there were gains to be made in attacking them and losses in protecting them. It was said that the Taiwan government was supporting the rebels in Sumatra and feeling mounted against the Chinese for that. It was said that Baperki, far from encouraging the assimilation of the Chinese, was an instrument of Peking and the Communist Party, and feeling mounted against them for that also. A law was passed in 1958 enabling the several hundred thousand alien Chinese (that is, immigrants not born in Indonesia, mostly from mainland China) to apply for citizenship; but this was accompanied in 1957 and 1958 by laws and regulations on taxes, employment, education and newspapers which afflicted Chinese citizens as much as aliens. Finally, in May 1959, a regulation was drafted banning foreigners from trade in towns and villages of less than 15,000 inhabitants, in short, in all rural areas. President Sukarno promulgated the regulation by decree on 16 November.

This decree, affecting it seems in theory about 300,000 Chinese, had in itself little lasting effect. The idea was that the Chinese traders would be replaced by co-operatives; but only in West Java apparently were serious attempts at implementation made, and with no success; trade was merely disrupted for a while until eventually the Chinese resumed business. The serious aspect was the unleashing of popular feeling against the Chinese in killing and looting in West Java. Internationally, the Peking government was moved to send a note of "serious protest" (December) and to statements inviting the Chinese in Indonesia to return to their homeland in China.

The quarrel intensified over the next few weeks as several thousand Chinese, totalling in the end about 90,000, responded to this call. In March 1960, the Peking government sent another note of strong protest against the treatment of these people by the Indonesian authorities, notably their "forcible evacuation" by the army into internment centres. In May, it protested against obstruction of ships sent from China to take them away. In July, it protested against a second wave of "forcible evacuation".

It seems clear, however, that the Chinese Government, while constrained to protest, was also constrained against complete rupture with the Indonesian Government. At this time, the Soviet Union was showing interest in strengthening its relations with Indonesia. Chairman Nikita Krushchev made a long tour of the country (18 February–1 March 1960). It may be surmised that the Peking government, now in growing (though as yet unpublicised) conflict and rivalry with the Soviet leadership, was not willing to see the prospects of influence under the new regime in Indonesia taken over by the Soviet Union. Moreover, as Soviet interest increased, as the standing of the Indonesian Communist Party grew, the United States began to reappraise its cool attitude of recent years to the Sukarno regime, and to consider new efforts in economic aid and influence.

All this gave good grounds for not allowing the problem of the overseas Chinese to disrupt Sino-Indonesian relations. On 20 January, as requested by the Chinese, the process of ratification of the 1955 treaty was completed. By the autumn, the ferment of harassment, evacuation and shipment of those Chinese returning to China had died down. On 19 December, an agreement was signed on procedures for the implementation of the treaty, that is, for the exercise of choice by the Chinese. Over the next few years, until the fall of Sukarno in October 1965 and the great massacres of the Communists and the Chinese,[1] the Peking government's relations with the Indonesian Government were fair and its opportunities for influence were considerable. Even the Chinese community enjoyed a few years of relative respite.

*   *   *

G. AMBEKAR and V. DEVEKAR: *Documents on China's Relations with South and South-East Asia (1949–62)*, Allied Publishers, Bombay 1964.

S. FITZGERALD: *China and the Overseas Chinese*, Cambridge University Press, 1972.

D. HINDLEY: *The Communist Party of Indonesia 1951–63*, University of California Press, Berkeley 1964.

L. MITCHISON: *The Overseas Chinese*, Bodley Head, London 1961.

V. PURCELL: *The Chinese in South East Asia*, Oxford University Press, 2nd ed., 1966.

L. WILLIAMS: *The Future of the Overseas Chinese in South East Asia*, McGraw Hill, New York 1966.

L. WILLIAMS: "Sino-Indonesian Diplomacy", *The China Quarterly*, No. 11, July–September 1962.

[1] See pp. 247–8.

Britain – Iceland 1958-62

IN 1958, nearly a quarter of Iceland's gross national product came from the fisheries around its coast and about nine-tenths of its exports. Britain's interest in these fisheries was also considerable. Thirty per cent of the cod, 26 per cent of the haddock, 33 per cent of the halibut and 25 per cent of the plaice landed by British trawlers came from the waters in dispute with Iceland.

A dispute had already occurred between the two countries following Iceland's decision of 15 May 1952 to adopt the straight base-lines system of demarcating territorial waters (similar to that adopted by Norway and upheld by the International Court of Justice in 1951) and to extend these from three to four miles. Relations rapidly deteriorated, Icelandic trawlers were banned from Hull and Grimsby and it was not until 1956 that the dispute was partially settled by an agreement worked out by the Organisation for European Economic Co-operation. It was always likely that the question of Iceland's waters would arise again.

International legal developments were another factor explaining the 1958 dispute. The law of the sea was in a state of flux and the need to clarify it was generally recognised. It was the first issue dealt with by the International Law Commission. The references in the Commission's report to the width of territorial waters indicated the uncertain state of the matter. It recognised that "international practice is not uniform as regards the determination of territorial waters". It considered that "international law does not permit an extension of territorial seas beyond twelve miles" but noted that "many states have fixed a breadth greater than three miles and, on the other hand, many states do not recognise such a breadth when that of their own territorial sea is less".

The Commission's report formed the basis of the discussions at the United Nations Conference on the Law of the Sea at Geneva in April 1958. At this conference, the Iceland delegation, headed by Hans Andersen, Ambassador to NATO, proposed that "under special conditions a coastal state which bases its existence on fisheries shall be granted complete control of fisheries as far out to sea as it considers necessary". This proposal made little impression on the conference. On the other hand, a majority expressed itself in favour of a twelve-mile limit, though not the requisite two-thirds majority.

With this encouragement, Iceland determined on unilateral action. A strong hint of this possibility was given in the final stages of the Geneva

Conference when, on 26 April, Andersen explained Iceland's abstention from voting on a Cuban proposal for another conference by saying that he did not wish to commit the Government of Iceland to the policy of not taking any action for the time being so far as Iceland's own fisheries jurisdiction was concerned. The conference was also influential in that it publicised the idea of a twelve-mile limit. Before this, Icelandic public opinion, although demanding the protection of the fishing industry, had been vague on specific proposals. The twelve-mile limit now became a catch-word.

Political developments in Iceland were also significant. After the 1956 elections, a coalition government under Hermann Jónasson was formed from the Progressives, the Social Democrats and the People's Alliance, that is, Communists. Having no clear electoral mandate, this coalition had considerable freedom of manoeuvre, while at the same time many interest groups represented in the three parties were united in favouring the extension of territorial waters. The Communists were the most vigorous supporters of this course of action and one of their ministers, Lúdvík Jósepsson, was Minister of Fisheries and Trade. It has been argued that "the 'fish war' . . . might well have been avoided if the Communists had not been in the government and controlled the strategic post of Minister of Fisheries".[1]

Many in Iceland saw that their country's membership of NATO, with its important airbase at Keflavik, gave them a powerful bargaining weapon against Britain. The latter would be wary of pressing Iceland too hard for fear of generating a strong neutralist movement, signs of which were never far from the surface in Iceland's politics and had become manifest in the 1956 election.

On 28 May 1958, the Iceland Government announced a decision in principle to implement regulations extending fisheries zones from four to twelve miles. On 3 June, Britain sent a protest note stating that unilateral action would be unacceptable. It urged negotiations and indicated that if the proposed action were taken, the possibility of the use of force could not be ruled out. The British Government would have the duty to prevent any "unlawful interference" with British vessels on the high seas. Undeterred, on 30 June, the Iceland Government promulgated regulations extending the fisheries limits to a distance of twelve miles from straight base-lines as from 1 September.

While the main protagonists in the dispute were Britain and Iceland, the British authorities were concerned about the influence of Iceland's action on other countries. If Iceland were successful, the Faroe Islands, Green-

[1] Nuechterlein, p. 195.

land and Norway might well follow suit. On 19 June, Norway stated that if Iceland went ahead, it would have to review its own position. Norway favoured a twelve-mile limit though changes should be made by international agreement. Later, on 20 January 1959, Norway made clear that it was thinking of protective measures if there was any consequential influx of foreign trawlers into its coastal waters.

Many other states protested against Iceland's proposed action, including Belgium, the Netherlands, Spain, Sweden and West Germany. Representatives of the fishing industries of Western Europe met at The Hague on 14 July 1958 and passed a resolution condemning Iceland's action as illegal and declaring their intention to fish up to the four-mile limit after 1 September. In general terms, the dispute can be seen as one between those states with long-range fishing fleets and those mainly concerned with their coastal waters and wishing special rights there. The exception was the Soviet Union, which joined the several countries voicing support for Iceland.

Between July and September, talks aimed at finding a solution were held within the North Atlantic Treaty Organisation. These were at various levels, including foreign ministers' discussions at Copenhagen, but were unsuccessful.

On 1 September, the Iceland regulations came into effect and from that date a series of incidents occurred between Icelandic coastguard gunboats and British trawlers protected by the Royal Navy Fisheries Protection Squadron. The Icelanders frequently fired warning shots and made use of boarding parties. On 3–4 September, anti-British demonstrations took place outside the British Embassy in Reykjavik, and at a well-attended meeting in the main square representatives of the main political parties denounced British "aggression". However, in this conflict, known colloquially as the "Cod War", there seems never to have been any threat of the use of force on a larger scale.

Early in September, Britain offered to take the dispute to the International Court but this was rejected by Iceland. It was not disputing the actual state of the law but was seeking to get the law changed so that it recognised the "special position" of countries such as itself. In the same month, Iceland protested to the United Nations about the activities of the British Fisheries Protection Squadron but the matter was not debated.

In 1959, NATO continued to be used as a forum for informal and formal discussions, including talks between the British and Icelandic Foreign Ministers, but without success. None the less, the dispute was becoming an embarrassment to Britain in a NATO context. There were incidents this year between Icelanders and United States personnel at the Keflavik airbase.

A further influence on Britain was the second United Nations Conference on the Law of the Sea held at Geneva on 17 March to 26 April 1960. This debated a Canadian–United States resolution urging the acceptance of a "six plus six" formula, that is, territorial waters of six miles with a contiguous fishing zone of a further six miles within which the coastal state would have special rights including the control of fishing. Nations which traditionally fished such zones would be allowed to do so for a certain time. Although this compromise solution failed to gain the required two-thirds majority, it did so by only one vote. This was a clear indication of the trend of international opinion.

In September 1960, Britain and Norway published a draft fisheries agreement (signed on 17 November) on a similar basis to the Canadian–United States formula. On 1 October, bilateral negotiations between Britain and Iceland began. As a sign of good intentions British vessels remained outside the twelve-mile limit and Icelandic vessels refrained from landing fish in British ports while the negotiations proceeded. The negotiations were adjourned on 10 October, resumed at the end of the month but later broke off in failure. However, in December, the British Foreign Secretary, Lord Home, took the opportunity of the NATO meeting in Paris to have a private discussion with Gudmundur Gudmundsson, the Icelandic Foreign Minister, and on 27 February 1961, a settlement was announced.

Britain accepted the twelve-mile fisheries limit but there was to be a three-year transition period during which its trawlers would be allowed to fish the greater part of the six- to twelve-mile area at specified seasons. Base lines were modified in Iceland's favour. Any future dispute was to be submitted to the International Court.

In the following years, the settlement worked satisfactorily, though for the longer term, Iceland retained its interest, as did other states similarly placed, in securing special rights over the whole "continental shelf" around its coast.

*   *   *

M. DAVIS: *Iceland Extends its Fisheries Limits*, George Allen & Unwin, London 1963.

D. NUECHTERLEIN: *Iceland, Reluctant Ally*, Cornell University Press, New York 1961.

L. GREEN: "The Territorial Sea and the Anglo-Icelandic Dispute", *Journal of Public Law*, No. 1, 1960.

Berlin 1958-62

AFTER the Berlin Blockade of 1948–49, the Federal Republic of Germany came into existence in the Western zones on 21 September 1949 and the German Democratic Republic in the Soviet zone on 7 October.[1] On 26 May 1952, the Western powers signed the Bonn Convention designed to restore sovereignty to West Germany and end its occupied status. Berlin remained a special case. The rights of the Allied powers in the city were to be retained and its political incorporation into West Germany remained prohibited. The Western powers were prepared, however, to relax their control so that Berlin could adopt similar legislation to that prevailing in West Germany, provided such legislation was not inconsistent with Allied rights or legislation. In an Annexe to the Convention, West Germany undertook to assist Berlin economically.

The Convention was conditional on West Germany's integration into a European Defence Community (whose other members were to be France, Italy, and the Benelux countries), the treaty for this being signed in Paris on the following day, 27 May 1952. In the event, the EDC project collapsed but the same purpose and provisions as the Convention were achieved by the London and Paris Agreements, signed 20–23 October 1954 and coming into effect on 5 May 1955, followed on 9 May by West Germany's entry into the North Atlantic Treaty Organisation.

The Soviet Union, for its part, having protested against these developments, established the Warsaw Pact including East Germany on 14 May 1955, and on 20 September signed a treaty with East Germany ending its occupied status. In an exchange of letters it was agreed that East Germany should assume control over its frontiers, including the frontier with West Germany and the Berlin frontier, and over the access routes from West Germany to Berlin. However, the control of Western military traffic with Berlin, which was to be allowed "on the basis of existing Four-Power decisions", was to be exercised for the time being by the Soviet military in East Germany.[2]

Early in the same month, September, Konrad Adenauer, the West German Chancellor, visited Moscow at the invitation of the Soviet Union, and on the 13th, the two countries announced the establishment of diplomatic relations. This marked a turning point in Soviet policy. For ten years, in its dealings with the Western powers, the Soviet Union had

[1] See pp. 28–31.
[2] US Department of State, p. 189.

168

emphasised the need to create an all-German government, adding latterly the neutralisation of the country. Now, it became an open exponent of a "two Germanies" solution and worked to strengthen East Germany and to achieve Western recognition of it, while maintaining its interest in a neutralised zone in central Europe.

The upheavals in Poland and Hungary in the autumn of 1956, together with the memory of the Berlin riots of 1953, may well have quickened the Soviet Union's desire to consolidate the position of East Germany. In 1956–58, it seems also to have been under increasing pressure in this direction from the Polish and East German governments.

The Poles were anxious to see East Germany consolidated because it had recognised the Polish–German Oder-Neisse frontier as permanent (whereas West Germany had refused to commit itself pending the signature of a German peace treaty). They accompanied this with a security proposal, endorsed by the Soviet Union, the Rapacki Plan for a nuclear-free zone in central Europe.

The East Germans were increasingly concerned at the deteriorating economic situation, in which Berlin played an indirect part. Although the city was divided into two, some freedom of movement remained and by 1958, some three thousand people were fleeing weekly from East to West Germany, mostly through Berlin.

By the autumn of 1958, the Soviet Union had made little progress towards achieving recognition of East Germany or as regards its security proposals. On the other hand, since the launching of the first artificial earth satellite (sputnik) a year previously, there had been a widespread feeling that the military balance had ceased to be heavily in the West's favour. Against this background, the Soviet Union touched off a new crisis over Berlin. In a speech of 10 November 1958, Nikita Krushchev, Chairman of the Council of Ministers, said: "The time has obviously come for the signatories of the Potsdam Agreement to renounce the remnants of the occupation regime in Berlin and thereby make it possible to create a new situation in the capital of the German Democratic Republic. The Soviet Union for its part would hand over to the sovereign German Democratic Republic the functions in Berlin that are still exercised by Soviet agencies." On 27 November, the Soviet Union sent notes to the three Western powers demanding that the occupation of Berlin be ended and that West Berlin be converted into a demilitarised free city, guaranteed by the four powers and possibly under United Nations observation. East Germany would take control over access to West Berlin. If after six months no action had been taken, the Soviet Union would conclude its own agreement with East Germany.

In the interval between Krushchev's speech and the detailed Soviet proposals, the United States Secretary of State, John Foster Dulles, caused some stir by speculating that the Western powers might be prepared to accept control over the access routes by East Germans as "agents" of the Soviet Union. This episode apart, the reaction of the Western powers was negative. At the NATO meeting in Paris in December, the Soviet plan was considered unacceptable and Western rights in Berlin were reaffirmed. On the 31st, the three Western powers sent separate notes to the Soviet Union rejecting unilateral Soviet Union action. They offered negotiations on Berlin in the wider framework of negotiations on the German problem and European security but only if it was clear that the Soviet Union was not intending a threat. In West Berlin itself, the Socialist Party (Communist) won only 1·9 per cent of the votes in the municipal elections of 7 December and the Christian Democrats pledged support for the Social Democrat Mayor, Willy Brandt, in a new term of office. "The Communist assault had caused the city to close its ranks and unanimity prevailed which had not been seen in Berlin since the days of Ernst Reuter."[3]

On a visit to the United States in January 1959, Anastas Mikoyan, the Soviet Deputy Premier, indicated that the six months ultimatum referred only to the opening of negotiations. In February, the Western Powers suggested a Foreign Ministers' Conference while the Soviet Union countered by proposing a "summit" meeting of heads of governments. After the British Prime Minister, Harold Macmillan, had visited Moscow (21 February–3 March) and Krushchev had admitted (19 March) that the Western powers had "lawful rights for their stay in Berlin", the tension eased further. The Soviet Union accepted the Western proposal for a Foreign Ministers' Conference (looking to a later "summit" conference) and this met at Geneva between 11 May and 5 August. Though it eventually reached deadlock, the more relaxed atmosphere continued.

Then followed, in September 1959, Krushchev's official visit to the United States and the announcement after the Camp David talks with President Dwight D. Eisenhower that negotiations on Berlin would be resumed, not to be "prolonged indefinitely" but with "no fixed limit". It was later announced that a "summit" conference would be held in Paris the following May. The only jarring note in the public harmony was occasional incidents in Berlin and East Germany. On 6 October, during anniversary celebrations of the founding of the Democratic Republic, East German flags were placed on S-bahn (overhead railway) stations in West Berlin and the police removing them were assaulted by Communists. On 3 February 1960, the East German Government announced that henceforth the Allied Military Missions in Potsdam would be ac-

---

[3] (Mayor during the Berlin Blockade, 1948–49.) Smith, p. 187.

credited to East Germany, not the Soviet Union, but this move was successfully resisted.

As the "summit" conference date approached, relations once again deteriorated sharply. Repeated statements by Krushchev of the need for a peace treaty and new arrangements for Berlin were met by repeated Western assurances to the Germans and the world at large that they would not surrender to Soviet threats. In March, President de Gaulle made plain to Krushchev on his visit to France that France was firm on the maintenance of Western rights. An especially strong speech by the US Under-Secretary of State, Douglas Dillon, in New York on 20 April was countered by an equally vehement speech by Krushchev in Baku (5 April). On 5 May, eleven days before the conference, Krushchev announced the discovery of United States U-2 flights over the Soviet Union. When the conference opened he demanded a prior apology from President Eisenhower. This was refused and the conference broke up.[4]

The ultimatum on Berlin was not revived, however; Krushchev stated that negotiations had merely been postponed until after the inauguration of a new United States president. From John F. Kennedy's inauguration on 20 January 1961 until his meeting with Krushchev in Vienna on 3–4 June there was a further lull. At Vienna, Krushchev once again demanded that the Berlin situation be "normalised" but little agreement was reached on this or any other subject, the conference communique merely recording a useful exchange of views.

Tension rose sharply once more when, in a broadcast of 15 June 1961, Krushchev stated that "the conclusion of a peace treaty with Germany cannot be postponed any longer. A peaceful settlement in Europe must be attained this year." In making this renewed challenge, Krushchev may have been influenced by the new United States Administration's fiasco in Cuba (the Bay of Pigs invasion) and by the need for a success in view of the growing quarrel with China. Probably his main concern, however, was the deteriorating economic situation of East Germany. The refugee drain was now seriously undermining the regime of Walter Ulbricht.

Following a formal diplomatic note of 17 July, President Kennedy declared in a broadcast of 25 July that the freedom of West Berlin was "not negotiable". He outlined a programme of military preparations, including the call-up of reservists, to meet any crisis. In the first days of August, the Warsaw Pact countries held a meeting in Moscow and the Foreign Ministers of the United States, Britain, France and West Germany met in Paris. Simultaneously, the rush of refugees from East Germany became a torrent; some 22,000 left in the first twelve days of August.

[4] See pp. 179–81.

Early on the morning of 13 August, East German troops and police erected a wall along the dividing line between East and West Berlin. On 15 August, the Western commandants in Berlin protested against this action to their Soviet counterpart as a breach of the four-power status of the city, and on the 17th the Western powers protested formally to the Soviet Government. East Germany and the Soviet Union declared that the wall was "a defensive measure" to counter subversive activities emanating from West Berlin. From the 18th, the East Germans began to build the wall into a more permanent structure. Henceforth German civilian movement across the division of Berlin was checked and only permitted occasionally. There was no serious attempt, however, to limit Allied access to East Berlin.

To raise West Berlin morale, the Vice-President of the United States, Lyndon Johnson, and the hero of the 1948 blockade, General Lucius Clay, visited the city and the garrison was reinforced by a battle group which travelled along the Helmstedt autobahn on the morning of 19 August. At the end of the month, Clay went to West Berlin as President Kennedy's personal representative.

Meanwhile, the United States and Britain, in face of opposition from Adenauer and President Charles de Gaulle of France, were seeking to resume talks with the Soviet Union. Initial soundings were taken with the Soviet Foreign Minister, Andrei Gromyko, when he attended the UN General Assembly in September and these continued through the ambassadors in Moscow.

In March 1962 the US Secretary of State, Dean Rusk, and the British Foreign Secretary, Lord Home, took the opportunity of the disarmament conference at Geneva to begin informal discussions with Gromyko and on 16 April a new round of negotiations opened in Washington between Rusk and the Soviet Ambassador, Anatoly Dobrynin. The United States put forward package proposals including an international access authority for Berlin, an exchange of non-aggression pledges by NATO and the Warsaw Pact countries, an agreement for the "non-proliferation" of nuclear weapons, and the formation of bilateral governmental committees between East and West Germany. These proposals did not, however, satisfy the Soviet Union.

Throughout these months, Soviet harassment continued in the air corridors to Berlin. In the summer and during the Cuba missiles crisis of October, tension over Berlin was again high. From then on, however, the situation cooled and Berlin was free of serious crisis for the rest of the decade. On 25 June 1963, President Kennedy visited West Berlin and reaffirmed the United States commitment. "All free men, wherever they may live, are citizens of Berlin and, therefore, as a free man, I take pride in the words 'Ich bin ein Berliner'." On 12 June 1964, the Soviet Union signed a separate peace treaty with East Germany but without denying the continued rights of the Western powers in the city.

*   *   *

M. BALFOUR: *West Germany*, Benn, London 1968.

W. HUBATSCH (ed.): *The German Question*, Herder Book Centre, New York 1967.

E. MCINNIS and others: *The Shaping of Postwar Germany*, Dent, London 1960.

M. SHICK: *The Berlin Crisis 1958–62*, University of Pennsylvania Press, Philadelphia 1971.

J. E. SMITH: *The Defense of Berlin*, Johns Hopkins Press, Baltimore 1963.

H. SPEIER: *Divided Berlin*, Praeger, New York 1961.

P. WINDSOR: *City on Leave, A History of Berlin 1945–1962*, Chatto and Windus, London 1963.

US DEPARTMENT OF STATE: *Senate Committee on Foreign Relations: Documents on Germany 1944–61*, USGPO, Washington, D.C., 1961.

E. BARKER: "The Berlin Crisis 1958–62", *International Affairs*, January 1963.

Cuba – The United States 1959–61

FROM 1933 to 1959, the "strong man" of Cuban politics was General Fulgencio Batista y Zaldívar, President from 1940 to 1944 and from 1952 to 1959. On 26 July 1953, a small group of revolutionaries led by Dr Fidel Castro launched their Revolutionary Movement with an attack on Fort Moncada. After trial, imprisonment, amnesty and exile, Castro landed again in Oriente Province on 2 December 1956 and began a guerrilla campaign in the hills against the Government. On 1 January 1959, Batista fled from the country and Castro entered Havana. Dr Manuel Urrutia Lleo was made President with Dr José Miró Cardona as Prime Minister. On 13 February Castro took over as Prime Minister.

The United States watched these events with mixed feelings. Since their liberation of the island from Spain in 1898, Americans had adopted a paternalistic attitude to the Cubans, maintaining a military base at Guantánamo Bay, influencing politics actively or passively, and developing the economy so that they owned most of the utilities, the cattle ranches, the iron and petroleum reserves and some 40 per cent of the sugar industry, the largest in the world. The cruelties of the Batista regime had been little publicised and it was at least a known quantity and gave no serious trouble. Castro and his followers, on the other hand, with their revolutionary ideals, their guerrilla warfare, their outlandish beards, boots and denims were plainly not conventional Latin American rebels but an unknown quantity. Throughout January and February, United States opinion was affronted by the trial of hundreds of Batista's henchmen and the execution of 450 of them. Some within the United States Government and Administration counselled co-operation with Castro, others a search for alternatives. In the event, when Castro visited the United States from 15 to 20 April, the Administration's attitude was coolly correct.

Then followed on 17 May the promulgation of the Agrarian Reform Law, operative from 3 June. According to this, the maximum land holding would henceforth be 30 caballerías (1 caballería is $33\frac{1}{6}$ acres) with exceptions for cattle, sugar and rice holdings which might extend to 100. Excess land would be taken over by the National Institute for Agrarian Reform which would distribute it to the peasants in basic units of 2 caballerías or, where there was not enough, organise it into co-operatives. Compensation would be paid to the present owners in the form of bonds, payable in twenty years' time, bearing $4\frac{1}{2}$ per cent interest. The amount due would

174

be the value which the owners had placed on the land for tax purposes in previous years.

The landowners immediately protested vehemently against these measures. The fragmentation of the sugar estates would ruin the industry; the compensation proposed was derisory. There were also deep fears of the growth of power of the State through its control of the land. The position of foreign landowners was in some degree unclear in that the law provided that the NIAR might allow them larger holdings if the Government considered this to be in Cuba's interest. None the less, the broad picture was clear enough. In a note of 11 June to the Cuban Government, the United States touched on the danger to the efficiency of the Cuban economy and, while admitting the right of expropriation, urged that it must be accompanied by "prompt, adequate and effective compensation". In later formal exchanges, the United States Government confined itself to this international legal point exclusively. In the United States Congress, on the other hand, and in the news media, the growth of the power of the State and the "collectivism" of the agrarian reform were seized on. Talk of "Communism in Cuba" began.

In the exchanges on compensation over the following months, the Cuban Government continued to insist that it wanted good relations with the United States but equally that it had not the resources to pay quicker, greater compensation. Meanwhile, talk of "Communism in Cuba" found further material. There was first the resignation of the moderate President Urrutia (17 July, succeeded by Dr Osvaldo Dorticós Torredo) and the prominence in Cuban affairs of extreme radicals such as Castro's younger brother, Major Raúl Castro, Minister of the Armed Forces, and Dr Ernesto "Ché" Guevara, Argentinian by extraction, President of the National Bank. There was next the uneasy growth of an alliance between Castro and the Cuban Communist Party and his government's willingness to make use of Communists as administrators of the great new social programmes.

In these months also, Castro on his side found material for complaint against the United States. Many Batista supporters had fled to the United States and in August, occasional air attacks from Florida and similar incidents began. Castro's accusations against the United States of complicity in these episodes became increasingly sharp. The United States Government answered that it was taking all the preventive measures in its power and implied that Castro was deliberately making trouble.

On 2 November 1959, sooner than the companies had been led to expect, certain United States cattle, iron ore and petroleum land-holdings were taken over and on 6 January 1960, the first United States sugar estates. In the United States Congress, open agitation for a deterrent cut in Cuba's sugar export quota began. The Administration responded with public statements which still expressed sympathy with the general aims of the Cuban revolution but also, it seems, began to consider taking powers to cut the sugar quota.

Then on 13 February, the Cuban Government took a step which created a vast sensation in the United States. For some years Cuban governments had sought new outlets for sugar exports. The Castro government now signed an agreement with the Soviet Union to barter sugar for Soviet goods, accompanied by a $100 million Soviet loan.

Relations between Cuba and the United States now worsened rapidly. The United States Administration began to accuse Castro of betraying the Cuban Revolution to Communism. Castro's marathon harangues to his people, to Latin America and to the world became increasingly bitter against "Yanqui imperialism". Measures and counter-measures mounted. In March, the United States Administration secretly authorised the training and equipping of Cuban *emigrés* for eventual guerrilla action in Cuba. In April, the Cuban Government made a trade agreement with Poland; in May, it established formal diplomatic relations with the Soviet Union; in June, it took over the country's oil refineries (Standard Oil, Texaco and Shell) because of their refusal to accept Soviet oil arriving under the Soviet–Cuban barter agreement. On 3 July, the United States Administration secured powers from Congress to alter sugar quotas. On the 6th, the Cuban Government took powers to expropriate United States banking, industrial and trading concerns. On the same day, the United States Administration abolished the remainder of Cuba's sugar quota for the year. On the 20th, the Soviet Union announced that it would purchase the sugar concerned and on the 23rd, China announced that it too would make purchases.

Cuba's defiance of the United States and breach of Western hemisphere solidarity went beyond economic affairs. At this time, Cuban spokesmen began to express fears of a United States attack and on 9 July, in the course of a speech, the Soviet leader, Nikita Krushchev, made an obscurely worded remark which seemed to suggest that the Soviet Union would defend Cuba with missile power. Despite the popular exaggeration of Soviet missile capability at this time, few in the United States took this remark literally but it dramatised the Cuban–Soviet threat to the Monroe Doctrine tradition. Cuba also approached the United Nations Security Council. When the matter came up on 18 July, it was adjourned without discussion on the argument of Argentina and Ecuador that it was already being investigated by the Organization of American States. After lengthy discussions in the OAS in August in which the majority of Latin American states resisted outright condemnation of Cuba, the Organization issued the

Declaration of San José (28 August), reaffirming traditional opposition to intervention or threats of intervention by external powers in the affairs of the hemisphere. On 2 September, Castro denounced the Declaration and repudiated the Inter-American Treaty of Mutual Assistance (the Rio Treaty, 1947).

Castro appeared in New York on 18 September for the opening of the UN General Assembly session and throughout the autumn, Cuba continued its efforts to involve the UN in the question of its relations with the United States. Meanwhile, the revolutionary transformation of Cuba continued. The Cuban Government took powers to nationalise the banks and major industrial concerns (13 October). The United States embargoed exports to Cuba except medical goods and foodstuffs (19th). The Cuban Government nationalised the principal United States companies (24th).

In November, Cuba became more specific in its charges that the United States was planning an invasion. The United States denied this and warned Cuba against action against the Guantánamo base. It also made naval movements in the Caribbean which it explained as necessary for the protection of Guatemala and Nicaragua. Castro explained them as part of an invasion plan. On 2 January 1961, at the United Nations, Cuba formally charged the United States with planning aggression. On the same day, it requested the United States to reduce its embassy staff in Havana to eleven. The next day, the United States broke off diplomatic relations.

John F. Kennedy became United States President on 20 January. During his election campaign in the autumn, he had denounced the Republican Administration for failure to prevent a "Communist take-over" of Cuba and shortly after his victory on 8 November, he had been informed of the training and equipping of Cuban *emigrés* by the Central Intelligence Agency in Guatemala. By March, he was ready to give tentative endorsement to the CIA plan, though continuing President Eisenhower's condition that the United States must not be directly involved in fighting. Early in April, he ordered the launching of the operation.

The plan had apparently developed considerably since its inception. Originally, it seems, Batista *emigrés* were to be landed clandestinely to create pockets of guerrilla activity. Over the past year, however, as Castro's policies developed, disillusioned or disgruntled liberals had also taken refuge in Miami and Guatemala and finally, in March, a Cuban Revolutionary Council had been formed with Dr José Miró Cardona, the first Prime Minister after Batista's fall, as provisional President. There was a vague but strong idea in many sections of the United States Government that the Cuban people must secretly resent "Castro's Communist tyranny" and be ready to rise against him in the cause of the true Cuban revolution. The plan now was, therefore, that an *emigré* force should make a frontal assault on the beaches of the island. If an uprising followed, well and good. If not, they would "melt into the hills" to begin guerrilla warfare.

On 15 April, eight United States aircraft from Nicaragua bearing Cuban insignia – they were supposed to be Cuban defectors – attempted to destroy the Cuban air force on the ground. On the 17th, a force of 1,400 *emigrés* landed on beaches in the Bay of Pigs from United States assault craft or were parachuted further forward. Little surprise was achieved, the Cuban Army was rapidly in action, the Cuban Air Force had control of the air, the Cuban Government made mass precautionary arrests throughout the island, there was no sign of an uprising. Over the next few days, as the assault faltered, the Cuban Revolutionary Council, which had always believed despite repeated denials that the United States would in fact give armed support, pleaded for United States intervention. This was not forthcoming except for a short period of carrier-borne air support on the 19th. By the 20th, about eighty of the invaders had been killed and most of the rest captured.

The assault on Cuba coincided with the discussion by the UN Political Committee of Cuba's long-standing charges against the United States. The ill-informed United States delegation led by Adlai Stevenson was in confusion. However, on the 21st, seven Latin American countries sponsored a resolution in the General Assembly whereby the affair should be left to the Organisation of American States. Other allies of the United States, notably Britain and Canada, using as an argument the uncertainty at that time on the extent of United States involvement, were active in preventing any movement in the Assembly to condemn the United States for aggression. This was the easier in as much as it was already clear that the assault on Cuba had failed.[1]

*   *   *

T. DRAPER: *Castroism, Theory and Practice*, Pall Mall Press, London 1965.

B. GOLDENBERG: *The Cuban Revolution and Latin America*, Praeger, New York 1965.

R. SCHEER and M. ZEITLIN: *Cuba, An American Tragedy*, rev. ed., Penguin Books, Harmondsworth 1964.

A. SCHLESINGER: *A Thousand Days*, André Deutsch, London 1965.

R. F. SMITH: *The United States and Cuba, Business and Diplomacy 1917–60*, Bookman Associates, New York, 1961.

[1] For subsequent developments in Cuba–United States relations, see pp. 233–7.

The U-2 Incident 1960

AT the Geneva "summit" conference of July 1955, President Eisenhower made an "open skies" proposal whereby the United States and the Soviet Union, for their greater security, would allow aerial photography of each other's territory. The Soviet Union rejected this proposal. Covert flights by United States Lockheed U-2 photo-reconnaissance aircraft over the Soviet Union apparently began the following year.

The Soviet-American quarrel over these secret flights erupted early in May 1960. In 1959, the crisis over Berlin had eased, Chairman Krushchev had visited the United States and held friendly talks with President Eisenhower at Camp David, and a new summit conference had been agreed for May 1960. As the date of the conference approached, however, relations deteriorated. Continual statements by Krushchev on the need for a peace treaty with Germany and new arrangements for Berlin were matched by Western pronouncements that they were not going to surrender to Soviet threats.[1]

On 5 May 1960, Krushchev stated with little detail during a speech to the Supreme Soviet that, on the 1st, the Russians had shot down a United States plane flying across the Soviet Union. The US National Aeronautics and Space Administration had made a routine announcement on the 3rd that one of its U-2 research planes "being flown in Turkey in a joint NASA-US Air Force Air Weather Service Mission apparently went down in the Lake Van, Turkey, area, at about 9.00 a.m., Sunday 1 May". Now, on 5 May, in response to Krushchev, the US State Department made a statement saying that an oxygen failure could have made the pilot of this plane unconscious and the plane could have continued under the control of the automatic pilot, accidentally violating Soviet airspace.

On the 7th, however, Krushchev stated that the aircraft had been brought down by Russian rockets near Sverdlovsk, more than twelve hundred miles inside the Soviet Union. Moreover, he had proof that it had been on a photo-reconnaissance mission across the Soviet Union from Pakistan to Norway. The pilot, Francis Gary Powers, was alive and well and the plane's equipment had been recovered.

On the same day, the State Department replied that "insofar as the authorities in Washington are concerned, there was no authorisation for any such flight as described by Mr Krushchev. Nevertheless, it appears that in endeavouring to obtain information now concealed behind the Iron

[1] See pp. 168–71.

Curtain, a flight over Soviet territory was probably undertaken by an unarmed civilian U-2 plane."

On the 9th, Secretary of State Christian Herter made a longer statement. He recalled the secretiveness of the Soviet Union and its rejection of the "open skies" proposal. The United States Government would be failing in its responsibility if it did not take its own measures to gather information. At the outset of his presidency, President Eisenhower had ordered the gathering "by every possible means (of) the information required to protect the United States and the free world against surprise attack. Under these directives, programmes have been developed and put into operation which have included extensive aerial surveillance by unarmed civilian aircraft, normally of a peripheral character but on occasions by penetration." However, "specific missions of these unarmed civilian aircraft have not been subject of Presidential authorisation". On 11 May, President Eisenhower at a news conference acknowledged his personal responsibility and said that such activities were "distasteful but of vital necessity".

Eisenhower, Krushchev, de Gaulle and Macmillan gathered in Paris for the summit conference on 16 May. At a private meeting before the official opening, Krushchev demanded a statement by the United States condemning the U-2 flights, undertaking to punish those directly responsible, and cancelling them for the future. While indicating that he had already ordered the suspension of the flights, President Eisenhower would not submit to these demands. The conference broke up.

The official Soviet view of the episode was that United States violations of Soviet airspace and unwillingness to repudiate them at a delicate moment in East–West negotiations indicated a fundamental lack of interest in any *détente* and the worthlessness of the "spirit of Camp David". Accordingly, the summit conference or any other negotiations would be useless until after the United States elections and a change in its Administration.

Much Western comment simply stressed that, according to his own speeches, Krushchev had known of the U-2 flights for a considerable time. He had used them now as a mere pretext to disrupt the summit conference with the maximum propaganda embarrassment to the United States. He had done this because he realised that his campaign of threats about Berlin had not moved the Western powers and that the summit conference would produce no gains.

Others took the more complex view that Krushchev had been under pressure to make much of the 1 May incident from the military and others in the Soviet Government and from China, who had no faith in the policy of *détente* with the West, but had balanced this with his own conviction that something was to be made of "the spirit of Camp David". He had therefore revealed the incident but initially quite mildly, saying, moreover (7 May), that President Eisenhower might not have known of the flights. What tilted the balance was the United States response and especially President Eisenhower's acceptance of responsibility for the actions of the United States espionage agencies. This transformed an unpleasant fact of international life into an open affront to the Soviet Union. It was no longer possible for Krushchev to urge his picture of Eisenhower as a man of wise statesmanship to be differentiated from the "Pentagon militarists". He was thus obliged to bow to those who had long opposed the policy of *détente* with the West.

No explicit settlement of the affair was reached but little more was heard of it. It appears that the U-2 flights over the Soviet Union were not resumed and that there was soon less need to do so in relation to the Soviet Union in view of the development of artificial earth satellites.

*   *   *

E. CRANKSHAW: *Krushchev*, Collins, London 1966.

E. HUGHES: *The Ordeal of Power*, Macmillan, London 1963.

ROYAL INSTITUTE OF INTERNATIONAL AFFAIRS: *Documents on International Affairs 1960*, Oxford University Press, 1964.

D. WISE and T. ROSS: *The U-2 Affair*, Cresset Press, London 1963.

Q. WRIGHT: "Legal Aspects of the U-2 Incident", *American Journal of International Law*, October 1960.

Somalia 1960-69

THE three and a half million Somalis are a Hamitic people, Sunni Muslim, and for the most part nomads, following the grazing seasonally over many miles. From about the year 1000, they expanded from the tip of the Horn of Africa until they reached as far as Djibouti in the north, the River Tana in the south, and high up the Juba and Shebelle rivers in the centre, some 400 miles from the coast, where they met the counter-pressure of the Christian kings of Ethiopia.

In the second half of the last century, various northern powers came on to the scene in competition with one another. In 1884 and 1886, the British made protection agreements with the clans of the coast and hinterland opposite Aden; the French did the same with the clans around Djibouti (1885); and the Italians also, with various sultans on the Indian Ocean coast (1889).

The three powers then came to agreements with one another delimiting their respective spheres, the British and French in 1888, the British and Italians in 1894. The last two also reached agreement (1891) regarding the far south, where the Juba was to be the line between the British in East Africa and the Italians in Somaliland. (Jubaland, to the south of the river, was transferred to Italy by a treaty of 1924.)

At the same time, the three powers also had to reckon with the growing strength of the Emperor Menelik of Ethiopia, who laid claim (1891) to the whole of the Horn of Africa. After his victory over the Italians at Adowa (1896), Italy and Britain made agreements with him (1897) drawing back substantially the line of their protectorates in the Haud and Ogaden respectively, and so in effect ceding territory inhabited by Somali tribes whom they had taken under protection.

Most of the details of this partitioning seem to have been unknown to at any rate the inland Somalis. From 1900 to 1920, Sayyid Muhammad 'Abdille Hassan led a sporadic *jihad* against British, Ethiopians and Italians alike, but for the rest, life went on much as before. The 1897 agreements preserved grazing rights across the borders and in any case these had as yet little practical significance of any sort. The Ethiopians and the Italians were in standing dispute over the location of their line in Ogaden (placed by their 1897 agreement irreconcilably, thanks to an erroneous map, at 180 miles from the coast and at various specified points, and little clarified by their treaty of 1908). In practice, at that time, neither side had extended its control to the area. In the Haud, the British did not tell the tribesmen of their 1897 agreement with the Ethiopians; but as yet the Ethiopians troubled them little.

By the 1930s, the Ethiopians were making themselves felt in both the Haud and Ogaden. In the Haud, an Anglo-Ethiopian Commission sought to demarcate the 1897 line, rousing the opposition of the tribesmen. In Ogaden, the Italians, who had meanwhile used some force to convert their protectorate into a direct-rule colony, were likewise advancing. The outcome was the Walwal Incident (1934), the Italian conquest of Ethiopia (1935–36) and the joining of Ogaden to Italian Somaliland. Then followed the Second World War, the brief Italian conquest of British Somaliland (1941) and, from the end of 1941, a situation in which, with the exception of French Somaliland, the British administered all the lands inhabited by the Somalis.

After the war, in April 1946, the British proposed in the four-power commission set up to consider the matter (Britain, France, Soviet Union, United States) that the whole area currently under its administration should be unified into a Greater Somalia under British trusteeship.[1] However, the three others opposed this solution and so did Ethiopia, to which Britain had restored full sovereignty by a treaty of 31 January 1942 following the ejection of the Italians. Accordingly, in 1948, the British returned Ogaden to Ethiopia; in 1950, the Italians began a ten-year trusteeship of Italian Somaliland; and in 1954, the British returned the Haud to Ethiopia. Legally speaking, therefore, little had changed for the Somalis after the twenty-year upheaval, except that there was now a ten-year limit on the Italian presence. Even the border dispute in Ogaden continued, though in practice the Italians and Ethiopians observed a compromise line established by the British. Despite United Nations pressure, an agreement in principle to go to arbitration came to nothing.

Within Somali society, on the other hand, there had been considerable change. Following the first stirrings of modern nationalism in the 1930s, the Somali Youth Club (later renamed League) was founded in 1943. This movement, eventually to become the leading political party of independent Somalia, protested strongly in the name of Somali independence and unity against the return of the Italians and the Ethiopians. When in 1960, British Somaliland (26 June) and Italian Somaliland (1 July) became independent and amalgamated (1 July) in a jubilant, if in practice somewhat uneasy, union, their new constitution declared (Article VI) that "the Somali Republic shall promote, by legal and peaceful means, the union of Somali territories . . .".

Somalia focused its attention first on Kenya where great changes were

---

[1] i.e. British and Italian Somaliland, the Haud and Ogaden. No mention was made, it seems, of the Somali-inhabited Northern Frontier District of Kenya.

anyway impending and where the prospects seemed best. The Northern Frontier District, in which the Somalis concentrated in the eastern part were in the majority, had always been separately administered. From 1948, the SYL was banned there but when the ban was lifted in 1960, it promoted the formation of the Northern Province People's Party which agitated for secession and union with Somalia.

The outlook seemed at first moderately promising. In Africa at large, opinion had not yet set firm on the issue of colonial borders. The All-African People's Conference had passed a resolution at Tunis in January 1960 supporting Somali unity. Opinion in the Conference turned against Somalia in 1961 but there was still no decisive stand for the maintenance of colonial borders. In 1962, there was much talk among African statesmen of solving the problem by a wider pan-Africanism of one sort or another.

In February 1962, at the constitutional conference in London looking towards Kenya's independence, the British Colonial Secretary, Mr Reginald Maudling, faced with the demands of the leaders of the Somalis in the NFD, in the end announced that a commission of enquiry would be sent to the District to "ascertain public opinion regarding its political frontier". In talks with President Adan Abdulla Osman at Mogadishu, the two Kenyan party leaders, Jomo Kenyatta (July) and Ronald Ngala (August), were not encouraging, raising at most the idea of obliterating all such local issues in a wide East African federation; but neither did they state flat opposition and the talks were friendly. In December, the commission of enquiry produced a report which may be summarised as saying that the great majority of the population of the NFD were in favour of joining Somalia.[2]

In the event, the British Government rejected secession, deferring apparently to Kenyan and Ethiopian views and to the development of African opinion generally. This was now setting firm against Somalia, both in particular and as a matter of principle. If the inherited colonial borders of Africa could be questioned on ethnic grounds, few would stand and the whole continent would be in turmoil. On 8 March 1963, the new Colonial Secretary, Mr Duncan Sandys, announced that the predominantly Somali areas of Kenya would be formed into a seventh (North-Eastern) Region of the country, so giving "its inhabitants greater freedom in the management of their own affairs".

Somali disappointment was intense; Somalia broke off diplomatic relations with Britain on 18 March; there were incidents in the NFD. In an effort to maintain good will between the Kenyans and Somalia, the British called a meeting in Rome on 25–29 August, but they and the

[2] HM Stationery Office, *Kenya, Report of the Northern Frontier District Commission*, Cmnd. 1900, 1962, London 1962.

Kenyans were unresponsive to the Somali proposal that the NFD should be placed under joint Kenyan–Somali or United Nations administration. On 12 December, Kenya became independent with the area still part of it.

The previous month Somalia had broken off negotiations with Britain for an arms supply agreement (on the grounds that the arms offered were inferior in quantity and quality to those supplied to Ethiopia) in favour of an agreement with the Soviet Union. (It had accepted economic assistance from the Soviet Union as well as from the West for the past two years in line with its foreign policy of neutralism.) From Kenya's independence in December and for four years thereafter Somali *shiftas* carried out frequent guerrilla raids against Kenyan security forces in the Somali area. It seems clear that Somalia, while admitting only its propaganda support, supplied arms to them.

In the following year (1964), Somalia's relations with Ethiopia came to a crisis. Since Somalia's independence in 1960, Ethiopia had conceded as before that the Ogaden border was in dispute and had stated its willingness in principle to embark on the necessary procedures for border demarcation in accordance with the 1897 and 1908 treaties; but it would not discuss the wider contention that the nineteenth-century treaties were wholly invalid and that the future of the Somalis in Ethiopia was an open question, to be decided by self-determination. *Shifta* attacks began and a Somali Liberation Movement developed in Ogaden which Ethiopia accused Somalia of fomenting and which Somalia declared was a spontaneous local movement against Ethiopian oppression and restrictions on grazing rights.

In May 1963, the Organisation of African Unity was inaugurated at Addis Ababa. Somalia took the opportunity to state its claims but this was received coldly. In August, Ethiopia carried out a large-scale campaign in Ogaden in an effort to stamp out the Liberation Movement. In November, it alleged that Somali regular army units had entered Ethiopia, and in January 1964, Somalia counter-alleged that Ethiopian planes had bombed Somali villages. In February, serious border clashes began.

Both sides called for an extraordinary meeting of the Council of Ministers of the OAU and this recommended a cease-fire and bilateral negotiations to be followed by a report to the Organisation. Negotiations began in Khartoum with the good offices of Sudan, and on 30 March an agreement was reached. There was to be a cease-fire and a demilitarised zone of 10–15 kilometers, to be supervised by a Mixed Military Commission drawn from both sides, and a cessation of hostile propaganda and an exchange of notes on the vexed issue of grazing rights.

Somalia wanted the negotiations to extend to the wider issue of the future of the Somalis in Ethiopia but Ethiopia would not agree to this interpretation of the OAU recommendation. Further talks were held in

Cairo in July immediately before the OAU meeting but came to nothing. At the meeting, Ethiopia successfully promoted a resolution (with Somalia dissenting) in which the members "pledge themselves to respect the borders existing on the achievement of national independence".

In Ogaden, over the next few years, incidents continued and Somalia continued to complain of restrictions on the grazing rights of the nomads and various forms of Ethiopian oppression. Ethiopia answered that it was merely taking the measures necessary to curb the *shiftas* and Somalia's request to the OAU (April 1965) for a fact-finding commission made no progress.

Somalia hoped for greater support from the OAU, especially its Liberation Committee, in its call for self-determination in French Somaliland but was again disappointed. Ethiopia had a broad common interest with France in resisting Somalia's claims and a particular common interest in the development of the Addis Ababa–Djibouti railway, and the only actions of the OAU were occasional expressions of solidarity with the French Somalis. Somalia also sought to interest the United Nations Committee of Twenty-Four,[3] proposing that the UN should sponsor a plebiscite, but without success.

In August 1966, President Charles de Gaulle visited French Somaliland and was greeted by independence demonstrations. In March 1967, the electorate of the territory were confronted with the choice of either the continuation of Overseas Territory status, greater local autonomy and increased development aid; or independence and no aid. The outcome was a 60 per cent vote in favour of continuing the link with France (only achieved, Somalia alleged, by disenfranchising many Somalis on the grounds that they were nomads). The name of the territory was changed from Côte Française des Somalis to Territoire Français des Afars et des Issas.[4]

In the course of 1967, Somalia's policies towards its neighbours began to change. Its claims had made no progress, and not merely had its quarrel with Ethiopia, Kenya and France and its aid relations with the Soviet Union and China made it unpopular with the Western powers, but it was isolated and unpopular in Africa also. At the OAU meeting at Kinshasa in September 1967, the Prime Minister of the new Government of Somalia elected in June, Mr Mohammed Haji Ibrahim Egal, asked President Kenneth Kaunda of Zambia to mediate between Somalia and Kenya, and this was agreed. On 22 September, Ethiopia and Somalia issued a joint communique stating that they had agreed to eliminate all forms of tension,

---

[3] See p. 211 (Angola).
[4] The Afars, about half the population, being an Ethiopian people, the Issas a Somali clan.

to establish a joint commission to examine any complaints, and to hold quarterly meetings of administrative authorities. On 28 October, Kenya and Somalia signed a Memorandum of Understanding establishing diplomatic relations, restoring trade links, promising to maintain peace and security and to end hostile propaganda, and setting up a committee to supervise the achievement of these objectives.

From that time, the state of emergency in Ogaden and the north-eastern region of Kenya was ended, the borders were opened, and the restrictions on nomad movements were eased. In these two areas, Somali dissatisfaction apparently continued and Somalia did not formally renounce the idea of Greater Somalia; but incidents died away and fair relations between the governments were maintained.

As regards French Somaliland, on the other hand, tension continued. In July 1969, the OAU Liberation Committee interviewed the Somali Coast Liberation Front at Dakar and in September, the OAU Foreign Ministers, meeting at Addis Ababa, advised France to pay heed to the call for independence. In short, in the autumn of 1969, there were some small signs that new diplomatic alignments might be in the making. Then, in October 1969, with the military and police *coup d'état* in Somalia and the installation of the Supreme Revolutionary Council, the outlook became more uncertain once again.

*　　*　　*

J. DRYSDALE: *The Somali Dispute*, Pall Mall Press, London 1964.

C. HOSKYNS: *The Ethiopia–Somalia–Kenya Dispute 1960–67*, Oxford University Press, 1969.

I. M. LEWIS: *The Modern History of Somaliland*, Weidenfeld & Nicolson, London 1965.

S. TOUVAAL: *Somali Nationalism*, Harvard University Press, Cambridge 1963.

I. M. LEWIS: "Recent Developments in the Somali Dispute", *African Affairs*, April 1967.

South Africa 1960-70

SOUTH AFRICA in the period 1960–70 had a population (1960 census figures) of 3 million Whites, predominantly Afrikaners of Dutch descent; 10·8 million Natives; 1·4 million Coloured; and nearly half a million Asiatics. White supremacy and responsibility and social segregation had been the tradition since the beginnings of European settlement and this continued after independence from Britain in 1910. As the post-Second World War period opened, however, the White population began to feel that its future was less secure. Within the Union, rapid economic growth was bringing more and more Natives into the towns and into industrial labour, creating both social problems and the prospect of eventual competition. Externally, the climate of world opinion was changing, evidenced in the United Nations Charter, the Declaration of Human Rights (1948) and above all in the success of the independence movements in Asia. Might not such changes begin to affect southern Africa also?

These anxieties were the main cause of a drastic swing among the White electorate away from Field-Marshal Jan Christian Smuts's United Party in favour of the Nationalist parties. The United Party Government passed the Asiatic Land Tenure Act 1946 designed to prevent further Indian penetration into White areas and yet seemed to many to be indecisive on the racial question. Jan Hendrik Hofmeyr, with Smuts, the outstanding member of the Government, was believed to wish to grant considerable political representation to the Coloured community. The Nationalist parties, on the other hand, were single-mindedly devoted to the preservation of White standing and culture. Following the 1948 elections, a Nationalist Government came to power under Dr Daniel Malan with this as its principal commitment.

The intellectual under-pinning of this movement of White opinion was provided by a group of Nationalist intellectuals, including Dr Hendrik Verwoerd, later Prime Minister, at Stellenbosch University in the years 1945–47. They worked out a policy of "separate development" of Whites and Natives under which each would live in distinct areas, dotted about the total territory of the Union, there to govern their own affairs and develop their own cultures and forms of economy. The great towns and industrial belts would be in the White areas.

It was this policy, commonly called, together with social segregation, *apartheid*, that the Nationalist Government now began to put into effect. Notable stages were, first, the passing in 1951 of the Bantu Authorities Act

188

which established the Native areas, called Bantustans, giving them tribal, regional and territorial authorities with executive, administrative and judicial powers. Simultaneously, the old Natives Representative Council was abolished. In 1959, the Promotion of Bantu Self-Government Act provided for the evolution of the Bantustans into self-governing states within the Union.

Meanwhile, as regards the Coloured population, the Separate Representation of Voters Act of 1951 gave those of Cape Province (the majority), provided they had certain property and educational qualifications, four seats in the House of Assembly, elected on a separate roll. The Senate Act of 1960 laid down that at least one of the two senators from each province of the Union should be informed of Coloured affairs and able to voice their interests.

Step by step with the policy of *apartheid*, opposition to it within South Africa strengthened. Just as the Indians had protested against the Land Tenure Act and had been supported in this by the Government of India, both before and after independence, so now in the 1950s small groups among the urban, educated Natives grew in numbers, echoing the demands of the independence movements in the rest of Africa. The most prominent of these were the African National Congress (founded in 1912) led by Chief Albert Luthuli and Nelson Mandela, and a splinter-group from it, the Pan-Africanist Congress, led by Robert Sobukwe. The denial of political demands, coupled with resentment at social discrimination and some economic unrest, led to more and more frequent disturbances as the 1950s progressed. These culminated in March 1960 in riots in Durban and a great incident at Sharpeville when police opened fire on demonstrators, killing at least 67 and wounding over 180.

From now on, the implementation of *apartheid* was accompanied by the perfecting of a network of legislation and governmental and police measures designed to prevent such outbreaks. In 1963, the Transkei Bantustan reached the stage of limited internal autonomy with its own Cabinet and Parliament. In 1968, three more were given the first rudimentary precursors of autonomous institutions. Simultaneously, labour enactments, notably the Bantu Labour Act of 1965, gave the District Labour Bureaux extensive powers of regulation over Natives working in White areas. Other legislation, such as the General Law Amendment Act, gave the police wide powers of detention of suspects. The African National Congress and the Pan-Africanist Congress were banned after the Sharpeville affair. Nelson Mandela and Robert Sobukwe and others were imprisoned.

The two organisations continued to operate in a small way from neighbouring countries and there were occasional guerrilla incidents throughout the 1960s, the most extensive in 1963 being mounted by Poqo, the guerrilla group of the Pan-Africanist Congress. Such incidents and the occasional internal incident apart, the South African Government was successful in keeping the country at peace throughout the decade.

On the other hand, there was continual publicity turmoil over detentions, trials and censorship. There was also some growth of doubt among the White population about the whole *apartheid* policy. A main argument of urban Native leaders and outsiders had always been that one of its most unjust features was also in the long run impracticable: the White population needed the Natives as a labour force in their areas and yet treated them as aliens there. There were now signs that this line of thought was beginning to tell among the White population, particularly the younger generation. On 6 September 1966, Verwoerd died (assassinated by a demented White) and his successor, Dr Balthazar Vorster, seemed to have a somewhat less rigid approach to the doctrine of *apartheid*. Those like him within the National Party were now called the *verligte* as opposed to the *verkrampte*, who stood fully by the old doctrine.

The other difficulty about the policy of *apartheid* was the growing embarrassment to South Africa's international relations. *Apartheid*, internal opposition, repression and external odium, grew in step over the years, each fostering the others. As the African countries came to independence in the 1960s, they kept the world in a state of continual rhetorical uproar on the South Africa question. They felt that the dignity of their peoples was not complete so long as anywhere on the continent Africans were suffering White domination. They were supported in this by the Asian countries on "anti-colonialist" grounds and by the Communist countries. Many in the West also abhorred *apartheid* and their governments expressed this, so that at the end of the period there were no overtly sympathetic countries but Portugal and Rhodesia. All this seems to have done little material damage to South Africa's·external relations but the spiritual pressure was strong and it made the world a less comfortable place for South Africans.

The campaign first began at the United Nations in 1946 when the Indian Government raised the question of the treatment of Indians in the Union of South Africa. On 8 December 1946, the General Assembly passed a resolution condemning racial persecution and discrimination. In 1952, the Assembly set up a Good Offices Commission on the matter but South Africa denied the UN's competence and the Commission was unable to function.

In September 1952, thirteen Afro-Asian states placed the broader question of "Race Conflict . . . resulting from the policy of *Apartheid*" on the Assembly's agenda and in December it established a Commission to report on "the racial situation in the Union of South Africa . . . with due regard to the provisions of Article 2, paragraph 7 . . . ,[1] Article 1, paragraphs 2 and 3, Article 13, paragraph 1 (b), Article 55 (c) and Article 56[2] of the Charter and the resolution of the United Nations on racial persecution and discrimination." In 1954, it was also bidden to have regard to Article 14,[3] and from 1953–55 (when it was wound up) it produced three reports criticising South Africa's racial policies and discussing the question of UN intervention, each followed by a further Assembly resolution condemning South Africa and calling upon it to abandon these policies.

Similar resolutions were passed in 1957–59 but the atmosphere became markedly hotter as the 1960s opened. The Sharpeville affair of March 1960 caused world-wide shock; the African states were now making their voices heard in the United Nations and they were impatient for strong action.

This posed a dilemma of varying degrees of acuteness for the permanent members of the Security Council, most of all for Britain. Like the others, especially France, it had some need of good relations with the African states. Still more than France or any other power, it was expected by its former African colonies to take a lead against South Africa.

On the other hand, there were many of British extraction in the White community there; Britain had a great economic interest in the connection and some strategic interest; it was responsible for Swaziland and for Bechuanaland (Botswana) and Basutoland (Lesotho) until 1966; policy towards South Africa had great implications for the handling of the Rhodesia question both before and after it seized independence in November 1965. Moreover, like the other permanent members of the Security Council (except the Soviet Union), it had grave doubts about whether pressure on South Africa would work and about where it would lead.

On 3 February 1960, the Conservative Prime Minister, Harold Macmillan, bluntly warned the South African Parliament that "the wind of change is blowing through this continent"; when South Africa became a republic and left the Commonwealth on 31 May 1961, Britain made little fuss; the Labour Government which took office in 1964, after some hesitation, refused to sell armaments to South Africa; and the Conservative Government which followed in 1970, again after some hesitation and great Commonwealth acrimony, adopted a restrictive policy. But this was as far as Britain was willing to go.

By way of detail on this issue, on the news of the Sharpeville affair, the Afro-Asian group urged a meeting of the Security Council, and in a

---

[1] Non-interference in domestic affairs.

[2] All concerned with human rights.

[3] ". . . the General Assembly may recommend measures for peaceful adjustment of any situation, regardless of origin, which it deems likely to impair the general welfare of friendly relations among nations. . . ."

resolution of 1 April 1960 the Security Council, without going so far now or later as to find the South African situation "a threat to the peace" under Chapter VII of the Charter, did declare that "the situation in the Union of South Africa is one that has led to international friction and if continued might endanger international peace and security". In 1961 the Assembly passed a series of condemnatory resolutions, but there was also a slight temporary thaw when the Secretary-General, Dag Hammarskjöld, had talks with the South African Government which they described as "constructive". In the following year, the Assembly passed a resolution (6 November 1962) requesting member states to take various steps including breaking off diplomatic relations with South Africa and: "Boycotting all South African goods and refraining from exporting goods, including arms and ammunition, to South Africa." In the following year (7 August 1963), the Security Council did not go so far but: "Solemnly calls upon all States to cease forthwith the sale and shipment of arms, ammunition of all types and military vehicles to South Africa."

The majority of member states complied with this request but pressure continued within the Assembly for complete, mandatory economic sanctions. At the end of the year, under a Security Council resolution of 4 December, the Secretary-General, U Thant, appointed a Group of Experts to consider further measures and they reported on 20 April 1964 that sanctions were feasible provided they were agreed by all and complete. Thereupon, by a resolution of 18 June 1964, the Security Council set up an Expert Committee composed of representatives from each of its members to report what they thought on the "feasibility, effectiveness and implications" of further measures. The Committee reported its conclusion on 2 March 1965 that feasibility and effectiveness would depend on universality of application and that there would be serious implications for individual countries. This conclusion was supported by Bolivia, Brazil, Britain, China, Norway and the United States. Czechoslovakia, Ivory Coast, Morocco and the Soviet Union dissented, roundly declaring that a total commercial boycott was feasible and should be imposed; but they had been outvoted.

At the end of the year attention focused on Rhodesia and, after a period of lesser measures, the Security Council resolved on selective mandatory sanctions against Rhodesia at the end of the following year (December 1966).[4] The comparative failure of these pressures intensified the desire of many states to see South Africa, whose support for Rhodesia was crucial, sanctioned as well but the Western members of the Security Council remained reluctant. On 2 December 1968, the General Assembly drew the attention of the Security Council to the grave situation in southern Africa

[4] See p. 200ff.

and requested mandatory sanctions against South Africa. The voting was 85–2 in favour but there were 15 abstentions, including Britain, France and the United States.

The remaining action against South Africa within the United Nations during these years was its ejection from the International Labour Organisation and the World Health Organisation. It also left the Food and Agricultural Organisation and, though it remained a member of the Economic Commission for Africa, active co-operation was suspended in 1963. Most Asian countries and the Communist countries broke off diplomatic and commercial relations with South Africa. For the rest, the African states were left to their own organisations for hope of stronger action. In May 1963, the Addis Ababa Conference committed the Organisation of African Unity to a commercial boycott and to direct involvement in the liberation struggle against White racialism in southern Africa. The boycott had little effect because most African states had few commercial links with South Africa, and those that had – for instance, Malawi and Zambia – found difficulty in severing them. The Addis Ababa conference established an African Liberation Committee at Dar-es-Salaam to channel support to guerrilla groups and co-ordinate their attacks but, by 1970, with little success.

* * *

D. Austin: *Britain and South Africa*, Oxford University Press, 1966.

A. H. Hepple: *South Africa, A Political and Economic History*, Pall Mall, London 1966.

E. Louw: *The Case for South Africa*, MacFadden, New York 1963.

C. and M. Legum: *South Africa, Crisis for the West*, Pall Mall, London 1964.

J. E. Spence: *Republic under Pressure, A Study of South African Foreign Policy*, Oxford University Press, 1965.

Rhodesia 1960-70

THE population of Southern Rhodesia at the 1961–62 census consisted of some 3·6 million Africans, 17,000 Asians and Coloureds, and 221,000 Europeans, mostly of British extraction.

From the arrival of the first European settlers in 1890 until 1923, the territory was administered by the British South Africa Company, founded by Cecil Rhodes and incorporated by royal charter. In 1923, it became a British Colony but self-governing under a constitution granted to it.

The European settlers believed in the superiority of European culture, in the social separation of the races and in European responsibility. As the country developed, these beliefs received legal expression. Under the 1923 constitution, the franchise was restricted by income, property and educational qualifications. By the time of federation in 1953 (see below) the total electorate for the thirty-member Legislative Assembly was 50,475, of whom 594 were Asian, 570 Coloured, and 441 African. The Land Apportionment Act of 1930 gave statutory form to the division of the land into racial areas, under which the Europeans had the larger share. They justified this on the grounds that their kind of farming required it. A new Act of 1941 enlarged the Native Reserves somewhat in response to population pressures. Under the Industrial Conciliation Act (1934) Africans were excluded from the legal category "employees" and the rights and duties pertaining to it and were instead legally "servants", regulated by the Masters and Servants Act of 1901.

From time to time in the 1920s and '30s, the idea was discussed of merging Southern Rhodesia with the adjoining Protectorates controlled by the British Colonial Office, Northern Rhodesia and Nyasaland. After the Second World War, this idea became more attractive to the Europeans in Southern Rhodesia. For though Nyasaland remained poor, Northern Rhodesia, thanks to the discovery of copper there, was enjoying economic development even greater than Southern Rhodesia's. The main doubt on the part of the Southern Rhodesian Europeans was that in the new entity they would be outnumbered by Africans even more markedly. The British Government, however, hoped that this very fact might on balance help to promote acceptance of racial equality. Its greatest reason for desiring the amalgamation, apart from solving the problem of the future of Nyasaland, was the vision of a great multi-racial society in southern Africa which should show an alternative to the racial-separatist policies of the Union of South Africa.

194

The Federation of Southern Rhodesia, Northern Rhodesia and Nyasaland (the Central African Federation) was created by an Order in Council of 1 August 1953. Each of the territories retained its existing constitution, including a British Governor. Under the Federal Constitution, the Queen was represented by a Governor-General. Extensive powers were given to the Federal Government: external affairs, defence, major communications, economic planning, income tax. The franchise for the Federal Assembly was on much the same basis as in Southern Rhodesia. Sir Godfrey Huggins, formerly Prime Minister of Southern Rhodesia and leader of the United Federal Party, became federal Prime Minister (succeeded in November 1956 by Sir Roy Welensky). The federal capital was Salisbury, the capital of Southern Rhodesia.

The federation lasted only ten years. The African nationalist leaders in the three territories disliked it from the outset, fearing that it would merely strengthen the Southern Rhodesian system economically and spread it to the other two territories. Admittedly, there was a handful of Africans in the Federal Assembly, and the United Federal Party adopted a policy of partnership between the races. In 1957 in Southern Rhodesia and in 1958 in the Federation, a "special" electoral role was established alongside the "ordinary" role, and this increased the potential African electorate. Greater effort was put into African education in Southern Rhodesia from this time onwards and a new Industrial Conciliation Act in 1959 included Africans within its terms. However, the underlying idea of a slow evolution to racial equality was unacceptable to the African nationalist leaders. In line with nationalist feelings throughout the continent, they wanted majority rule rapidly and independence.

In 1959, there were African riots in Nyasaland and from this time onwards, the attitudes of the Southern Rhodesian Europeans and the British Government began to diverge markedly. The Southern Rhodesians passed a Preventive Detention Act and an Unlawful Organisation Act and banned the Southern Rhodesian African National Congress. The British Governor of Nyasaland proclaimed a state of emergency and called in federal troops. Dr Hastings Banda, the leader of the Nyasaland ANC, was detained. But, in January–February 1960, the British Prime Minister, Harold Macmillan, descended on southern Africa and warned that "the wind of change is blowing through this continent" (South African Parliament, 3 February). In July, a conference in London resulted in a new constitution for Nyasaland which greatly advanced the position of the Africans there.

Though not enough to satisfy the Nyasas, this, against a background of African riots at Sharpeville in South Africa in March[1] and the explosion

[1] See p. 189.

of the Congo[2] and riots in Southern Rhodesia itself in July, went too far, too fast for the Southern Rhodesian Europeans. The Federal Government now began to press for steps towards the independence of the Federation before British concessions to the Africans in Nyasaland and Northern Rhodesia led to its break-up or undermined European rule within it. A Royal Commission headed by Lord Monckton recommended in October the continuance of the Federation but stressed the need for a voluntary basis with African advancement and right of secession. This solution satisfied neither Africans nor Europeans and the subsequent conference (December) was fruitless.

Over the next two years, the Federal Government struggled to hold the Federation together and to advance it towards independence; but to all others, its survival was increasingly in doubt. Meanwhile, parallelling the evolution of Nyasaland and Northern Rhodesia, a constitutional conference on Southern Rhodesia was held in Salisbury in February 1961. The aim of the Southern Rhodesian UFP Prime Minister, Sir Edgar Whitehead, was to achieve greater independence of Britain or, as it was commonly put more bluntly, to reduce Britain's powers of interference. The aim of the National Democratic Party (the ANC under a new name) led by Joshua Nkomo was "one man, one vote".

Both sides won something in the new constitution. In return for a diminution of the powers of the British monarch, governor and parliament, the UFP accepted safeguards for African rights (a Declaration of Rights and a Constitutional Council) and the establishment of "A" and "B" rolls leading to African members of the Legislative Assembly. By June, the NDP had repudiated their delegation's concessions and reverted to an uncompromising "one man, one vote" and they boycotted the referendum the following month. The Europeans, their misgivings about the bargain somewhat allayed by this, endorsed the new constitution by a great majority.

The NDP, denouncing the constitution and forbidding Africans to register to vote, now took to violence. It was banned in December 1961 on this account; the Zimbabwe African People's Union was formed in succession; after a lull and the launching of a heightened campaign to mobilise international opinion at the United Nations and elsewhere, violence began afresh; ZAPU was banned in turn in September 1962.

The UFP Government meanwhile intensified its policy of partnership, seeking to woo the Africans from the nationalists, urging qualified Africans to register to vote, setting up Native Councils, building up the position of the traditional chiefs, promising to repeal the Land Apportionment Act. But many Europeans doubted or denied the necessity for such measures

[2] See p. 204.

and African violence hardened their attitudes still further. The opposition Dominion Party merged into a broad Rhodesian Front and in the elections of December 1962, from which most qualified Africans abstained, the Front was victorious. The UFP had failed to win the Africans and had lost the confidence of the majority of Europeans. A Rhodesian Front Government was formed with Winston Field as Prime Minister, standing for a slow, unforced evolution in race relations and meanwhile the firm maintenance of White rule.

The Federation, by this time, was plainly on the point of dissolution despite the efforts of the federal Prime Minister, Sir Roy Welensky, and his colleagues. Northern Rhodesia and Nyasaland, advancing rapidly to self-government with majority rule, had made plain their determination to secede with British acquiescence. Most Southern Rhodesian Europeans no longer desired such partners though they bitterly regretted the economic disruption. In March 1963, Britain announced the forthcoming independence of Nyasaland (Malawi) and Northern Rhodesia (Zambia) outside the Federation (accomplished on 6 July 1964 and 24 October 1964) and three months later arrangements for winding up the Federation were made at the Victoria Falls Conference (June 1963). It was formally dissolved on 31 December 1963 with some surviving economic co-operation. From March onwards, the Europeans began to press Britain to grant independence to Southern Rhodesia.

The Europeans desired independence from Britain because they were confident of their ability and duty to control the country and because they wished to end the possibility of British interference in doing so. They were not faced at this time with a strong, united, widespread African nationalist movement but rather with a threat to law and order arising largely from quarrels among the Africans themselves. ZAPU split down the middle, with a rival organisation emerging: the Zimbabwe African National Union, led by Rev. Ndabaningi Sithole. Throughout late 1963 and 1964, mob violence was endemic but by the end of 1964, it had been suppressed by draconian security legislation, deportations and detentions, including the detention of most of the leaders of both ZAPU and ZANU.

This situation in the country strengthened the Europeans in their determination to take over final responsibility from the British with their "unrealistic" assessment of Africans. The difficulty in the negotiations was the terms of independence. The Europeans expected that they would become independent on the basis of the 1961 constitution. The British, on the contrary, believed that they should not relinquish control until changes had been made which would somewhat accelerate the advance of the Africans and, above all, ensure that the advance was irreversible. This "interfering" attitude aroused the indignation of the Europeans and increased the ill-feeling which the events of recent years had generated. Moreover, the British were currently subject to great clamour from the Afro-Asian countries in the United Nations and the Commonwealth in the cause of majority rule in Southern Rhodesia; and though they resisted United Nations discussion in 1962–63 (on which account their delegate, Sir Hugh Foot, resigned in October 1962) they clearly shared the general world opinion and were sensitive to it. The Europeans saw this as a weak surrender to Afro-Asian nationalism, and, believing themselves to be a bastion of civilised standards in a country and a continent threatened by barbarism and Communism, were contemptuous and still further embittered.

The negotiations thus began in March 1963 not merely in disagreement but in an atmosphere of tension and low confidence. Over the next twelve months, the Southern Rhodesian Government conceded the gradual demise of the Land Apportionment Act, the ending of some forms of social discrimination and some expansion of the "A" and "B" voting rolls. But the British, seeking "a blocking third" of African members in the Assembly against unwelcome amendments of the constitution after independence, wanted a rather larger expansion. This proved to be the sticking-point and progress came to a halt.

On 14 April 1964, Winston Field was succeeded as Prime Minister by his deputy, Ian Smith. From now on, there were ministerial hints and much general talk in Southern Rhodesia of a unilateral declaration of independence ("UDI"). Many Europeans, however, shrank from so drastic a step and the United Federal Party, which had meanwhile been reformed as the Rhodesia National Party, was now reformed again as the Rhodesia Party under Sir Roy Welensky and Sir Edgar Whitehead in opposition to UDI.

In early September, Ian Smith held talks in London with the British Prime Minister, Sir Alec Douglas-Home, at the latter's invitation. The talks centred on Smith's assertion that the majority of the population of Southern Rhodesia supported independence on the basis of the 1961 constitution. How could he show that, the British asked. Smith proposed a referendum to the electorate and an *indaba* of the chiefs but the British said that this was inadequate as a way of consulting the Africans. On the other hand, tension eased on UDI. The British stated that neither Britain nor the United States would accept it and pointed to the economic consequences; to their relief, Smith stated that he was not threatening them with UDI.

This statement and Smith's general air of optimism were also greeted with relief in Southern Rhodesia, and destroyed the appeal of the new Rhodesia Party at two current by-elections.

On 14 October, the Southern Rhodesian Government informed the British Government that it proposed to hold an *indaba* and invited observers; and despite statements from both the outgoing Conservative Government and the incoming Labour Government that this was inadequate, the *indaba* of 622 chiefs and headmen opened on 22 October. On the 26th, it endorsed independence on the basis of the 1961 constitution. On the 27th, fearing that the Smith government after all intended UDI and that the *indaba* and the referendum announced for 5 November were preliminary steps, the new British Prime Minister, Harold Wilson, made a strong statement saying that UDI would be "defiance . . . rebellion . . . treasonable" and would lead to the isolation of Southern Rhodesia and "disastrous economic damage". The Smith government stated in response that a "yes" vote at the referendum would not be taken to signify approval of UDI. At the referendum, a great majority of the votes cast endorsed independence on the basis of the 1961 constitution.

These events brought relations between the two countries to their lowest ebb so far. When Ian Smith came to London in January 1965 for the funeral of Winston Churchill, discussions were held but a subsequent visit by the British Commonwealth Secretary, Arthur Bottomley, was fruitless (February). UDI was now once more the main topic of discussion in Southern Rhodesia. A government White Paper, *Economic Aspects of a Declaration of Independence* (April), took a sanguine view of the effect of economic sanctions though industrial opinion was generally gloomy. In the May elections, the government party won a total victory over the Rhodesia Party, the opponents of UDI. Feeling mounted in Rhodesia over the following months for a decision one way or the other. On 5 October, Ian Smith went to London in an effort to break the deadlock and on 25 October, Harold Wilson went to Salisbury. The British Government summarised its policy in five principles which must be satisfied before independence and the discussions proceeded on this basis.[3] The underlying position was that the British Government wanted to ensure majority rule within the foreseeable future whereas the Southern Rhodesian leaders had stated that this would not come about in their lifetime. The discussions and various last-minute exchanges were once again fruitless. On 11 Novem-

---

[3] (i) The principle and intention of unimpeded progress to majority rule, already enshrined in the 1961 Constitution, would have to be maintained and guaranteed. (ii) There would also have to be guarantees against retrogressive amendments of the Constitution. (iii) There would have to be immediate improvement in the political status of the African population. (iv) There would have to be progress towards ending racial discrimination. (v) The British Government would need to be satisfied that any basis proposed for independence was acceptable to the people of Rhodesia as a whole. (The British Government added a sixth principle in January 1966 after UDI: It would be necessary to ensure that, regardless of race, there was no oppression of majority by minority or of minority by majority.)

ber, the Southern Rhodesian Government issued a Proclamation of Independence of Rhodesia.

The British Government responded on the same day by denouncing the proclamation as illegal and declaring the Smith government dismissed. Resisting Afro-Asian views, it had repudiated the use of force at any time in the matter (1 November) but it now banned imports into Britain of Rhodesian tobacco, cut the country out of the sterling system and, over the next three months, progressively banned other imports and exports and secured the co-operation of the major international oil companies in ending the sale of oil. The UN General Assembly had called upon Britain to use force (5 November) and now, on 20 November, the Security Council recommended to all its members a trade boycott, especially in oil. The following 9 April (1966) it authorised the British naval patrol off the port of Beira in Mozambique (the head of the oil pipeline to Rhodesia) to intercept ships suspected of carrying oil to Rhodesia.

At the Commonwealth Conference in Lagos of 10–12 January 1966, the British Prime Minister reassured the Afro-Asian members that these measures would restore legality "within a matter of weeks rather than months". In the event, economic sanctions against Rhodesia, especially after they had become mandatory (see below), put great pressure on the country, most of all as regards tobacco exports, but the effects were mitigated in various ways. In particular, Rhodesia had had much time in which to prepare; South Africa and Portugal were sympathetic and provided channels for imports and exports; some other countries and companies evaded the British commercial surveillance system; Rhodesia's minerals were mostly indistinguishable from "legal" minerals on world markets; the country developed import-substitution industries. Moreover, the reverse strain of the boycott on Britain, on Rhodesia's smaller African neighbours and on other world importers was considerable.

As the summer of 1966 went by with the Smith government still unsubdued, the Afro-Asian countries intensified their demand that Britain cease reliance on "voluntary sanctions" and use force or at least take the affair to the UN Security Council. The communique of the further Commonwealth Conference in London on 5–14 September ordered the Smith regime to stand down in favour of "a broadly based representative administration" appointed by the Governor so that constitutional negotiations could be resumed; if it refused to do so, Britain would thenceforth deal with Rhodesia on the principle of no independence before majority rule (NIBMAR, for short). Moreover, it was agreed that if Britain failed to bring about the return to legality by the year's end, the matter would go to the Security Council.

The Smith government had stated its willingness from the outset to continue to talk with Britain; exchanges had begun in April; and now, on 2–4 December, Wilson and Smith met aboard HMS *Tiger*, cruising off Gibraltar. There was some apparent progress on constitutional questions, notably franchise expansion and a formula to achieve "a blocking quarter" of African legislative seats, but most of the frequently ill-tempered discussion turned on the prior question of the return to legality, the British demanding, in brief, that the Smith regime hand over power to the Governor. The Rhodesian Government gave its answer, as demanded by Britain, on the following day, the 5th: no.

Britain now accordingly appealed to the UN Security Council, which resolved on 16 December that the Rhodesia situation was a "threat to the peace" and that all members must end trade with it in selected key goods, including oil. These selective, mandatory sanctions intensified the pressure on Rhodesia but none the less 1967 passed with little change. On 29 May 1968, the Security Council adopted a British resolution ordering further measures to isolate Rhodesia, in communications, diplomatic representation and the like, amounting to an almost total boycott. The limited success of the sanctions and the part played in this by South Africa led to a climax in December 1968 of the long-standing pressure in the UN General Assembly for sanctions against South Africa. But, among others, three Security Council members, Britain, France and the United States, were opposed.[4]

Britain had by then held a further round of negotiations with the Rhodesians, beginning with talks between Wilson and Smith aboard HMS *Fearless* at Gibraltar on 10–14 October and lasting into November, but with no better success than before. Britain's proposals for the process of return to legality still involved the formation of a broadly based administration including Africans but this time the negotiations concentrated on the substantive question of Rhodesia's constitution. The British made no mention of NIBMAR, but in addition to "a blocking quarter" of African seats in the legislature against unwelcome constitutional amendments, they now wanted a second external safeguard, namely, the possibility of appeal to the Judicial Committee of the Privy Council or some equivalent outside body. They made plain, that is, that they did not trust the Rhodesians not to erode "the blocking quarter" by some dubious means or other. The Rhodesians, for their part, rejected the idea as an infringement of sovereignty. The negotiations failed.

The Rhodesians, meanwhile, had been studying and discussing a new constitution for the country on their own account. It was published on 12 February 1969. Rhodesia would become a republic. There would be near parity of seats between the races in the Senate and evolution to parity

4 See pp. 192–3.

over some unpredictable term of years in the Lower House. The new constitution was endorsed in a referendum to the electorate in June. The republic was proclaimed on 2 March 1970. The British Government moved a resolution in the UN Security Council calling on member states not to recognise the republic but, with the United States, vetoed a draft resolution calling for the use of force to suppress it.

* * *

J. BARBER: *Rhodesia, The Road to Rebellion*, Oxford University Press, 1967.

T. BULL (ed.): *Rhodesian Perspective*, Michael Joseph, London 1967.

M. DOXEY: *Economic Sanctions and International Enforcement*, Oxford University Press, 1971.

P. KEATLEY: *The Politics of Partnership, The Federation of Rhodesia and Nyasaland*, Penguin Books, Harmondsworth 1963.

C. PALLEY: *The Constitutional History and Law of Rhodesia 1888–1965*, Oxford University Press, 1966.

C. K. YOUNG: *Rhodesia and Independence*, new ed., Dent and Sons, London 1969.

The Congo 1960-63

BELGIAN policy in the Congo after the Second World War can be summarised as "expansion in social and economic fields with political advance postponed until some undefined threshold of maturity has been reached".[1] This policy enjoyed considerable international respect and was pursued peacefully in the years 1945–55. However, when independence came suddenly five years later, the country was ill-prepared politically.

The nationalist movement for independence accelerated rapidly from the end of 1955. Encouraged by similar developments in the rest of Africa, the small but growing number of Congolese "*evolués*" provided the leaders. Support came from the growing urban labour force, many of whom, on the decline of international copper prices in 1957, were facing unemployment. There was apparently considerable latent discontent in rural areas arising from Belgian efforts to promote social and economic change.

In January 1959, serious riots broke out in the capital, Leopoldville (nowadays, Kinshasa). The immediate cause was economic grievances but the whole edifice of Belgian rule was shaken and excitement in the country intensified. The Belgians hastily introduced measures of political advance but by the time of the Round Table Conference at Brussels in January 1960, it was clear that they must either concede immediate independence or shoulder a heavy burden of civil disorder. They decided on independence. Few of their 90,000 nationals in the country were settlers; they had little imperialist tradition; the task of keeping order would be thankless internationally and the cost large, perhaps enormous; they were determined that the Congo must not be allowed to become "another Algeria". A preliminary constitution was accordingly worked out and, after some Belgian vacillation in the ensuing months, the date of independence was finally fixed for 30 June 1960.

The preliminary constitution covered over serious rivalries and disagreements among the nationalist leaders. The Congo was a vast country, more than twelve hundred miles wide and long, divided into six provinces, each inhabited by numerous tribes, some dominating the others. The growth of nationalist feeling in the late 1950s did little to diminish tribal awareness, most of the newly-formed political parties being on a tribal basis. The first political movement to call openly for independence, Joseph Kasavubu's *Abako*, was dominated by the Bakongo of the Leopoldville

[1] Young, p. 60.

203

province. Other tribal groups, excluded from Abako, responded by forming rival movements.

Something of an exception to this pattern was Patrice Lumumba's *Mouvement National Congolais* which set out to appeal to all Congolese. Lumumba drew most of his strength from the tribes of the Oriental and Kivu provinces and at the same time attacked tribalism in favour of national unity. In Western constitutional terms, he wanted a centralised state. Kasavubu and his like, on the other hand, inclined towards a looser, federal arrangement.

At independence on 30 June 1960, Kasavubu became President, Lumumba Prime Minister. Trouble began immediately. The Armée Nationale Congolaise (the former Force Publique) continued to be Belgian-officered, and disappointment at this led to mutiny on 4 July. By the 8th, the army was an uncontrolled mob. As disorder spread throughout the country and Belgian residents began to flee, Belgium, which retained bases at Kitona (Leopoldville province) and Kamina (Katanga province), reinforced them with paratroops and requested permission to help restore order. Lumumba refused. On the 10th, the Belgians none the less intervened "to protect lives and property".

On the 11th, the Prime Minister of Katanga, Moise Tshombe, declared its secession from the Republic. Tshombe's party, Conakat, had long aimed at sufficient autonomy for Katanga to prevent, as they saw it, the exploitation of its mineral wealth by the rest of the Congo. Conversely the other provinces felt a strong need of Katanga; the Belgians before independence had strongly resisted separatist moves; and, it seems, the mining companies had also favoured a unitary Congo, if this should prove possible. Now, with the breakdown of order and Lumumba's refusal to invoke Belgian assistance, Tshombe received much sympathy and support from the Belgian public and the companies.

Faced with Belgian intervention and Katanga's secession, Kasavubu and Lumumba appealed in all directions for aid against Belgian "aggression". They appealed first informally to Dr Ralph Bunche, the Special Representative of the United Nations Secretary-General (11th). They repudiated an appeal by their Foreign Minister to the United States, which in any case referred him to the UN, and appealed formally to the UN (12th). They also appealed to the Soviet Union, which promised "resolute measures to end aggression" if the UN failed (14th).

After rapid negotiations, the Security Council passed a resolution (14th) which, without condemning Belgium, called upon it to withdraw its troops and authorised the Secretary-General to provide "such military assistance as may be necessary, until, through the efforts of the Congolese Government with the technical assistance of the United Nations, the national security forces may be able, in the opinion of the Government, to meet fully their tasks".

Under this resolution, the Secretary-General, Dag Hammarskjöld, rapidly established ONUC (Organization des Nations Unies au Congo) with a force eventually numbering 20,000, drawn from African and neutral states, with the United States and Britain providing transport equipment. However, disorder had not subsided, the Belgians were reluctant to withdraw, Tshombe announced that UN troops would not be allowed in Katanga, and the Soviet Union began to send arms and transport equipment to Lumumba's stronghold, Stanleyville, the capital of Oriental province.

By mid-August, ONUC had persuaded the Belgians to agree to withdraw to their bases and Tshombe to accept a Swedish contingent (12th) but by this time was seriously at odds with Lumumba. For Lumumba wanted the UN force to be used to end Katanga's secession, whereas ONUC interpreted the Security-Council resolution as empowering only the maintenance of civil order and necessary self-defence, not intervention in the Congo's politics and offensive action.

On 5 September, Kasavubu announced the dismissal of Lumumba and the appointment of Joseph Ileo. Lumumba replied by charging the President with high treason and ordering troops from Stanleyville in their Soviet transport planes to the capital. Believing that the outcome would be tribal warfare, ONUC foiled Lumumba by closing the airports at the capital and elsewhere. On the 12th, Kasavubu arrested and then released Lumumba. On the 14th, with some sort of acquiescence from the President, Colonel Joseph Mobutu, commander of the ANC since its mutiny, announced that the army had taken over the government of the country.

These events provoked an outcry at the United Nations from those states in Africa and elsewhere who sided with Lumumba. Following a Soviet veto in the Security Council, the General Assembly passed a resolution (20 September) amounting to endorsement of ONUC's handling of the situation but the Soviet Union maintained its outright opposition. On the 23rd, Chairman Krushchev of the Soviet Union attacked the Secretary-General in a speech of extraordinary vituperation in the General Assembly, proposing the substitution for the secretary-generalship of a "*troika*" from Eastern, Western and Neutralist states, and emphasising his opposition to the contrary views of the Filipino delegate on the 26th, by banging on his desk with his shoe.

In the Congo, meanwhile, Mobutu was seeking to establish control and a form of government. On 11 October ANC troops tried to seize Lumumba but they were prevented by UN troops. However, on 27 November,

Lumumba left this protection in an effort to reach Stanleyville and was caught by the ANC (1 December). Thereupon in Stanleyville, Antoine Gizenga, Lumumba's deputy, announced that he had taken over as head of the lawful government of the Congo. Lumumba was handed over to the custody of the Katangans on 17 January 1961, and on 13 February they announced that he was dead, killed, they said, by tribesmen while seeking to escape. The following day, the Soviet Union called for the dismissal of Hammarskjöld and the withdrawal of the UN from the Congo and announced that it was considering aid (i.e. overt aid) to the Stanleyville government. Egypt, Guinea, East Germany and Yugoslavia recognised this government in the next few days.

Over the following months, the Stanleyville government, with this international support, continued to denounce Katanga and, controlling Kivu as well as Oriental, to attack it across its northern border. Simultaneously, the attitudes of the new Kennedy Administration in the United States and the development of opinion at the United Nations were such that ONUC increased its pressure on Katanga. Against this background, the Leopoldville government (Kasavubu reappointed Ileo on 9 February, Mobutu being somewhat discredited by his inability to control even the ANC) was able to draw Tshombe into negotiations.

On the other hand, Tshombe had considerable resources for resistance. He had the tax revenues of the Union Minière de Haut Katanga; he was recruiting Belgian and other foreign mercenaries to command his troops; he enjoyed much sympathy from international business in Katanga, neighbouring Rhodesia, Europe and the United States where the Katanga Information Center found considerable support in Congress; international business and many governments (most actively Belgium, Britain and France) believed that drastic pressure on Katanga would not solve the Congo's troubles and would lead only to disorder and destruction in the province. Tshombe was thus able to bargain hard.

On 21 February 1961, the Security Council passed a resolution calling for "the immediate withdrawal and evacuation from the Congo" of all Belgian and other foreign military and political personnel and mercenaries. Gradually ONUC strengthened its presence in Katanga. Meanwhile, representatives of the various Congo factions, including Katanga but not the Stanleyville and Kivu governments, came together on 8 March at Tananarive (Madagascar) and, in constitutional terms, decided that the Congo should be a confederation. This outcome reflected the strong position of Katanga at that time. When the discussions were resumed at Coquilhatville (Equateur province) on 24 April to 28 May, however, the position of the Leopoldville government was improving (not least in bringing the ANC under some degree of control with ONUC assistance) and now a federal principle was generally favoured. Tshombe resisted, was arrested by the Leopoldville government, was released (22 June) with apparently some agreement to co-operate, but once back in Katanga, continued his opposition.

Simultaneously, however, the Leopoldville government improved its position still further by reaching an agreement with the dissident authorities in South Kasai district and above all with Stanleyville (13 June). The two sides which had been trying to convene Parliament at rival places, now agreed through ONUC's good offices that it should meet in the Lovanium (the University of Leopoldville). At its meetings in July–August, it endorsed a new government of the Congo with Cyrille Adoula as Prime Minister and Gizenga as one of the vice-premiers. The relatively close harmony weakened in the autumn but, for practical purposes, the existence of a rival Congo Government at Stanleyville and international (notably, Soviet) support for it, were at an end.

Thus strengthened, the Congo Government released a Presidential Ordinance (24 August) ordering the expulsion of non-Congolese from Katanga's forces and calling for the assistance of ONUC. With this authority and in accordance with 21 February resolution of the Security Council, the UN forces began a full-scale operation on 28 August to arrest and evacuate the mercenaries. At first successful, it led in mid-September to an attempt to arrest Katangan ministers and to heavy fighting. ONUC thereupon sought a cease-fire. The UN Secretary-General, Dag Hammarskjöld, himself set out to meet Tshombe at Ndola (Northern Rhodesia) but was killed when his plane crashed (17 September). A cease-fire was concluded on the 21st between ONUC and the Katanga government. The Congo Government was not a party to this, and the ANC launched its own operation, unsuccessfully however.

Belgium, Britain and France in particular had opposed the extension of the ONUC operation into an apparent attempt to break Katanga's resistance by force but, following ONUC reports of attacks on its units despite the cease-fire, the majority of the Security Council were determined on the contrary to strengthen ONUC's powers. In a resolution of 24 November, passed 9–0–2 (Britain and France), the Council authorised the Secretary-General (U Thant was Acting Secretary-General) "to take vigorous action, including the use of requisite measures of force, if necessary", to arrest and deport the mercenaries.

Heavy fighting followed from 5–18 December in which the UN forces had considerable success. On the 19th, through the good offices of Mr Edmund Gullion, the United States ambassador, and Dr Ralph Bunche, the UN Special Representative, Tshombe and Adoula met at Kitona. Here, Tshombe accepted an eight-point statement, including recognition of the unity of the Congo, the authority of the central government, and the position of President Kasavubu as head of state (21st).

Over the following months, however, no progress was made towards implementing this agreement. Tshombe and Adoula held further talks at Leopoldville from 18 March to 10 April 1962 and again from 25 May to 26 June but to little effect.

In this impasse, the Acting UN Secretary-General worked out a Plan for National Reconciliation (August) similar to proposals already made to Katanga, notably, a federal constitution and, during a transitional period, a half share of mining revenues for Katanga, but coupled with deadlines. If a draft constitution was not agreed within thirty days and the other matters within ninety days, economic sanctions would be organised against Katanga.

The Congo Government accepted the Plan on 23 August and Katanga on 3 September, but subsequently the deadlines passed without progress. On 10 December, accordingly, the UN Secretary-General informed Katanga that sanctions would be imposed, and on the following day the Congo Government appealed to seventeen governments to embargo imports of Katangan copper and cobalt. Britain, while favouring the Plan, had made clear its opposition to sanctions since mid-August, but Belgium, the United States and others were responsive and the Union Minière, though fearful of Katangan retaliation against its installations, was also disposed to co-operate.

However, the full development of this policy was abruptly cut short at the end of December. In the Congo, the Adoula government was in danger of overthrow by such opponents as Gizenga; the Soviet Union had become active once more, this time in Leopoldville, and might emerge as the central government's new ally in dealing with Katanga; Tshombe, for his part, was reported to be strengthening his mercenaries once more. Such factors disposed the UN Secretariat and the United States Administration to quicker action than sanctions, and when attacks on the UN forces multiplied in late December, and when a counter-attack on 28 December scored a substantial success, the UN forces pursued their advantage. Tshombe repeated his threats of a "scorched earth" policy, and some sections of public opinion in some countries remained sympathetic to Tshombe. However, ONUC with United States backing and Soviet acquiescence held to its course and seized the principal centres in Katanga rapidly one by one. On 16 January 1963, Tshombe announced that Katanga's secession was at an end.

*   *   *

J. GÉRARD-LIBOIS: *Katanga Secession*, University of Wisconsin Press, Madison 1966.

R. HILSMAN: *To Move a Nation*, Dell, New York 1964.

C. HOSKYNS: *The Congo since Independence*, Oxford University Press, 1965.

E. LEFEVER: *Crisis in the Congo, A United Nations Force in Action*, The Brookings Institution, Washington D.C., 1965.

CRAWFORD YOUNG: *Politics in the Congo, Decolonization and Independence*, Princeton University Press, 1965.

Angola 1961-64

THE Portuguese arrived on the coast of Angola in the mid-fifteenth century; they extended their control to the interior in a purposive fashion in the late nineteenth century at the time of the European partition of Africa; they had pacified the whole country by 1915. The Portuguese Government gave strong encouragement in the 1950s to Portuguese immigration so that the number of settlers rose from some 80,000 (1950) to 200,000 (1960). The attraction was the plantation and mineral wealth of a country five times the size of Portugal.

The African population, the *indígenas*, numbered in 1950 about 4 million. The social attitudes of the Portuguese settlers were not opposed to racial mixing and their constitutional policy was that anyone could become a citizen provided he had a certain degree of property and education. An African or person of mixed race who attained this was called an *assimilado*. However, in practice there were few of these. Until the 1950s, the Government's assistance to education was limited; thereafter, in view of the experience of other countries in Africa, it devoted its efforts mainly to producing technicians, that is, agriculturalists, engineers, doctors and the like. On the economic side, most Africans were poor and those who worked for the plantation and mining companies did so generally for low pay in bad conditions which the Government did little until the 1960s to rectify. There were, moreover, disincentives to the African to becoming a citizen: it meant separation from his own people; it meant higher taxes; it brought only remote political benefit, since the colony did not have local self-government. In 1950, there were 30,000 African *assimilados*; in 1966, out of a total population of some 4·9 million, there were 48,000.

Small African nationalist groups had existed in Angola since the inter-war years but, as in the rest of Africa, their significance grew in the 1950s. The União das Populaçoes de Angola was formed in 1954 under the leadership of Holden Roberto at Leopoldville, the capital of the Belgian Congo. The principal group of tribes of the Leopoldville province, the Bakongo, extended over the border into north-western Angola and it was from these people that the UPA drew most of its support. In 1956, a rival Movimento Popular de Libertação de Angola was formed under the chairmanship of Dr Agostinho Neto with Communist participation. Its headquarters were at Conakry (Guinea).

Simultaneously, at the United Nations and elsewhere, the African and Asian states mounted a campaign against Portugal along with the other

European colonial powers. Portugal, emulating France, changed the legal status of its overseas possessions in 1951 (the principal ones in Africa were Angola, Guinea and Mozambique) from "colony" to "overseas territory". When it was admitted to the United Nations in 1955, it refused to transmit information about them to the Secretary-General under Article 73 (e) of the Charter on the grounds that they were not "non-self-governing territories"; under the Portuguese constitution, there was one unitary Portuguese nation with undivided sovereignty and organs of sovereignty extending over all the national territories, including the overseas territories. The African and Asian states, for their part, were determined to have it accepted that the territories were in colonial bondage. A bitter quarrel ensued on the information issue.

At length, on 12 December 1959, the Afro-Asian group caused the General Assembly to pass a resolution setting up a Committee of Six on the Transmission of Information under Article 73 (e) of the Charter; and on 15 December 1960, in the light of the Committee's report, a further resolution pronouncing the overseas territories non-self-governing and declaring Portugal's obligation to transmit information. This resolution formed part of a general great debate on colonialism at the 1960 Assembly session of which the highlight was a resolution passed on the previous day called the Declaration on the Granting of Independence to Colonial Countries and Peoples. A Special Committee of Seventeen (later Twenty-Four) was set up by an Assembly resolution of the following year (27 November 1961) to enquire into the implementation of the Declaration, and this thenceforth harassed Portugal and other European colonial powers continuously.

Meanwhile, in Angola, against this heated international background, the Portuguese authorities were determined to put an end to the increasing activities of the nationalist groups. In 1959–60, they made a series of arrests, including the arrest of Dr Neto of the MPLA. Demonstrations followed and were vigorously repressed. The excitement was intensified by the rapidly approaching independence of Angola's northern neighbour, the Belgian Congo. On 30 June 1960, it became independent and within a few days collapsed into prolonged disorder.[1] That winter, unrest developed in the cotton-growing areas of northern Angola (Baixa de Cassange).

On 22 January 1961, Captain Henrique Galvao seized a Portuguese liner, the *Santa Maria*, off Curaçao. He had once been a Portuguese colonial inspector, had denounced African working conditions on the plantations, had become an opponent of the Salazar regime in Portugal, and now acted in this spectacular fashion to draw world attention to the affairs of Portugal and its possessions. There was some expectation (there

[1] See pp. 203–4.

may indeed have been a plan) that the seized liner would dock at Luanda; in the event, it docked at Recife in Brazil on 3 February. On the following day, under the eyes of assembled reporters of the world press, the MPLA, now led by Mario de Andrade, organised an attack on the prison, the police barracks, and the radio station in Luanda.

This attack was rapidly beaten down but the excitement continued. At the United Nations, on 10 March, Liberia complained to the Security Council that Portuguese repression was a threat to international peace. Its attempt to place the matter on the Council's agenda was defeated but there was a great stir when the United States voted in favour. The new Kennedy Administration was seeking in general to place the United States on the side of African nationalism and in particular to prevent the Congo's history being repeated in Angola.

On 15 March, serious trouble erupted in the north-west of Angola. Instigated by the UPA, African workers on the coffee plantations attacked police posts and settler houses and massacred 200 to 300 Europeans. The Europeans responded by indiscriminate killing of Africans to the number of several thousand. At the United Nations, the Afro-Asian group carried a resolution in the General Assembly establishing an investigatory committee (29 April) but the Portuguese refused to admit it to the country. In May, the Portuguese army launched a major pacification campaign. On 9 June, the Security Council passed a resolution declaring the situation "likely to endanger the maintenance of international peace and security" and calling on Portugal to "desist forthwith from its repressive measures".

The Portuguese military campaign continued and at the same time certain reforms were introduced. On 8 September 1961, the *Estatuto dos Indígenas* was rescinded so that all Africans could now claim Portuguese citizenship. Angola and Mozambique were given three additional seats each in the Portuguese National Assembly (14 September). Reforms of labour and living conditions for the Africans and increased educational programmes were put in hand.

These measures were beside the point to the African and Asian countries and the pressure at the United Nations continued. In December 1961, the investigatory committee reported that the grievances which had touched off the uprising were well-founded and that Portuguese allegations of Communist subversion were exaggerated. The Indian invasion of Goa intensified the excitement.[2] As the 1962 Assembly session approached, the United States persuaded Portugal to agree to the appointment of a UN representative to gather information in Angola (and another in Mozambique). The Afro-Asian group was dissatisfied with this; the United States dropped the proposal; and resolutions condemning Portuguese colonialism

[2] See p. 218.

and giving responsibility to the Committee of Twenty-Four were passed instead. In July 1963, at the request of the UN Economic Commission for Africa, the Economic and Social Council expelled Portugal. On 31 July 1963, the Security Council recommended a ban on the sale of armaments which could be used for the suppression of the indigenous people in Portuguese African territories.

All this time, guerrilla warfare had continued in north-western Angola (UPA) and in some other areas, notably still further north up the coast in the Cabinda enclave (MPLA). The MPLA had moved its headquarters to Leopoldville (September 1961) where it enjoyed the favour of the Soviet Union. The UPA had gathered in another smaller group in a common front and had formed a government-in-exile in Leopoldville (April 1962). It enjoyed the support of the Congolese Prime Minister, Cyrille Adoula, and of the United States, still heavily involved in the affairs of the Congo.

By the end of 1964, however, it was clear that the progress of the guerrilla campaign was faltering. The Organisation of African Unity, at its inaugural meeting at Addis Ababa in May 1963, called upon its members to end diplomatic relations and boycott trade with Portugal and set up a Committee of Liberation to sponsor guerrilla activities against the colonial powers. This committee sought to end the quarrels among the leaders of the MPLA (Dr Neto escaped from Portugal to Leopoldville in July 1962), the persistent intrigue and recurrent fighting between the MPLA and the UPA, and the divisions among the African states as to which to support. By the end of 1964, two major efforts at this had failed.

By this time, moreover, Cyrille Adoula, the UPA's patron in the Congo, was no longer Prime Minister, and with the ending of the Congo crisis, the presence of its other supporter, the United States, had diminished. Even under the Kennedy Administration, favour for African nationalism had been tempered with need of Portugal as a NATO ally; now, under the Johnson Administration, the United States was turning away from Africa.

As to Angola's other neighbours, South Africa was friendly to the Portuguese, and Zambia, independent of the British on 24 October 1964, had need of Portuguese co-operation for trading access to the sea and was thereby inhibited from strong assistance to the guerrillas. The Soviet Union maintained its assistance to the MPLA, the campaign at the United Nations went on, the Portuguese continued to have a serious security problem in the north and in the province bordering on Zambia for the rest of the decade and beyond; none the less, the acute internal and international crisis in the affairs of Angola had eased.

*　　*　　*

D. Abshire and M. Samuels: *Portuguese Africa, A Handbook*, Pall Mall Press, London 1969.

J. Duffy: *Portugal in Africa*, Penguin Books, Harmondsworth 1962.

Institute of Race Relations, London: *Angola, A Symposium*, Oxford University Press, 1962.

D. Wheeler and R. Pélissier: *Angola*, Pall Mall Press, London 1971.

G. Chaliand: "Problèmes du nationalisme angolais", *Les Temps Modernes*, August 1965.

R. Pélissier: "Nationalismes en Angola", *Revue Française de Science Politique*, December 1969.

Goa 1961

FROM the early sixteenth century, the Portuguese ruled several small enclaves on the west coast of India: Goa, Damão and Diu and their still smaller appendages. The total population in 1950 was some 600,000, almost entirely indigenous, 37 per cent Roman Catholic in religion. The trade through the port of Marmagão was mostly transit trade but there were also considerable exports from iron and manganese mines.

British India became independent in 1947. By this time, most of the princely states had already signified their intention to accede to the Indian Union. The Indian Government settled the troubles of Junagadh (November 1947) and Hyderabad (September 1948) by moving in troops. The remaining problems were Kashmir[1] and the French and Portuguese enclaves.

In 1950, the Indian Government formally requested the handing over of the enclaves. It took the view that they were part of the country and nation of India and should therefore come under the Republic of India. Continued rule by the French and Portuguese was a vestige of colonialism. The French had already held referenda to decide the future of their enclaves at Karikal, Mahé, Pondicherry, and Yanaon, and at length handed them over *de facto* in November 1954. The Portuguese, however, took the view that their enclaves were part of the Portuguese nation and state, as laid down in Portugal's constitution. In deference to the sentiments of the time, they changed the legal name of their "colonies" to "overseas territories" in 1951 but otherwise saw no good reason for a change of status. They valued the Estado da India, in Salazar's words, as a "memorial of Portuguese discovery and a small hearth of the Western spirit in the East".

Diplomatic exchanges having produced no result, a Goan liberation movement began to form in 1954 and incidents and arrests began. The Portuguese Government proposed impartial observation, the Indian Government accepted, but the two sides could not agree on how to manage it. Free Goa Volunteers seized control of Dadrá and Nagar Haveli, appendages of Damão (July), and the Indian Government refused passage across Indian territory to Portuguese troops to restore the position. Propaganda became embittered. There was much talk in Goa that the Indians would disfavour Catholics if they took over, hotly denied by the Indians, including Catholic spokesmen.

Feeling came to a head on 15 August 1955. Large numbers of *satyagrahis*,

[1] See pp. 68–73.

215

non-violent demonstrators, moved across the border from India. The Portuguese police, unable to stem the tide by other means, opened fire. Some of the demonstrators were killed. Opinion throughout India was outraged.

In this crisis, the Indian Government decided to damp down the situation. Since independence, it had stated the conviction that international disputes should not be settled by force. This belief was closely linked with the general doctrine of international relations which it had proclaimed to the world, Panchsheel.[2] Correspondingly, it had made plain that it would not use force to take Goa.

At the same time, as Pandit Nehru, India's Prime Minister and chief exponent of these ideas, admitted, there were also serious difficulties for a government in the idea of non-violence and serious perplexities for all in the *satyagraha* method now that the Portuguese, in contrast to the British in their time, had been driven to respond to it with shooting. In the weeks before 15 August, the Indian Government had made statements deprecating *satyagraha* against the Portuguese authorities. It now decided to ban any further use of it and to quieten the situation generally.

Pandit Nehru had the habit of "thinking aloud" in his speeches to the Indian Parliament and the state of Indian official doctrine on the use of force in these years can be illustrated by extracts from these. In a speech of 25 August 1954, when tension was mounting over Goa, he said:

> The policy that we have pursued has been, even as in India under British rule, one of non-violence and we have fashioned our approach and conduct accordingly. This adherence to non-violence means that we may not abandon or permit any derogation of our identification with the cause of our compatriots under Portuguese rule; and equally we may not adopt, advocate or deliberately bring about situations of violence. We regard and base our position on the fact that the liberation movement is Goan and spontaneous, and that its real strength lies in this fact.
>
> The Government of India, and I am confident the great majority of our people, have no intention of adopting any policy or methods which depart from these principles, which are the foundation on which our very nationhood rests and which are the historic and unique legacy of Gandhiji and the pioneers of our freedom.[3]

On 26 July 1955, as the stream of *satyagrahis* into Goa was beginning, Nehru said in disclaiming government support for them:

---

[2] See p. 80.
[3] Jawaharlal Nehru, *India's Foreign Policy, Selected Speeches September 1946– April 1961*, The Publications Division, Government of India, Delhi 1961, pp. 108–9.

(Acharya Kripalani) put a straight question: whether our government was pledged to non-violence. The answer to that is no, the Government is not. As far as I can conceive, no Government can be pledged to non-violence. . . . One may have an ideal. One may adhere to a policy leading in a certain direction and yet, because of existing circumstances, one cannot give effect to that ideal. . . . Even (Gandhiji) in certain circumstances admitted the right of the State, as it is constituted, to commit violence in defence. The Government of India obviously cannot give up that right in the existing circumstances. Nevertheless, we have made it perfectly clear that we shall use force only in defence and that we shall not provoke a war or start a war or adopt any aggressive tactics in regard to a war. That is our policy.[4]

On 17 September 1955, after the August bloodshed, Nehru said in justification of the decision to ban *satyagraha* against the Portuguese:

The question also arises: what after all is satyagraha? I have stated elsewhere that the ideology of satyagraha is dynamic, but that sufficient research has not been conducted into its nature. How far can it go and what are the limits beyond which it cannot go? I for one cannot answer that question. I can, however, say that at any rate it is not appropriate at the present moment, and that it would be a blunder to embark on it at this juncture, because it would be harmful for the country.

You should also take into account the policy and methods followed by Dr Salazar and his Government; keeping them in view you should consider how far satyagraha against such a Government and such a person can prove successful.[5]

In the next few years, tension over Goa subsided. The Indian Government's attitude was simply that one day Goa would revert to the motherland. It had other great preoccupations at this time which made trouble with Portugal inappropriate. The one development of note was the confirmation of a *fait accompli*. In December 1955, Portugal took the issue of the denial of passage of its troops across Indian territory to the International Court of Justice. In 1960, the Court decided that Portuguese sovereign rights had not been infringed in that it could only claim right of passage for private citizens and not for armed forces. Following this, Dadrá and Naga Haveli were officially incorporated into India (16 August 1961).

In 1961, tension over Goa rose rapidly once more. Part of the background to this was the increasing bitterness of the African and Asian countries

---

[4] *Ibid.*, p. 115.
[5] *Ibid.*, p. 123.

against Portugal at the United Nations in the late 1950s, culminating in the storm over the Angola massacres in March 1961.[6] The world-wide publicity given to these events stirred Indian opinion against Portugal. In October, an Afro-Asian seminar on Portuguese colonialism was held in Delhi. To the dismay and irritation of the Indians, the Africans showed that they doubted India's claims to leadership in anti-colonialism in view of its continued tolerance of the situation in Goa. The Indian philosophy of non-violence was in no state to withstand African arguments on the need for violence, especially in the current heated atmosphere against Portugal.

A further part of the background in 1961 was the widespread dissatisfaction among the Indian public with the Government's handling of the border dispute with China[7] and the Opposition feud with the Minister of Defence, Krishna Menon. Menon and the army command began covert military moves towards a stronger line against China and were similarly ready to take a stronger line against the Portuguese.

The signal for the onset of crisis came on 13 November when the UN General Assembly debated Portugal's overseas possessions yet again and Krishna Menon stated that India had never renounced all use of force in international relations and that Portugal should not assume that India would tolerate its colonialism for ever. Journalists descended on Goa in the expectation of Indian action. Then followed Indian allegations that the Portuguese had fired on Indian fishing boats. Incidents occurred along the border. The Portuguese proposed an impartial observer group, the United States offered its good offices, but to no effect. Indian troops moved to the border. Nehru, privately it seems in turmoil over the course of events, stated on 11 December that Indian patience was at an end. On the 17th, Indian troops crossed the border. The Portuguese made only brief resistance and Goa, Damão and Diu were all rapidly taken over. They were formally incorporated into India a year later, 19 December 1962.

Western opinion was shocked by India's action, believing that it breached all its past professions and the Charter of the United Nations. At the Security Council on 18 December, the United States, Britain, France and Turkey introduced a resolution calling for a cease-fire, Indian withdrawal and a peaceful settlement. However, this resolution, though it won seven votes, was lost through the opposition of the Soviet Union together with Ceylon, Liberia and Egypt. To the bitter disappointment of the Portuguese public, the Western powers did nothing further to assist Portugal, though the affair contributed to the souring of relations between the Western powers and India in the following years.

[6] See p. 212.
[7] See pp. 156–7.

India's defence against its critics, in which it had the support of the majority of African and Asian states, was that it was not in fact the aggressor; Portuguese colonialism, like other colonialism, constituted "permanent aggression". Specifically, it argued in the Security Council on 18 December, that Portugal's presence in Goa had always been illegal, that it had consistently refused to negotiate, and that its continued presence was a breach of the UN General Assembly's Declaration on Colonial Independence.[8] Its four supporters in the Council introduced a counter-resolution rejecting the charge of aggression, declaring that the Portuguese enclaves constituted a threat to international peace and calling on Portugal to end hostilities and to negotiate with India on their transfer. This resolution was lost by the contrary votes of the other seven members.

*   *   *

M. BRECHER: *India and World Politics, Krishna Menon's View of the World*, Oxford University Press, 1968.

H. KAY: *Salazar and Modern Portugal*, Eyre and Spottiswoode, London 1970.

Q. WRIGHT: "The Goa Incident", *The American Journal of International Law*, July 1962.

[8] See p. 211.

Iraq-Kuwait 1961

In 1897, Turkey sought to give substance to its nominal authority over the sheikhdom of Kuwait. Moreover, in 1899, to the disquiet of the British, it granted a concession to a company owned mainly by the Deutsche Bank to build a railway across Turkey and Mesopotamia to Basra. There were also reports of Russian interest in a railway and a coaling station. The interests of the Sheikh and the British thus ran parallel and in the same year they signed an Exclusive Agreement whereby the Sheikh would not alienate any of his territory without British consent. They in return, it was understood, would give him protection. On the outbreak of war with Turkey in 1914, Britain announced that it considered the sheikhdom to be an independent government under British protection.

On 19 June 1961, the Agreement was terminated by mutual consent as inconsistent with the sovereignty and independence of Kuwait. In an exchange of letters between Sheikh Abdullah and the British Political Resident in the Persian Gulf, Sir William Luce, the British declared their continued readiness "to assist the Government of Kuwait if the latter requests such assistance".

Six days later (25 June), the Prime Minister of Iraq, General Abdul Karim Qassim, announced that Kuwait was "an integral part of Iraq". It was a district of Iraq and the Sheikh would be appointed official in charge.

Rulers of Iraq had made this claim from time to time in the past, notably King Ghazi in the 1930s. Iraq's historical argument was that Kuwait had been part of the Basra province of the Ottoman empire which Iraq had inherited. General Qassim in addition made his claim in the name of Arab unity and of the return of Iraq's natural port.

The motives ascribed to General Qassim by commentators at the time were various. There was first the enormous wealth of this minute state of 321,000 people, envied throughout the Arab world. An oil concession had been granted in 1934; production had begun in 1946 at 6 million barrels; by 1961 this figure had passed 600 million, far greater than Iraq's own considerable output. The on-shore concession in Kuwait proper was held by the Kuwait Oil Company, a 50–50 consortium of British Petroleum and Gulf Oil (United States), the off-shore rights by Royal Dutch Shell (Dutch and British). The Sheikh had half the profits. In addition, there were the oil revenues from the Kuwait–Saudi Arabia Neutral Zone. Much was spent on welfare. The rest was banked with Britain and was an important item in sterling area finance.

Another motive widely ascribed to General Qassim concerned the internal situation of Iraq. General Qassim had led the revolution of 14 July 1958 which overthrew the monarchy but the large promises made at that time (notably land reform) were far from fulfilment. The country was deeply divided: "the Shi'ite majority jealous of the power of the Sunni minority; the Kurdish demands for autonomy; tribal unrest; the aspirations of those who favoured Arab unity versus those who favoured Iraq for the Iraqis; merchant versus peasant".[1] According to many commentators, General Qassim's aim was to divert and unite the country by a foreign adventure and bolster his regime by a foreign victory.

Finally, there was the question of Iraq's standing in the Middle East. Since the Suez *débâcle* of 1956, Britain's power in the region had been in decline. Egypt, Saudi Arabia and Iraq were all in varying degrees rivals for leadership. Any one of them might manoeuvre to succeed to the British position in Kuwait for the prestige of a further blow against Britain and in relation to each other. Saudi Arabia shared with Iraq the advantage of proximity; Egypt might engineer a link with Kuwait in the name of Arab unity and of placing its wealth at the disposal of all Arabs. Along these lines, whether the stake was wealth or prestige, General Qassim's move could be seen as "an attempt, on the one hand to forestall other claimants and to warn them and, on the other hand, to test the reaction of the British".[2]

In reply to General Qassim's move, Sheikh Abdullah reaffirmed the independence of Kuwait, protested to the Arab League and asked fellow Arab rulers for support. Saudi Arabia immediately informed Iraq through its ambassador in Baghdad that it would resist any attack on Kuwait.

Britain also immediately confirmed its support. It first tried to persuade either Turkey, Pakistan, India or Iran to act as a mediator but when Iraqi troop movements were reported, the Sheikh asked Britain for military assistance (30 June) and British troops arrived in the first days of July. Saudi Arabia sent a small contingent at the same time.

At the Security Council, on 1 July, Kuwait complained about the "situation" arising from "the threat by Iraq to the territorial independence of Kuwait". Iraq countered by complaining of the "situation" arising "out of the armed threat by the United Kingdom to the independence and security of Iraq". Kuwait's complaint could not be received, it said, because Kuwait was not independent. The Council debated the issue between the 2nd and 7th of July. A resolution calling on "all states to respect the territorial integrity of Kuwait" and urging that "all concerned should work for peace and tranquility in the area" was defeated only by a

[1] D. Peretz, *The Middle East Today*, Holt, Rinehart & Winston Inc., New York 1963, p. 394.
[2] Shwadran, Part 1, p. 6.

Soviet veto (with Ceylon, Ecuador and the United Arab Republic of Egypt and Syria abstaining). A UAR resolution to the effect that Britain should immediately withdraw gained the support only of Ceylon and the Soviet Union.

While Egypt was strongly opposed to Kuwait's link with Britain, it was equally opposed to the pretensions of Iraq. During the Security Council debates, the Arab League sent its Secretary-General, Abdul Khaliq Hassunah, to Baghdad, Kuwait and Taif to attempt mediation. Afterwards, the League met in Cairo (12 July) and on the 20th it agreed, first, to accept Kuwait as a member and, second, to substitute Arab assistance for British. Iraq withdrew in protest before the vote and afterwards announced that it would boycott the League.

Negotiations for an Arab Defence Force were completed on 12 August and a military mission drawn from the UAR, Saudi Arabia, Lebanon and Jordan arrived in Kuwait. Difficulties persisted on paying for the force, however, and some Arab countries, headed by Egypt, began to develop reservations about the precedent being created. On 10 September, the first contingents (3,300 men) arrived in Kuwait with a Saudi Arabian in command and a Jordanian second-in-command.

The British force now began to withdraw and by 10 October the change-over was complete. Despite the Arab opposition aroused, Iraq persisted in its claim. It boycotted Arab League meetings at which Kuwait was present and declared that it would "reconsider" its relations with any country which established diplomatic relations with Kuwait. Under this Iraq broke off diplomatic relations with Jordan, Japan, Iran, Lebanon, Tunisia and the United States at various times. The Soviet Union vetoed Kuwait's application for UN membership in November 1961. However, after 1961 less was heard of the claim and after the overthrow of General Qassim on 8 February 1963 and the ensuing six months of Baath Party rule, it was abandoned by the new government of Colonel Abdul Salam Aref. Iraq formally renounced its claim, Kuwait made an interest-free loan of KD 30 million, and the two countries established diplomatic relations (4 October).

*   *   *

Royal Institute of International Affairs: *Survey of International Affairs 1961*, Oxford University Press, 1965.

A. G. Mezerik: "The Kuwait–Iraq Dispute", *International Review Service*, Vol. VII, No. 66, 1961.

E. Monroe: "Kuwait and Aden, A Contrast in British Policies", *The Middle East Journal*, Winter 1964.

B. Shwadran: "The Kuwait Incident", *Middle Eastern Affairs*, two parts, January and February 1962.

Aden 1961-67

THE port of Aden, originally seized by the British in 1839 and attached to the Bombay Presidency, was designated a Colony in 1937. The desolate hinterland was ruled by numerous emirs, sultans and sheikhs as the British Protectorate of Aden, divided into Western and Eastern sections. Further north still was the independent Kingdom of Yemen. In 1950, its ruler, the Imam, had revived ancient claims to rule the whole region. There were some 90,000 Yemenis in the town of Aden out of a population of some 230,000.[1]

The intricate politics of Aden can be given some shape in terms of two periods of British policy. From 1958 to 1966, the British sought to create a federation of the Protectorate and of the town which would eventually receive independence but which would continue to accept a British military base. They established an Integrated Aden Command in 1958 and later, when it became clear that Britain would be unable to retain a large base in Cyprus or Kenya, they transferred the headquarters of the Middle East Command there. This involved a heavy investment in military installations with every appearance of permanence, the base being regarded as vital to the carrying out of Britain's global, regional and local security commitments. In 1966, a new period opened when the British decided that they did not after all want a base in Aden. The problem now became, who would succeed them in power when they withdrew, the Federal Government or someone else.

The British idea for a federation was accepted in principle by the Protectorate rulers as early as 1954 but for some years made no further progress in view of the tribal rivalries. In March 1958, however, Yemen announced its association with the two most radical Arab countries, Egypt and Syria, in a United Arab State, and many of the Western Protectorate rulers feared that the Imam would now get Egyptian support in his claims to their territory. On 11 February 1959, six of them formed the Federation of the Emirates of the South, later renamed the Federation of South Arabia, with the objectives of mutual defence and economic development. The rest of the Western Protectorate rulers soon joined in but those of the Eastern Protectorate, despite continual British urging, stood aloof.

Meanwhile, in the town of Aden, nationalist sentiment was growing. Compared with the tribesmen of the Protectorate, the Adenis had a

[1] For events in the Kingdom of Yemen, see pp. 228–32.

relatively high standard of living and were affected by modern political ideas, notably through their trades union movement. The growing nationalist feeling in part reflected world-wide attitudes but more particularly the anti-British reaction which had swept the Middle East since the Suez crisis of 1956. It was continually stimulated by radio propaganda from Egypt and Yemen. There were moderate nationalists who were content to press for constitutional advancement and there was a smaller number of extremists who advocated direct action to get rid of the British immediately and entirely.

The situation came to a head in 1961 when the British made known their intention of bringing the town into the Federation. Some moderate Adenis, notably several of the twenty-three member Legislative Council of the Colony, seem initially to have favoured the merger as a defence against an eventual take-over by Yemen. On the other hand, they shared the widespread fear that it would place the town and its wealth in the hands of the sheikhs of the Protectorate and the equally widespread suspicion that the move was simply a device of the British to strengthen their sheikh allies and so themselves and their base.

The British appear to have been aware of the likely strength of popular opposition but could see no practicable alternative arrangement for the future. They have been criticised for rushing the merger through rather than working longer to try to achieve wider consent.[2] When the terms finally agreed by the Adeni Ministers in London (July–August 1962) were put to the Legislative Council on 24 September 1962 in an intense atmosphere of propaganda and counter-propaganda, only three of the Adeni nominated or elected members joined the five ministers, the five British *ex-officio* members and the two European nominated members in voting in favour.

Aden now reverted for a few months to relative calm but in Yemen on 27 September there was a *coup d'état* against the new Imam and a Republic was proclaimed. This strengthened the case of those Adeni nationalists whose recipe for the future was immediate independence followed by some form of union with Yemen. Moreover, Egypt sent troops to support the Republican Government in the civil war with the Imam and these gave training and supplies to militant Adeni organisations. The National Liberation Front of South Yemen (i.e. Aden and the Protectorate) was formed at this time in Sana.

In 1963, there were a number of political strikes as in previous years. A grenade attack on the British High Commissioner, Sir Kennedy Trevaskis, in December 1963, marked the opening of terrorism. The British responded by declaring a state of emergency. Simultaneously (winter of 1963–64)

[2] Little, pp. 87–8.

British troops were used in support of the Federal Army against dissident tribesmen in the Radfan mountains on the Yemen border.

Over the next two years, the British held continual discussions with the Federal Ministers and Protectorate rulers on constitutional advance, notably a Constitutional Conference under the chairmanship of the Minister of State for the Colonies, Duncan Sandys, in the summer of 1964. Here it was agreed that the Federation should receive independence not later than 1968. Then followed the visit of the new Labour Government Minister, Anthony Greenwood, and efforts to arrange a further constitutional conference in 1965. All these discussions assumed the maintenance of the Federation and of the British base. The militant nationalists, on the other hand, were exerting increasing pressure for the immediate complete withdrawal of the British and for elections on the basis of universal suffrage, leading, it seemed likely, to the destruction of the Federation. In August 1965, the British Speaker of the Legislative Assembly and the Superintendent of Police were murdered. Sir Richard Turnbull, High Commissioner since December 1964, thereupon suspended the constitution and exercised direct rule. The Federal Ministers, he said, had refused to condemn terrorism and had assisted the NLF.

These events exposed the weakness of support for the federal concept within Aden; confidence was soon to crumble among the Protectorate rulers also. On 22 February 1966, the British Government published a Defence Review which contained the statement that all British forces would be withdrawn from Aden by the time of independence, two years ahead. This *volte face* by Britain, based on a reassessment of its role in the world "East of Suez", opened a new stage of the South Arabia conflict. The British appointed new Federal Ministers and continued until the following summer to try to breathe life into the federal structure, but their intention to withdraw militarily suggested even to the Protectorate rulers that it was doomed. Events now centred on a struggle for power between factions with quite different plans.

In their continued efforts in 1966–67 to create a broadly-based federal government in peaceful succession to themselves, the British considered what assistance they could get from the United Nations. The UN "Committee of Twenty-Four"[3] had established a sub-committee in May 1963 to investigate the Aden question but the British had rejected this as unwarranted interference and had refused it entry to the territory. Now, however, they accepted various UN resolutions and, in the autumn of 1966, asked for a UN Mission to facilitate the territory's progress to independence. This was supplied by the "Committee of Twenty-Four" and visited Aden in April 1967. However, it quarrelled with the High

[3] See p. 211 (Angola).

Commissioner, the Federal Ministers and one of the principal nationalist factions, FLOSY, and retired ineffectively.

FLOSY, the Front for the Liberation of South Yemen, had been formed in January 1966 out of the Organisation for the Liberation of the Occupied South, sponsored by Egypt, and the National Liberation Front. This unhappy partnership had finally broken down in December 1966, leaving FLOSY and the NLF as rivals for the succession to the British.

In May 1967, Sir Humphrey Trevelyan became High Commissioner with the task of organising the British withdrawal on time and in good order. In June, as a first stage, British troops were withdrawn from the Western Protectorate. Efforts to bring the militants and the Federal Ministers together were disrupted by a mutiny of the Federal Army and Police on 20 June. This had to be dealt with by the British and was the final exposure of the weakness of the Federal Government and especially of its inability to control and protect the rulers. In the next two months, the NLF rapidly extended its control over the greater part of the Protectorate, expelling or overawing the rulers. Its rival, FLOSY, lost this contest partly because it had weaker roots in the Protectorate and partly because Egypt began to withdraw from the Yemen civil war at this time and was less able to support it.

By September, the Federal Government had plainly collapsed, and on the 5th, the High Commissioner invited FLOSY and the NLF, which were continuing the struggle in Aden, to join in talks aimed at the formation of a new government. They refused, however. The Arab League also sought a cease-fire and called for a conference of all "nationalist forces" in South Arabia. This was rejected by both FLOSY and the NLF because representatives of more moderate parties had also been invited.

The British had now reached the stage of handing over security responsibility in Aden to the Federal Army. On 7 October the NLF and FLOSY began talks in Cairo, each claiming the major share in a new government. On 2 November, the British announced that they would complete their withdrawal at the end of the month. Fighting broke out again in Aden, and by force and diplomacy the NLF completed the defeat of its rival and was acknowledged by the Federal Army.

Bilateral negotiations between the British and the NLF over arrangements for independence took place in Geneva, agreement of necessity being quickly reached to keep pace with the British withdrawal. On 29 November 1967, the withdrawal was completed and the Southern Yemen People's Republic came into being. A matter left outstanding, subsequently causing some friction, was the amount of British financial aid to the new republic.

*   *   *

G. KING: *Imperial Outpost, Aden,* Oxford University Press, 1964.

T. LITTLE: *South Arabia,* Pall Mall Press, London 1968.

B. REILLY: *Aden and The Yemen,* HM Stationery Office, 1960.

H. TREVELYAN: *The Middle East in Revolution,* Macmillan, London 1970.

J. B. KELLY: "The Future in Arabia", *International Affairs,* October 1966.

Yemen 1962-68

THE kingdom of Yemen in the early 1950s was one of the most archaic countries in the world. The people were divided into tribes, settled in villages and a few small towns, Moslem in religion, Zeidi (Shia) in the north, Shafi (Sunni) in the south. There was a northern aristocracy, the Seiyids, but the religious and secular ruler, the Imam, also from a northern dynasty, was a complete autocrat. Politics were personal, treacherous and cruel. Many old inventions, banking, administrative records, and most new ones, railways, telephones, were unknown; others, a handful of cars and aeroplanes, were still a marvel. The country had little representation abroad. Foreigners were rare and suspect.

In the mid-1950s, the pace of change quickened. The latest of successive groups of foreign technicians brought in on occasion over the years were the Russians and the Chinese who improved the port of Hodeida and the road from there to Sana. They gained no influence, however, and indeed, when they had finished the work, no payment. More significant was the development of closer links with Egypt.

Since the mid-1940s, a group of Free Yemenis, disgusted with the backwardness of their country, had intrigued and made propaganda, mostly from the neighbouring British Colony, Aden. From the Egyptian revolution of 1952, they took Egypt as their inspiration and sponsor. From 1956, Egypt under President Nasser was at the peak of its influence throughout the Middle East as leader in the cause of anti-Zionism, anti-imperialism, anti-monarchism, social revolution and Arab unity. Syria joined Egypt in a United Arab Republic in February 1958 and there was high excitement that year at the prospect that Lebanon and Jordan might also be swept in.[1] To placate Egypt, to counter the propaganda of the Free Yemenis, to seem generally progressive, and to gain Egypt's support in Yemen's long-standing and recently active claims to Aden and the surrounding Protectorate,[2] Imam Ahmed in March 1958 formed a link with the new UAR known as the United Arab States.

This union had no constitutional significance but it was accompanied by an influx of Egyptians to train the feeble army and to develop secular schools and by a general stirring of ideas. The Imam was soon alarmed and quarrelled with President Nasser. The UAS was dissolved (31 December 1961). However, the activities of the Egyptians continued, sponsored by

[1] See pp. 137, 140.
[2] See pp. 223ff.

228

the heir to the throne, Prince Mohammed al-Badr, and now backed by a renewed torrent of Egyptian propaganda calling for social revolution in Yemen.

On 18 September 1962, Imam Ahmed died and Prince Mohammed al-Badr, his son, succeeded. Though he said that he would continue social reforms, the Free Yemenis and many army officers were determined to have done with the Imamate and there seems to have been a multiplicity of plots. It was also doubtful whether, as Imam, Prince Mohammed's respect for Egypt would continue. The Egyptian Government recognised him on the 23rd but it also had close contacts with enemies of the Imamate, notably Colonel Abdullah as-Sallal, a moderniser of long standing and appointed Chief of Staff by the new Imam. On the night of the 26th, an armoured unit at Sana began a *coup d'état*. Colonel Sallal took charge and on the 27th proclaimed the Yemen Arab Republic with a government of officers and Free Yemenis. A first contingent of Egyptian troops, some 3,000, arrived the following day and with this assistance, the Republican Government swiftly secured the allegiance of the main towns of the country. Various foreign governments, notably the Soviet Government, gave recognition over the next few days.

The Republican Government proclaimed the Imam killed in the *coup* but, in fact, he made his way a fortnight later to Najran, just over the northern border with Saudi Arabia, where princes of the royal family had already gathered and had proclaimed a government-in-exile. The kings of Saudi Arabia had no love for the Imams of Yemen but on the other hand King Saud, like other Arab monarchs, was in bitter feud with President Nasser of Egypt. Early in November, the Imam and the princes returned to various points in the mountains in northern Yemen and, with the financial assistance of Saudi Arabia, began to compete with the Republican Government for the allegiance of the mountain tribes. They were helped in this by the tribesmen's dislike of the Egyptians.

Skirmishing began between the rapidly reinforced Egyptian troops and the Imam's tribesmen but, internationally, the most alarming feature of the situation was the possibility of direct conflict between Egypt and Saudi Arabia. Egyptian aircraft attacked the camps near Najran early in November and again in late November. The United States offered its good offices between the republicans and Egypt on the one hand and the kings of Saudi Arabia and Jordan on the other (27 November). After great deliberation and consultation in view of its friendship with Saudi Arabia, the United States recognised the Republican Government on 19 December and with this added support, its credentials were accepted by the United Nations the following day. The United States Administration remained anxious, however, and set out in co-operation with the UN Secretary-

General, U Thant, to try to end the fighting. It sent Mr T. Ellsworth Bunker to talk with the Saudi Arabian Government; Dr Ralph Bunche of the UN Secretariat had talks with the Republican Government; and both of them held discussions with President Nasser.

On 29 April 1963, at which time the Egyptian forces were engaged in a heavy and promising spring offensive against the Imam's tribesmen, the UN Secretary-General announced that a Disengagement Agreement had been reached. The Egyptian forces would leave the country; Saudi Arabia would cease aiding the Imam; a demilitarised zone would be established on the northern border with UN observers to be paid for by Egypt and Saudi Arabia. In fact, however, neither country observed the withdrawal part of the agreement and the fighting continued, each side putting the blame on the other. The UN Yemen Observer Mission was duly sanctioned by the Security Council on 11 June and began to arrive on the 13th, but then spent fifteen dangerous, frustrating and ultimately fruitless months in and around Sana until its withdrawal on 4 September 1964. The other arrival in the summer of 1963 was a handful of European mercenaries, paid to advise the Imam's tribesmen.

At the beginning of 1964, Egypt was, it seems, already tired of the strain of maintaining some 50,000 troops in Yemen; at the same time, it could not accept a victory for the Imam and Saudi Arabia. Saudi Arabia, for its part, seems to have been reluctant to go on aiding the Imam; but it could not give Egypt the victory by abandoning him. There was just enough mutual interest to arouse deep suspicions in the two *protégés* of the intentions of their respective masters and to get contacts and intrigues going between all four, but not enough, as it turned out, to reach agreement.

President Nasser and King Saud and King Hussein talked amicably at the Arab Summit Conference in Cairo in January; King Hussein withdrew support of the Imam; the other two began continuous negotiations. President Sallal visited Moscow in March and Peking in June and successfully secured additional armaments and other aid; but he was not successful in getting it direct; it came via Egypt.

At length, on 1–3 November, Algeria and Iraq having acted as the principal intermediaries, delegates of all four parties came together at Erkowit in Sudan. They announced that there would be a cease-fire on the 8th to be followed by a peace conference on the 23rd. Over the next few days, statements made by the Imam's party were adamant for the preservation of the Imamate and the immediate withdrawal of the Egyptians; the republican party were as adamant for the opposite. The proposed conference was not held.

Much the same pattern was repeated in 1965, though on the whole it was a better year for the Imam's cause. King Faisal, who succeeded his brother

King Saud in November 1964, gave the Imam enough support to take the offensive and strengthen his military position. President Sallal was now in serious trouble with the Shafis of the south who, while favouring the Republican Government as opposed to the northern Imamate, were bitterly disappointed by their exclusion from office in it. He was also in trouble with a growing number of members of the Government and other notables who were weary of the Egyptians and increasingly eager to be rid of them.

President Sallal was able to master these difficulties, however, and the deadlock continued as before. On 22–24 August, President Nasser and King Faisal met at Jiddah and agreed on an immediate cease-fire to be supervised by a joint force; the ending of Saudi Arabian aid; the withdrawal of the Egyptian forces within a year; and a conference of all Yemeni factions to be held at Harad (northern Yemen) to form a provisional government which would hold a plebiscite on the constitution. Moreover, President Nasser held President Sallal in Cairo and allowed the republican delegation to the Harad Conference to consist mostly of those who wished to see Egypt withdraw if possible; King Faisal, for his part, secured the exclusion of members of the royal family from the Imamate delegation in favour of more moderate personages of that faction. Even so, the two sides could not bridge the gap. At the Conference which began on 24 November, the Imamate delegation pressed for an immediate Egyptian withdrawal but the republicans were mistrustful. The Imamate delegation talked of a neutral provisional government whereas the republicans wanted one largely republican. The Conference broke up in failure on 24 December.

President Nasser had meanwhile begun to reduce his forces in line with the Jiddah Agreement, but at the beginning of 1966 he reversed this policy, whether because, as he said, the Harad Conference had failed or because, as has been speculated, Britain's startling announcement (February) that it proposed to withdraw from Aden raised new reasons to remain strong in the area.[3] At all events, he announced a "long-breath strategy" according to which Egyptian forces would hold the centre of the country and the towns on behalf of the republicans for as long as need be. In the summer, he put a stop to private discussions between the moderate republicans and the moderates of the Imamate faction by sending President Sallal back to Sana, who formed a new government with himself as Prime Minister, manoeuvred for a while against the moderates, and held a "purge" in the autumn. President Nasser had his own negotiations with King Faisal in June–July with the Sheikh of Kuwait as intermediary, and on 17 August their delegates met in Kuwait; but still fruitlessly.

The deadlock was at last broken by the defeat of Egypt, Syria and

[3] See pp. 225.

Jordan in the Six Day War with Israel in June 1967.[4] President Nasser's prestige was lowered; the pressure within Egypt to end the costly intervention was now difficult to counter; King Faisal had leverage in the form of a subsidy to Egypt needed to replace the revenue from the closed Suez Canal. The Khartoum "summit conference" of Arab Governments (29 August–1 September) produced, *inter alia*, an agreement on Yemen whereby Egypt would withdraw, Saudi Arabia would cease support of the Imamate faction and Iraq, Morocco and Sudan would form a Tripartite Committee to seek to bring about a national coalition in the country. This time, both interveners carried out the agreement and, despite the bitter complaints of President Sallal, the last Egyptian forces had gone by the end of the year. Immediately, President Sallal's position became desperate. He hoped that the Soviet Union would step into the breach; he left for Moscow on 3 November; on the 5th, the moderates among the republicans declared him deposed and set up a three-man Presidential Council which appointed a new government.

King Faisal secured the promise of the Imam to co-operate with the Tripartite Committee and to negotiate with the new republican regime, but by this time the Imam was a sick man in Jiddah and the effective leadership had passed to his cousin, Prince Mohammed Hussein. Prince Mohammed and other members of the family, and perhaps the Imamate faction generally and certainly the tribesmen, believed that with the withdrawal of the Egyptians and the fall of Sallal their chance had at last come for victory. Gathering together, they advanced on Sana in December, encircling and besieging it. The defence was vigorous. The Soviet Union poured in armaments. The new rulers of Aden, who had been assisted by the Yemeni republicans during their struggle with the British (whence various border incidents and some guarded British support for the Imam), now did their bit in return. The season was the wrong one for tribal campaigning. By the beginning of February (1968) the siege had been broken and the tribesmen withdrew. The conflict in the country now died down, with the Republican Government controlling the central and southern areas, and with the northern area still somehow to be pacified.

*   *   *

H. INGRAMS: *The Yemen*, John Murray, London 1963.

E. O'BALLANCE: *The War in the Yemen*, Faber and Faber, London 1971.

R. STEPHENS: *Nasser*, Allen Lane, The Penguin Press, London 1971.

M. WENNER: *Modern Yemen 1918–66*, Johns Hopkins Press, Baltimore 1967

[4] See pp. 269–72.

The Cuban Missiles Crisis 1962

IN the relations between the great powers in 1962 which formed the background to the Cuban missiles crisis of October, the most clearly defined features were the tension between the United States and the Soviet Union and their allies over Germany and Berlin;[1] the intensification of the now scarcely concealed quarrel between the Soviet Union and China; and, coinciding with the missiles crisis, the Chinese invasion and humiliation of India.[2] Less clearly defined was the issue of nuclear power in the world: the controversy over the testing of nuclear weapons; the opposition of the Soviet Union to a Chinese nuclear weapons programme; the Geneva discussions on a "nuclear non-proliferation" treaty; the popular impression in the West promoted by the Soviet Union that it equalled the United States in nuclear missile capacity contrasted with the reality of its inferiority. Putting all these issues together in the broadest terms, it was fairly evident even at the time that the United States, the Soviet Union and China and their leaders personally were engaged in 1962 in a struggle for psychological supremacy in world politics.

The precise connections between this wider background and the Cuban missiles crisis remain largely a matter of speculation, however. Confining this account solely to Cuba and the events of the crisis, after the failure of the Bay of Pigs attack in April 1961,[3] Cuba continued to express fears of invasion by the United States, raising the matter at the opening of the United Nations General Assembly session in September and pursuing it there into the new year. In fact, however, it seems that the Kennedy Administration had now decided to handle the Cuba problem by isolating the country diplomatically and economically. At the Punta del Este conference of January 1962, the Organisation of American States expelled Cuba and on 3 February, the United States embargoed all trade with Cuba (except medical goods) and pressed its Western allies to do likewise. The aim was to mobilise Latin American opinion against Cuban propaganda and subversion, to create havoc in the country's finances, and to make the Soviet Union carry the full cost of supporting its *protégé*.

Though this aim was largely fulfilled, many in the United States remained restless at the continued presence of a "Communist regime" in the Caribbean and the Republican Party showed that it would make Cuba

[1] See pp. 168–72.
[2] See p. 158.
[3] See pp. 177–8.

233

a major issue in the November Congressional elections. Throughout the summer, there was talk of a Soviet military build-up in Cuba. On 2 September, the Soviet Union confirmed that, in view of "imperialist threats" to Cuba, it was supplying armaments and military training personnel. This gave rise to the charge that Cuba was being converted into a Soviet strategic base, which the Administration set out to refute. It did not believe that the Soviet Union would place long-range offensive weapons on Cuba and, on the basis of intelligence reports, including aerial reconnaissance, said on 4 September that there was no evidence of "offensive ground-to-ground missiles". President Kennedy repeated this in a news conference of 13 September, adding the assurance that if such weapons were introduced, the United States would act.

Then followed in October a strong condemnation by the Organisation of American States of Soviet attempts to turn Cuba into an armed base for penetration and subversion of Latin America (3rd); a denial by the Soviet Ambassador in Washington, Anatoly Dobrynin, that the Soviet programme included offensive missiles (13th); and the first clear intelligence of six sites for medium range ballistic missiles on the island (14th).[4]

The United States Administration kept this information to itself for seven days while it decided what to do.[5] Some are said to have argued (notably Robert McNamara, Secretary of Defense) that Soviet missiles on Cuba made little strategic difference; others (Paul Nitze, currently one of his assistant secretaries) that they made a considerable strategic difference, drastically reducing the warning time of a Soviet missile attack. All, however, believed or were soon persuaded that the Soviet action would have a profound effect on the standing of the United States in the western hemisphere and the world and were agreed that the missiles must somehow be removed.

As to how this was to be done, diplomatic action seemed too weak and inconclusive, invasion of Cuba too slow and drastic, and an air attack on the sites was at first favoured. The objection to this was that it might not work, that it would be repugnant to world opinion, and that it would engage Soviet prestige too clearly, perhaps ensuring a drastic response. Gradually the idea emerged of an embargo on shipments of the missiles and a naval blockade to enforce it (to be called, in a euphemism reminiscent of Franklin Roosevelt, "a quarantine") and on 20 October this was decided upon. The objection to this tactic was that it did not remove the missiles already on Cuba but its supporters argued that, in Robert McNamara's

[4] The later full United States estimate was that 42 MRBMs and 24–32 IBRMs (Intermediate Range Ballistic Missiles) arrived in Cuba or were on their way.
[5] For the membership of the Executive Committee of the National Security Council and the groupings within it, see D. C. Watt, *Survey of International Affairs 1962*, Oxford University Press, 1970, pp. 55–6.

subsequently fashionable phrase, "it maintains the options". An air-strike could follow, if necessary.

During these deliberations, the Soviet Foreign Minister, Andrei Gromyko, assured President Kennedy personally that offensive weapons were not being installed on Cuba (18 October). On 22 October, the world crisis began. That evening, having notified the principal allies of the United States the previous day, Secretary of State Dean Rusk handed a note of the proposed United States measures to the Soviet Ambassador, President Kennedy made a broadcast to the nation, and the United States delegate, Adlai Stevenson, appealed to the United Nations Security Council. In his broadcast, President Kennedy denounced the Soviet action as a "deliberately provocative and unjustified change in the status quo"; called on Chairman Krushchev to "halt and eliminate this clandestine, reckless and provocative threat to world peace"; warned that a missile attack on any western hemisphere state would call forth a "full retaliatory response against the Soviet Union"; warned the Soviet Union also against any offensive move anywhere else in the world, especially West Berlin; and declared: "Should these offensive military preparations continue, thus increasing the threat to the hemisphere, further action will be justified. I have directed the Armed Forces to prepare for all eventualities; and I trust that, in the interest of both the Cuban people and the Soviet technicians at the sites, the hazards to all concerned of continuing this threat will be recognized."

It became clear on the following day (23rd) that the majority of the NATO allies were solidly behind the United States. Britain and Canada had reservations; they believed that the United States had an *idée fixe* about Cuba and there had been friction over the trade embargo; however, public opinion in these countries was won by the publication of the aerial photographic evidence of the Soviet missile sites. The OAS passed a resolution (19–0–1) calling for withdrawal of the missiles and recommending to its members individual and collective measures, including armed force if necessary, to ensure that no further offensive military material reached Cuba. In the Security Council, the United States introduced a draft resolution calling for a withdrawal of the missiles under UN observation. The Soviet Union's counter-resolution condemned the intended blockade and proposed negotiations between Cuba, the Soviet Union and the United States, but the most that the Soviet Union got by way of general support was a draft resolution by the Afro-Asian states directing the Secretary-General to confer with the protagonists, who were meanwhile to do nothing to aggravate the situation.

On the evening of the 23rd, Chairman Krushchev said in a letter to President Kennedy that the Soviet Union would not observe the proposed blockade. Kennedy's reply to this was a firm appeal for observance. On the suggestion of the British ambassador, David Ormsby-Gore, the blockade line was drawn back from 800 miles to 500 miles off Cuba to give the Soviet Union more time for deliberation before a clash. The blockade was then proclaimed for 9 a.m. Caribbean time (2 p.m. GMT) on the following day (24th).

On the 24th, the Soviet Union formally rejected the United States note of the 22nd announcing the blockade. However, at 9 a.m., the twenty Soviet ships nearest to the blockade line stopped or altered course. (The oil tankers among them subsequently proceeded and were allowed to pass by the United States Navy, the only ship to be boarded during the entire affair (26th) being a Panamanian-owned cargo ship under charter to the Soviet Union.) U Thant, the UN Secretary-General, proposed to the Soviet Union and to the United States a three-week standstill on the delivery of arms to Cuba and a suspension meanwhile of the blockade. Bertrand Russell, in public letters to Kennedy and Krushchev, proposed a "summit conference". Chairman Krushchev accepted Lord Russell's proposal the same day and U Thant's the next (25th).

President Kennedy, on the other hand, replied to U Thant (25th) that the necessary step was for the Soviet Union to withdraw the missiles placed on Cuba. (He dismissed Lord Russell's suggestion, 26th.) U Thant thereupon proposed that the Soviet Union should hold back its ships for a limited time and that the United States should avoid clashes. This proposal, reflecting what the two sides were already doing, was accepted by the United States (25th) and the Soviet Union (26th). It did not, however, advance matters with regard to the missile sites actually on Cuba on which work was still continuing rapidly, and on the 26th, the United States was faced with the prospect that its menacing military preparations for direct action would have to be put into effect.

In the event, on the same day, Alexander Fomin, a Soviet embassy official believed to be the local head of Soviet intelligence, contacted John Scali, a newspaper correspondent assigned to the State Department, with the suggestion that the Soviet Union would withdraw its missiles from Cuba under UN inspection if the United States would give an undertaking not to invade the country for the purpose of overthrowing the Castro regime. The Executive Committee gave an encouraging response and the contact was followed by a letter from Chairman Krushchev to President Kennedy to the same effect (though without mentioning UN inspection).

The next day (27th), a formal note from the Soviet Union proposed a withdrawal of the missiles from Cuba in return for a United States withdrawal of its missile bases in Turkey, but President Kennedy decided to act on the previous message, and wrote to Chairman Krushchev accepting its terms though adding UN inspection. On the 28th, the Soviet leader stated that in view of President Kennedy's pledge not to attack Cuba, "the arms you have described as offensive" would be withdrawn and that discussions with the UN Secretary-General on arrangements for this would begin forthwith.

The proposal for UN inspection foundered on the opposition of the Cuban Government. Prime Minister Fidel Castro proclaimed on the 28th his own terms for an ending of the crisis, including the lifting of the United States trade embargo and the evacuation of the United States base at Guantánamo Bay. On the 30th, he informed the UN Secretary-General that he would not admit UN personnel.

President Kennedy, having lifted the blockade on the 30th, re-imposed it again on 1 November. The Soviet Union sought to appease the wounded feelings of the Cubans, the United States to appease criticism from the Latin American countries that it had not ended Cuban subversion. Meanwhile, the withdrawal of the missiles went ahead under United States aerial and naval surveillance. By 20 November, the missiles had gone and on that day the blockade was finally ended.

*　　*　　*

E. ABEL: *The Missile Crisis*, Lippincott, Philadelphia 1966.

A. GEORGE and others: *The Limits of Coercive Diplomacy, Laos, Cuba, Vietnam*, Little Brown & Co., Boston 1971.

D. LARSON (ed.): *The Cuban Crisis of 1962, Selected Documents and Chronology*, Houghton Mifflin, Boston 1963.

A. SCHLESINGER: *A Thousand Days*, André Deutsch, London 1965.

Gibraltar 1963-70

GIBRALTAR was captured by the British in 1704 during the War of the Spanish Succession and ceded to them by Spain under Article 10 of the Treaty of Utrecht of 1713.[1] Almost all the inhabitants withdrew to Spain in 1704, the present Gibraltarians being descendents of new immigrants from other parts of the Mediterranean and from Britain.

As the Treaty defined no border, a mile-wide no-man's land was established between the Rock and Spain. In 1838, the British placed a line of sentries at the half-way mark, replacing this with a fence in 1908, at which date the British Foreign Secretary, Sir Edward Grey, formally notified Spain that his government considered the enclosed area to be British-administered territory. Having built a racecourse there, the British converted this into an airstrip in 1938 and into a runway in the course of the Second World War.

When the dispute over Gibraltar became acute in the mid-1960s, Spain denied that the British had acquired rights by occupation to this "neutral ground" and argued that Spain had repeatedly protested against the encroachment. Britain argued, on the other hand, that Spain's occasional protests had concerned specific issues such as construction works and that it had acquiesced in British control of the patch of ground and had forfeited any title it may at one time have possessed.[2]

Spain also complained that Gibraltar was being used for large-scale smuggling into Spain (to which the British replied that their efforts to prevent smuggling would have been even more successful with Spanish co-operation) and protested against the military use of the aircraft runway and its links with the North Atlantic Treaty Organisation (though it should be noted in this connection that Spain itself accepted United States Air Force bases). Spain claimed overall that Britain had disregarded the limitations laid down by Article 10 of the Treaty of Utrecht on the exercise of its sovereignty and had thus "impaired the legal basis of the British presence on the Rock."[3]

As to why Spain decided to press its claim to Gibraltar in the mid-1960s, one explanation frequently given concerns Spanish domestic politics; the regime of General Franco, faced with internal discontents, would welcome

---

[1] The text is given in: House of Commons (Cmnd. 2632), p. 13; Ministerio de Asuntos Exteriores (1965), p. 155; Stewart, p. 267.
[2] House of Commons (Cmnd. 3131), p. 62.
[3] Fawcett, p. 239.

a national victory abroad. Another concerns developments in the relations of Britain with Gibraltar after the Second World War, as with its other similar possessions in the world.

Britain's interest in possessing Gibraltar had from the outset been strategic, especially naval; Gibraltar controlled the entrance to the Mediterranean. After the Second World War, with the changes in Britain's position in the world and the developments in strategy, this interest diminished. Simultaneously, Britain made constitutional changes in Gibraltar. This was stimulated by the birth of the Association for the Advancement of Civil Rights, which quickly became Gibraltar's main political party. In 1950 Gibraltar received a constitution by which the legislative powers previously held by the Governor were vested in a Legislative Council, half of whom were to be elected members.

In January 1954, the Spanish Government deprecated (unavailingly), as liable to jeopardise good relations, the proposed visit of Queen Elizabeth II to Gibraltar, "a piece of Spanish territory the reclamation of which our people does not renounce".[4] In April, it placed certain restrictions on movements between Spain and the Rock and occasionally over the next nine years reiterated its claim.

The acute phase of the dispute opened in September 1963 when the United Nations Committee of Twenty-Four on decolonisation[5] took up the case of Gibraltar. Spain decided to urge its case before the Committee. Gibraltar, it argued, was a colonial territory on Spanish soil.

In April 1964, Britain announced a new constitution for Gibraltar giving its inhabitants still greater autonomy. The Legislative Council was to consist of eleven members elected by proportional representation and two *ex officio* members; the Executive Council, transformed and renamed the Gibraltar Council, was to be responsible for government, subject only to certain powers reserved to the Governor and the British Government.

In the summer of 1964, the British Labour Opposition (which became the Government after elections in October) attacked the sale of frigates to Spain. At the September meeting of the Committee of Twenty-Four Spain denounced the new Gibraltar constitution as a sham decolonisation designed to deceive the world and cheat Spain of its rights. As in 1963, the Chief Minister of Gibraltar, Sir Joshua Hassan, and the Opposition leader, Mr Peter Isola, came before the Committee to testify to the wish of the Gibraltarians to remain British. Spain argued, however, that under cover of self-determination for some 18,000 people who had come to Gibraltar under the British occupation, Britain was perpetuating a colonialist situation in relation to Spain. The more Britain gave control of Gibraltar

[4] Ministerio de Asuntos Exteriores (1965), p. 285.
[5] See p. 211 (Angola).

to these people, the more a provision of Article 10 of the Treaty of Utrecht applied: "And in case it shall hereafter seem meet to the Crown of Great Britain to grant, sell, or by any means to alienate therefrom the propriety of the said town of Gibraltar, it is hereby agreed, and concluded, that the preference of having the same shall always be given to the Crown of Spain before any others."[6]

On 16 October 1964, the Committee of Twenty-Four adopted a consensus motion, noting that there was a "disagreement, even a dispute, between the United Kingdom and Spain over the status and situation of the territory of Gibraltar" and inviting the parties to "undertake conversations in order to find . . . a negotiated solution", bearing in mind the provisions of General Assembly Resolution 1514 of 14 December 1960 on the Granting of Independence to Colonial Peoples. The British representative objected to this, stating that there was no dispute because there was no conflict between the provisions of the Treaty of Utrecht and the application of the principle of self-determination to the people of Gibraltar. The British Government was not prepared to discuss the question of sovereignty over Gibraltar with Spain. They could only be guided by the wishes of the Gibraltarians themselves.

On the day after the consensus motion, Spain began to reduce its trade links with Gibraltar and to restrict traffic across the frontier. Two thousand Spanish women who worked on the Rock were forbidden to continue doing so, although for the time being the several thousand Spanish men who worked there were allowed to continue.

In the diplomatic exchanges which followed, Britain said that it was willing to discuss ways in which good relations could be maintained but not so long as the restrictions continued. In December 1965, the UN General Assembly passed a resolution "inviting Spain and the United Kingdom to begin, without delay" the talks envisaged under the Committee of Twenty-Four consensus motion. The Assembly was to be informed of their outcome.

Talks were held in May, July, September and October 1966 but with little result. The atmosphere was intensified by Spain's continued tightening of the restrictions on Gibraltar. All traffic was prohibited and all imports into Gibraltar by land were cut off. These restrictions had a great effect on the Gibraltarian economy which had grown up on the basis of interdependence with the neighbouring areas of Spain. Nevertheless, the economy was successfully adapted to the changed circumstances. Early in 1965 the Senior Economic Advisor to the British Colonial Office had visited Gibraltar and by mid-June the Gibraltar Government had completed their studies of his report and informed the Colonial Secretary of

[6] Ministerio de Asuntos Exteriores (1965), p. 442 ff.

their plans to adjust the economy to the new situation. In this they were assisted by the British Ministry of Overseas Development and by a Colonial Development and Welfare Grant of £1 million. Further British assistance was made available in the following years.

On 10 October 1966, the United Kingdom proposed that the dispute be referred to the International Court of Justice for adjudication but Spain rejected this. In December the UN General Assembly adopted another resolution calling for the resumption of talks and asking the United Kingdom to "expedite without any hindrance and in consultation with the Government of Spain the decolonisation of Gibraltar".

In April 1967, Spain announced the imposition of a Prohibited Air Zone in the Algeciras area. This affected the air routes into Gibraltar and led to the postponement of talks scheduled to begin on 18 April. Talks were resumed in June but little progress was made. Spain adhered to its proposal, unacceptable to Britain, for a convention transferring Gibraltar to Spain, after which Spain would allow Britain to retain its military base in Gibraltar and would give certain guarantees to the Gibraltarians, who were to be allowed to remain British if they wished.

In September 1967 Britain held a referendum in Gibraltar, in which the inhabitants were given the choice of either passing under Spanish sovereignty on the basis of Spain's proposals or of retaining their links with Britain. In the event, 12,138 voted "for Britain" and 44 for Spain. In December, the UN General Assembly's Trusteeship Committee condemned the referendum as contrary to the UN resolutions.

In March 1968, talks were again held in Madrid but quickly broke down. In July, new constitutional discussions were held in Gibraltar against which Spain protested. In December, the UN General Assembly passed a resolution calling on Britain to end the "colonial situation" in Gibraltar not later than 1 October 1969. The voting was 67 votes to 18 with 34 abstentions, the main supporters of the resolution being non-Commonwealth Afro-Asian, Latin American and Communist states. Britain voted against this resolution as against that of 1967, on the grounds that it ignored the wishes of the Gibraltarians whose interests, according to Article 73 of the UN Charter, must be paramount. In a conflict between the Charter and a General Assembly resolution, the former must prevail.

In May 1969, Gibraltar received a new constitution under which it remained "part of Her Majesty's dominions" as a self-governing community. The Governor was to remain responsible for foreign affairs, defence and internal security. Spain protested strongly and on 8 June closed the land border completely with the result that the some 5,000 Spanish workmen could no longer work in Gibraltar. The deficiency was in part remedied by the use of Moroccan labour and supplies. On the

27th, the Algeciras–Gibraltar ferry service was suspended, so virtually isolating Gibraltar from the mainland. During the rest of 1969, Anglo-Spanish tension over Gibraltar persisted. At the turn of the year, behind-the-scenes attempts were being made by the British and Spanish authorities to end the deadlock. Later in 1970, internal political troubles in Spain reduced the attention paid to the problem, which continued unresolved.

*   *   *

HOUSE OF COMMONS: *Parliamentary Papers: Gibraltar, Recent Differences with Spain*, Cmnd. 2632, April 1965; *Gibraltar, Talks with Spain, May–October 1966*, Cmnd. 3131, November 1966; *Further Documents on Gibraltar, October 1966–June 1967*, Cmnd. 3325.

MINISTERIO DE ASUNTOS EXTERIORES: *A Red Book on Gibraltar*, Non-official translation, Madrid 1965; *Negotiations on Gibraltar, A New Spanish Red Book*, Non-official translation, Madrid 1968.

J. D. STEWART: *Gibraltar*, John Murray, London 1967.

A. BOYD: "Gibraltar", *The Quarterly Review*, January 1967.

J. FAWCETT: "Gibraltar, The Legal Issues", *International Affairs*, April 1967.

Indonesia - Malaysia 1963-66

NORTH BORNEO and Sarawak, hitherto British protectorates, the one administered by the British North Borneo Company, the other ruled by the Brooke family, became British Crown Colonies in 1946. The Sultanate of Brunei remained a British protectorate. In the late 1950s, the British encouraged greater administrative and economic co-operation between the three territories in preparation for their eventual independence. Some progress was made between North Borneo and Sarawak but the Sultan of Brunei stood aloof.

In the course of a speech on 27 May 1961, the Prime Minister of Malaya, Tunku Abdul Rahman, made the unexpected and momentous remark that a plan should be sought whereby Malaya, Singapore and these three territories could be "brought closer together in political and economic co-operation". The origins of this idea and the motives behind it are not yet known publicly but the broad explanation is generally said to be as follows.

The Singapore, Malayan, British and, in the background, the United States governments were all anxious about the future of Singapore, which had achieved internal self-government on 3 June 1959. Lee Kuan Yew, its Prime Minister, had long been pledged to re-creating the links between Singapore and Malaya, ended by the British at the behest of the Malayans after the Second World War. This was the way to secure complete independence of the British and the future prosperity of the island. Lately, he had further grounds in the growing strength of the Communists among the predominantly Chinese population. Merger with Malaya might help to counter them. For its part, Malaya, independent of Britain since 31 August 1957 after prolonged Communist insurrection, was alarmed at the possibility of Communism on its doorstep; Britain was worried about the Communist threat to Singapore as a great strategic and commercial centre; both agreed that merger with Malaya might be the answer.

As to the inclusion of North Borneo, Brunei and Sarawak, the British Government had to provide somehow for the future of these territories. The slow process of forging them into a unit capable of separate, independent statehood was looking steadily less attractive. At this time, Indonesia was at the height of its "anti-colonialist" campaign to drive the Dutch out of West New Guinea[1] and the three territories might well be its next target. The best course might be to associate them with Malaya forthwith.

[1] See pp. 85–6.

243

The Malayan Government had little love for Indonesia, at least under President Sukarno. The Malayan leaders remembered Sukarno's old dream of uniting all the Malays under one rule as in the days of the mediaeval Javanese empire. They disliked his brand of "neutralism" between the Communist and Western powers and his general style in foreign policy. The Indonesians maintained links with the largest of the opposition parties in Malaya, the Pan-Malayan Islamic Party. The Malayans had their links in Sumatra, chronically discontented under Javanese rule and lately in rebellion.

However, so far as is known, competition with Indonesia was not the reason why Malaya agreed to take North Borneo, Brunei and Sarawak under its wing. Rather, it is said, the reason was yet again Singapore. The Malays in previous years had pressed the British to end Malaya's link with Singapore because they feared that the Singapore Chinese joined to the Malaya Chinese would swamp them. They were still apprehensive of this aspect of the merger with Singapore. Bringing in the three territories would help to create a counterbalance.

Beyond this there was more general reasoning. A high proportion of the population of the three territories was of similar Malay or Chinese culture; all concerned had experienced British rule; the distance of several hundred miles of water was after all as nothing compared with the archipelagian spread of Indonesia; the moderate commercial links with the three territories might burgeon into a great common economic development. Still wider ideas may have been influential. In these years, the British gave many other instances of a passion for improbable federations as a solution to the problem of small bits of empire. Again, schemes for associations were everywhere in the air in south-east Asia, often diplomatic in significance though pitched primarily in economic terms in emulation of the European Economic Community. An Association of South-East Asia was proclaimed by Malaya, the Philippines and Thailand in July 1961, two months after Malaya's initiative regarding Singapore and the three Borneo territories.

Having tested public reactions by the Tunku's speech, the governments concerned acted swiftly. The Singapore Government announced its agreement in principle in September and the British Government in November, subject to the views of the Sultan of Brunei and of the people of North Borneo and Sarawak. The Tunku would consult with the Sultan; a British–Malayan commission under Lord Cobbold would assess opinion in the other two territories. The following June (1962), the Commission reported that about a third of the population favoured the proposed union, a third found it acceptable subject to various safeguards, and a third objected in varying degrees. The British members favoured a transition period of three to seven years but the Malayan members argued for speed to avoid confusion and tension. The governments accepted this and announced (August) that the Federation of Malaysia would be established a year later on 31 August 1963.

Meanwhile, however, opposition to the plan had been growing in south-east Asia at large. In the autumn of 1961, the Singapore Communists launched a campaign against it. By the end of the following year, they had been beaten in the contest for Singapore opinion by the government of Lee Kuan Yew but their opposition continued. In December 1961, the Indonesian Communists also launched a propaganda campaign, declaring that the plan was a device to perpetuate colonialist influence and strategic strength in the region. For the time being, however, the Indonesian Government voiced no objection.

It was the Philippine Government which first decided to have its say in the affair. The new President, Diosdado Macapagal, revived a claim which he had mooted in 1950 that the cession of North Borneo in 1878 by the Sultan of Sulu (now part of the Philippines) was invalid. He was worried, he said, that the link with Singapore would lead to increased Communist penetration of the territories. A press campaign began in the Philippines early in 1962. The House of Representatives passed a resolution supporting the claim in April. The Philippine Government made it formally to Britain in June. In July, the President proposed that the Philippines and the countries of the projected federation should join together in an Asian, not a British scheme, a Confederation of Greater Malaya.

At this time also, serious opposition to the Malaysia plan began in the Sultanate of Brunei, though many of the details are obscure. Despite the persuasive efforts of Tunku Abdul Rahman and the British, the Sultan, it seems, had deep doubts about submerging his kingdom in the projected federation. A local leader of the non-Malays, Inche Azahari, whose People's Party won all the elected seats in the Legislative Council in August, developed a scheme for uniting the three Borneo territories in independence under the Sultan. He went off to Manila and his associates also angled for the support of Indonesian groups in Kalimantan (Indonesian Borneo). Finally, on 8 December, an insurrection broke out; the rebels tried to seize the person of the Sultan; Azahari in Manila proclaimed the Revolutionary State of North Kalimantan. The insurrection was disorganised and the British had suppressed it by the 17th. However, after hopeful negotiations the following spring (1963), the Sultan finally decided in the summer that Brunei would not join in Malaysia.

The development of opposition in Brunei gave impetus to the now growing opposition of President Sukarno of Indonesia. After a period of violent troubles in the late 1950s, politics in Indonesia consisted basically of a tense balance between three forces, the President, the Communists, and the Army. President Sukarno had perhaps long had covert reservations about the Malaysia plan: he had great aspirations for Indonesia; the Borneo territories might one day have passed to Indonesia; he did not like the Malayan Government and its friendliness towards the West; he detested Britain's sponsorship of schemes for the region. Besides, the Communists were against Malaysia, and the President and the Army had reason to follow suit in what was potentially a new, highly popular campaign against the colonialists. In August 1962, Indonesia won its long "confrontation" with the Netherlands over West Irian. During a United Nations General Assembly debate on that issue, the Indonesian Foreign Minister had stated publicly that Indonesia had raised no objection to the idea of Malaysia and wished it success (20 November 1961). Now in September 1962, the Indonesian Government stated that the idea of Malaysia was being reappraised. In February 1963, Sukarno declared that there must be a "confrontation" on the issue. On 12 April, the first clearly Indonesian guerrilla attack occurred at Tabedu in Sarawak.

By this time, the Filipino Government had begun to take on a conciliatory role in the triangular situation, Malaya, Indonesia, the Philippines. Following tripartite official talks, Tunku Abdul Rahman and President Sukarno met in Tokyo (31 May). The latter asked for delay in implementing the Malaysia scheme. On 11 June, the Foreign Ministers of the three countries met in Manila and discussed a still broader version of the Filipino Asian, non-British scheme: Maphilindo, an association of Malaya, the Philippines and Indonesia.

On 9 July, the Agreement establishing the Federation of Malaysia was signed in London. President Sukarno was furious, declaring that in Tokyo the Tunku had promised to delay final action on the scheme (the Tunku denied this) and that at Manila all had agreed to the holding of a UN enquiry in the three territories. In a mass-audience speech, he declared that Malaysia must be "crushed" (27th).

Under Filipino persuasion, Sukarno none the less came to a planned meeting of the three heads of government at Manila (1–5 August). Here, Tunku Abdul Rahman agreed to a short delay in the proclamation of Malaysia, pending a UN enquiry. With Britain's permission, a request was sent to the UN Secretary-General, U Thant; his enquiry team, with Indonesian and Filipino observers, began work on 16 August; his conclusion announced on 14 September was that "a sizeable majority" of the population of Sarawak and Sabah (the traditional and now official name for North Borneo) wished to join in Malaysia. The new Federation was thereupon proclaimed on 17 September.

Two days previously, however, the Indonesian Government queried the

UN findings and declared that it considered the Federation "illegal" and that it would not recognise it. The Filipino Government, which had reserved the right at the Manila Conference to pursue its claim to Sabah whether the Federation was established or not, also withheld recognition. In Djakarta, the British and Malaysian embassies were burned (18th) and British companies were taken under government "protection" and, by stages over the following year, under government control. Guerrilla attacks in Sabah and Sarawak intensified with increasing participation of Indonesian regular units.

Australia, Britain and New Zealand sent troops to assist the Malaysians. The Soviet Union sent increased armaments to Indonesia, and China gave propaganda support. In January 1964, as the Philippines continued its conciliatory efforts, the United States Attorney-General, Robert F. Kennedy, visited President Sukarno but to little effect. Following a meeting of the Malaysian and Indonesian foreign ministers at Bangkok in February, the UN Secretary-General requested Thailand to provide a cease-fire supervisor but there was at best a lull in the fighting. At a further meeting at Bangkok in March, the Malaysian Foreign Minister insisted that the guerrilla attacks must cease before political discussions could begin, whereas the Indonesian Foreign Minister insisted on the converse.

On 24 April, the United States announced the suspension of its economic aid to Indonesia so long as the confrontation lasted. However, at a meeting of the three heads of government at Tokyo in June, the same impasse was reached as at the Bangkok conference in March.

The confrontation widened that summer with bomb incidents in Singapore and the first of a series of attacks on the east coast of Malaya. Malaysia appealed to the Security Council but a mildly worded Norwegian resolution was vetoed by the Soviet Union (17 September). On 1 January 1965, Indonesia withdrew from the United Nations in indignation at the seating of Malaysia on the Security Council. Its relations with both the Soviet Union and China strengthened continually, as did the standing of the Indonesian Communist Party. Relations with the United States continued to deteriorate. Control of all foreign companies in Indonesia was completed in April 1965.

That summer, the Federation of Malaysia was shaken when a steadily growing quarrel between the Singapore and Malayan governments culminated in the withdrawal of Singapore (9 August). However, at this very moment, Indonesia was becoming less well placed to continue the confrontation. The crisis in Djakarta in the autumn marked the beginning of the end. On the night of 30 September–1 October, a group of middle-rank military officers organised the arrest and killing of six army generals who, they said, were plotting to seize power from President Sukarno. They then proclaimed a new revolutionary government. The extent to which this was an attempt by the Communists to seize power remains controversial.[2] The outcome was, however, that the high command crushed the movement, and over the next few weeks many thousands of Communists and Chinese in Indonesia were massacred.

From this time on, Indonesia's confrontation with Malaysia was at a standstill. President Sukarno was unable to re-establish his position and on 13 March 1966, surrendered wide executive powers to Lt.-General Suharto. Dr Subandrio, the Foreign Minister, a powerful protagonist of confrontation, was dismissed, and his successor Adam Malik straightway indicated that Indonesia wished to bring the affair to an end. Two rounds of discussion between the two countries in Bangkok led to an agreement which included the following formula: the people of Sabah and Sarawak would be given the opportunity of reaffirming "in a free and democratic manner through general elections their previous decision about their status in Malaysia". Among many other points covered on relations between the two countries, no mention was made of Western defence arrangements with Malaysia, long a principal point in the denunciation of it as a colonialist scheme. On the contrary, discussions began between the two countries on problems of security against Communism. The Philippines, which had redoubled its conciliatory efforts, now recognised Malaysia, though it still reserved its claim in relation to Sabah. After objections by Sukarno, still with some influence, the agreement was finally signed in Djakarta by the foreign ministers of Indonesia and Malaysia on 11 August.

*　　　　　*　　　　　*

R. Allen: *Malaysia, Prospect and Retrospect*, Oxford University Press, 1968.

A. Brackman: *Southeast Asia's Second Front, The Power Struggle in the Malay Archipelago*, Praeger, New York 1966.

B. Grant: *Indonesia*, Penguin Books, Harmondsworth, rev. ed., 1967.

G. P. Means: *Malaysian Politics*, University of London Press, 1970.

J. Pluvier: *Confrontations, A Study in Indonesian Politics*, Oxford University Press, 1965.

[2] See L. Palmier, The 30 September Movement in Indonesia, *Modern Asian Studies*, January 1971.

The Panama Canal 1964

In 1903, Panama declared itself independent of Colombia; the United States recognised it; and the two countries concluded the Hay-Bunau-Varilla Treaty establishing United States rights in relation to the projected Panama Canal. By Article II, the United States was granted "in perpetuity the use, occupation and control of a zone of land and land under water for the construction, maintenance, operation, sanitation and protection of the Canal". The width of the Zone was to be ten miles. Article III granted the United States "all the rights, powers, and authority within the Zone which the United States would possess and exercise if it were the sovereign of the territory . . . to the entire exclusion of the exercise by the Republic of Panama of any such sovereign rights".

Panamanian nationalists later argued that their country had been forced into this Treaty. They were also angered by what seemed to them a "colonialist mentality" on the part of the inhabitants of the Zone, United States citizens known colloquially as Zonians. The report of the International Commission of Jurists in 1964 said it was "unfortunate that the United States citizens who have lived all their lives in the Canal Zone and, perhaps more particularly, the second and third generation United States citizens who were born and raised in the Zone, have developed a particular state of mind not conducive to the promotion of happier relations between them and the people of Panama. Indeed, on the contrary, this particular state of mind has resulted in building up resentment over the decades".[1]

Panamanians felt that the annuity which their country received from the United States Government in return for control of the Canal (raised in 1955 to $1,930,000) was grossly insufficient. They compared this with the higher Egyptian earnings from the Suez Canal even before its nationalisation in 1956. They also alleged discrimination against them concerning wages and employment opportunities in the Zone. Until 1946, Zonians were paid in gold, Panamanians in silver; thereafter, there was a United States rate for a job and a Panamanian. Panamanians further felt that Panamanian private enterprise should have greater access to the markets of the Zone.

Strategic and commercial factors explain the United States interest in the control of the Canal. In the Second World War, it enabled the United States Navy "to rendezvous anywhere in the world in three weeks or

[1] International Commission of Jurists, p. 42.

less".[2] The Zone was also an important military base. The strategic value of the Canal was increasingly questioned in the nuclear age but the United States Defense Department none the less rated it important in the mid-1960s. As to its commercial value, it shortened the New York–San Francisco sea route, for example, by nearly 8,000 nautical miles and the New York–Yokohama by over 5,000.

Tension between Panama and the United States began to mount in the late 1950s, strengthened by the Suez Canal crisis of 1956. In May 1958, Panamanian students planted flags in the Zone, symbolising their country's rights and aspirations. On 3 November 1959, Panama's Independence Day, there were riots in Panama City on the flag issue. In April 1960, President Eisenhower announced a nine-point programme for improving United States–Panama relations and in September, despite the opposition shown by Congress to such a concession, directed that the Panamanian flag be flown with that of the United States at Shaler Triangle (in the Zone), apparently as a gesture to confirm recognition of Panama's titular sovereignty over the Zone.

In late 1961, President Roberto Chiari requested the renegotiation of the Canal Treaty. In discussions in Washington in June 1962, President Kennedy indicated, it seems, that renegotiation would be inopportune; United States public opinion was sensitive; current ideas for a new sea-level canal in the region would anyway require a review of the entire situation in a few years' time. It was agreed, however, that a joint commission should be established to look into the problems of the Zone.

On 10 January 1963, the Commission decided that wherever the United States flag was flown in the Zone, the Panamanian should be flown also. This concession irritated and alarmed the Zonians. On 7 January 1964, Zonian students at the Balboa High School, encouraged by some parents and in defiance of the Zone authorities, raised the United States flag outside their school. On the 9th, Panamanian students, incensed by this gesture, entered the Zone in an unsuccessful attempt to raise the Panamanian flag at the school. Then followed four days of violence. There was continuous sniping at Zone targets from Panama and some penetrations further into the territory. There were demonstrations in the Republic and riots in the Zone. The Zone Police were inadequate to deal with the situation and United States troops were used. Twenty people were reported killed, including four United States citizens, and several hundred were reported wounded. However, the troops were able to contain the rioters and the Canal itself operated almost normally.

In accounting for this outbreak, personalities may be important. Joseph Farland, the popular United States Ambassador to Panama, had resigned

[2] Sixth Hammarskjöld Forum, p. 9.

in the summer of 1963 (in disagreement with his government's policies). The International Commission of Jurists criticised the Zone authorities for weakness towards their students on the flag issue.[3] The availability of snipers and "Molotov cocktails" suggests a degree of premeditation in the affair but the leaders have never been satisfactorily identified. United States officials suspected that Communists were involved. Others have suggested that the riots were planned by Fidel Castro to divert the attention of the Organisation of American States from considering the accusation of President Rómulo Betancourt against him of subversion in Venezuela.

The riots ended on 12 January when the Panamanian army, the Guardia Nacional, finally took action. However, on the 10th Panama had broken off relations with United States, alleging "acts of aggression", and President Chiari had declared that they would not be resumed until the United States agreed to renegotiate the Canal Treaty. On the same day, Panama requested both the United Nations Security Council and the Council of the OAS to deal with the "unprovoked armed aggression" of the United States. President Johnson talked with President Chiari (by telephone) and sent a Special Mission to Panama under Thomas C. Mann, Assistant Secretary of State for Inter-American Affairs.

Panama's case was dealt with first by the Inter-American Peace Committee. For three weeks after the rioting, the Committee, consisting of representatives of Argentina, Colombia, the Dominican Republic and Chile (which replaced the United States in view of the latter's involvement in the dispute) tried to work out a peace formula and get diplomatic relations resumed. These efforts foundered on the issue of the Canal Treaty, Panama insisting that there be negotiations, the United States offering only discussions. Panama's attitude can be explained in terms of the presidential elections to be held in May. The events of 9–12 January had provoked the public to insist on renegotiation in a way which no candidate could afford to ignore.

On 29 January, Panama formally requested the Council of the OAS, under Article 6 of the Rio Treaty, to call a meeting of the Organ of Consultation. On 4 February, the Council heard Panama's complaint and resolved to constitute itself a provisional Organ of Consultation. On the 7th, a seventeen-nation committee (that is, all the OAS members not party to the dispute except Bolivia which withdrew) was established to investigate and mediate. This committee sent a five-nation sub-committee to Panama to investigate. No public report was issued but the members refused to find the United States guilty of the Panamanian charge of aggression. After the mission, the sub-committee mediated between the parties.

On 3 April, an agreement was reached. Diplomatic relations were to be

[3] International Commission of Jurists, p. 40.

resumed and the parties were "to designate without delay special ambassadors with sufficient powers to seek the prompt elimination of the causes
of conflict between the two countries, without limitation or preconditions
of any kind". The "ambassadors designated will begin immediately the
necessary procedures with the object of reaching a just and fair agreement
which would be subject to the constitutional process of each country".[4]

This agreement marked the end of the crisis. It was greeted as a victory
in Panama. Action on it later proved slow but the new Panamanian
President, Marco Robles, who had been supported by Chiari, was in a
better position than his predecessor. Although anxious for treaty revision
and aware of its importance for maintaining popular support, he did not
have the same constricting electoral considerations. When on 4 July,
Panamanian students protested against United States policies, they were
vigorously dispersed by the Guardia Nacional.

The dispute continued over the following years in a lower key. In the
talks between the special ambassadors, Robert Anderson and Jorge Illueca,
which began in May, the United States could not accept that it had agreed
to "negotiations", and Panama was, it seems, distracted by exploration of
the possibility of taking the lead itself in the building of a new sea-level
canal. At length, on 18 December, President Johnson announced two
decisions. The first was to press forward together with Panama and other
interested countries with studies of four possible routes for a new sea-level
canal (the line of the existing canal; to the south of it, in Darién; in
Colombia; in Nicaragua). The second was to negotiate a new treaty for the
existing canal.

Negotiations began in January 1965 and in September, President
Johnson announced that basic agreement had been reached. The new
treaty would abrogate that of 1903, recognise Panama's sovereignty,
terminate after a specific number of years or with the opening of the
proposed sea-level canal, whichever was sooner, and provide for the
assimilation of the Canal Zone into the economy of Panama. In June 1967,
it was announced that a draft treaty had been completed on this, another
on defence arrangements for the Canal, and a third on a new sea-level
canal across Darién. The drafts were not made public but the broad
provisions became known. That relating to the existing canal was understood to provide *inter alia* for a much smaller Zone to be administered
under Panamanian sovereignty by a Canal Authority consisting of five
United States and four Panamanian representatives. This was ill-received
by Panamanian public opinion. The country underwent a period of
political turmoil before and after the 1968 presidential elections, leading to
a *coup d'état* by officers of the Guardia Nacional. The successive regimes

[4] Sixth Hammarskjöld Forum, p. 6.

all declared that the treaties, and especially that relating to the existing Canal, were not sufficiently favourable to Panama.

*   *   *

J. Dubois: *Danger Over Panama*, The Bobbs-Merrill Company Inc., Indianapolis 1964.

Georgetown University, The Center for Strategic Studies: *Panama, Canal Issues and Treaty Talks*, Washington D.C., 1967.

International Commission of Jurists: *Report on Events in Panama, 9–12 January 1964*, Geneva 1964.

S. B. Liss: *The Canal: Aspects of United States–Panamanian Relations*, University of Notre Dame Press, Notre Dame 1967.

Sixth Hammarskjöld Forum: *The Panama Canal, Background Papers and Proceedings*, Oceana Publications Inc., New York 1965.

M. O. Tate: "The Panama Canal and Political Partnership", *The Journal of Politics*, February 1963.

The Dominican Republic 1965-66

IN the generations after independence from Spain (1821) and from Haiti (1844) the affairs of the Dominican Republic were often violent politically and increasingly chaotic financially. A climax was reached in the early years of this century and in 1905, the United States established a financial receivership and from 1916 to 1924 sent in Marines both to back this and to prevent civil war. Then followed from 1930 the long dictatorship of General Rafael Leonidas Trujillo, during which there was comparative peace and some growth in prosperity but no political freedom.

By the 1950s, the Trujillo dictatorship was widely considered in Latin America to be a hateful anachronism, and towards the end of the decade the United States Administration, fearing "guilt by association" in the popular mind, began to be concerned once more with the country's constitution. This concern was greatly intensified when Batista of Cuba fell to Castro's revolutionaries in January 1959;[1] unless Trujillo made concessions, he too might similarly be overthrown, followed by renewed chaos or perhaps another Castro. The Administration, together with the Organisation of American States as a whole, began to exert pressure on Trujillo for greater respect for human rights and for the holding of free elections. The climax of the quarrel came when Venezuela charged Trujillo with responsibility for a plot to assassinate its President, Rómulo Betancourt, and the OAS passed a resolution recommending the breaking-off of diplomatic relations, a ban on arms sales and a cut in United States sugar purchases (18 August 1960).

On 30 May 1961, Trujillo was assassinated by political enemies. In the tense period which then ensued, responsibility fell to Joaquín Balaguer, installed in the presidency by Trujillo the previous August. The United States was deeply involved in the course of events, in particular warning the Trujillo family that it would intervene with force to prevent a seizure of power by them. At length, on 20 December 1962, elections were held and Dr Juan Bosch, an exile under Trujillo and leader of the Partido Revolucionario Dominicano, won a great popular victory with United States approval.

Popular enthusiasm cooled rapidly when President Bosch's first pre-occupation proved to be, not social revolution, but austerity measures to get the Government's finances to rights. When the reform programme

[1] See p. 174ff.

254

began to get under way the following spring (1963), it was not of a kind to bring quick benefits to the people and meanwhile it alarmed the most powerful sections of the community. The new constitution (April) antagonised the Church by proclaiming the separation of Church and State and authorising divorce, and landowners by extending the powers of the State over property. After the announcement of a large public works programme (June), two measures of land reform were put forward (July), notably a Confiscation Bill which would give the Congress powers to confiscate land deemed to have been acquired illicitly under the Trujillo regime. Many landowners denounced this as a device to justify large-scale expropriation without compensation and, aided by rumours that some appointees to official positions were Communists, talk of the threat of Castroism and Communism began. The business community, apprehensive from the outset of Bosch's popular promises and dubious of his administrative competence, by now had no good word to say for him. On 25 September, the Army high command turned Bosch out of office and he went into exile in Puerto Rico.

The army commanders, headed by General Elías Wessin y Wessin, decided that their best course was not to rule directly but to instal instead a committee of civilians. The United States was at first cool towards this regime. It had been disappointed by Bosch and retained henceforth a low estimate of his capacity to control events. On the other hand, it deplored the setback to constitutional government involved in his overthrow by the military. After a while, however, it was mollified by the promise of free elections in September 1965.

As 1965 opened, political tension increased once more. The civilian committee had always been unpopular and Donald Reid Cabral, a businessman, now its chairman, deepened this unpopularity and at the same time antagonised the army by his manoeuvres regarding the proposed elections and by austerity and efficiency measures affecting the public generally and the trading privileges and the budget of the armed services.

On 24 April, a group of army colonels declared a revolt against the Government and the next day forced Reid Cabral to resign and proclaimed Rafael Molina Ureña provisional President. The army high command was at first unsure of its attitude but soon it became clear that some of the rebel colonels favoured bringing back Juan Bosch, if only because he represented constitutionality, and that the whole group was being pulled in that direction by the eruption of street demonstrations in Bosch's favour in Santo Domingo. The previous January, the Christian Socialists had reached agreement with Bosch to co-operate in a return to constitutionality and this had been endorsed by the three small left-wing parties (two Communist and one Castroist) and by a manifesto of two thousand intellectuals and professional men. Street demonstrators, armed by the "constitutionalists", now demanded his immediate return.

General Wessin and the senior commanders, opposed to the return of Bosch and determined to get control of the situation, moved their forces on the capital and fighting began. The constitutionalist leaders appealed to the United States Ambassador, W. Tapley Bennet, for support or mediation (27th) but he refused this. The United States favoured a return to constitutional government but did not equate this with the return of Juan Bosch. Most of the constitutionalist leaders thereupon gave up the struggle but not Colonel Francisco Caamaño Deñó. He reorganised the constitutionalist government in defiance of Wessin y Wessin's junta. His soldiers and various popular militias, including the Castroists, rapidly completed their control of the Ciudad Nueva (the business quarter), seized further stores of arms, and began to extend their control to other quarters of the city. Wessin's troops began to falter.

In this situation, the United States Administration ordered the landing of Marines and airborne troops (28th) standing by since the 25th. One motive was protection of the lives and property of United States citizens; another, the possibility that events might develop in a way favourable to the Castroists and Communists, whether immediately or if Bosch were once again in office.

In taking this action United States officials used language which helped to discredit rather than justify it in the eyes of many in Latin America, the United States, and the world at large. In a message to Washington on the 28th, the United States Ambassador said that "the issue here is now a fight between Castro-type elements and those who oppose them". Taking up this theme, President Johnson said in a broadcast (2 May) that the insurrection had been "taken over" by "a band of Communist conspirators. . . . The American nations cannot, must not and will not permit the establishment of another Communist government in the Western hemisphere." To the derision of liberal opinion, the United States Embassy and the Central Intelligence Agency produced a varying list of 53 to 75 "known Communists" supporting the insurrection which was soon shown to contain many absurdities.

Having landed its troops and secured the Hotel Embajador, where about a thousand United States citizens were gathered, and various tactical points inside and outside the city, the United States Administration sought to have its intervention endorsed at a meeting of the OAS Council on the 29th. The general temper of the meeting was adverse. It resolved to send the Secretary-General, Dr José Mora, to help negotiate a cease-fire; and to convene a Meeting of Consultation which in turn established (1 May) a Special Committee to use its "good offices" between the factions consisting of members from Argentina, Brazil, Colombia, Guatemala and Panama. On 6 May, the Council set up an Inter-American Peace Force to replace the United States force.

At the United Nations Security Council on 3 May, the United States was able to defeat a condemnatory resolution by the Soviet Union, but at the same time, the Council was not content to leave matters to the OAS and appointed its own representative.

The United States did not order its force to attack the constitutionalists in the Ciudad Nueva and a cease-fire between the factions was achieved on 30 April with the Papal Nuncio as intermediary. The United States force was thereupon used to form a cordon between the Ciudad Nueva and the rest of the city, a task taken over by the IAPF on 23 May, though the great majority of its troops continued to be those of the United States.

The OAS Special Committee attempted to use its good offices between the factions but retired ineffectually in mid-May, in part at least because the United States Administration at this stage wanted to retain control over what was done, sending Mr John B. Martin, formerly its Ambassador in the country, to act on its behalf.

As a result of his pressure and persuasion on the Wessin y Wessin junta, they announced (7 May) that a Government of National Reconstruction would be formed under Antonio Imbert Barrera, one of the heroes of the assassination of Trujillo and (because of this) an honorary general. However, the Caamaño faction remained adamant for a return to constitutionality and even moderate opinion proved to be unenthusiastic about the Imbert government.

Next, therefore, the United States Administration sent Mr McGeorge Bundy to talk with Juan Bosch in Puerto Rico, and the outcome was an agreement (15 May) according to which Silvestre Antonio Guzmán, a friend and party colleague of Bosch, should become President for the remainder of Bosch's term of office under the 1963 constitution, followed by elections. This in turn was unacceptable to the Wessin y Wessin faction and the Imbert government.

The United States now concluded that the most acceptable course would be to work through the OAS and to aim at a non-partisan provisional government charged with holding elections rapidly. Accordingly, on 2 June, the OAS Council set up an Ad Hoc Committee consisting of Ellsworth Bunker, United States representative on the Council since 1964, Ilmar Penna Marinho of Brazil and Ramón de Clairmont Dueñas of El Salvador. On the 18th, they published proposals which included an amnesty, the formation of a broadly-based provisional government, the withdrawal of the army from the political scene, and the holding of elections within nine months.

While the response of the Wessin y Wessin faction and the Imbert government was unfavourable, that of the constitutionalists and the public at large was encouraging. The Ad Hoc Committee therefore went ahead and proposed Héctor García Godoy, formerly a diplomatist and a member of Bosch's 1963 government, as provisional President. The constitutionalists voted to agree on 8 July and over the next weeks the United States pressed the Wessin y Wessin faction and the Imbert government to agree also, notably, as regards the Imbert government, by threatening to withdraw budgetary support.

On 3 September, García Godoy took office as provisional President. Over the next few days, Wessin y Wessin showed renewed hostility but, with the assistance of the IAPF, he was removed from his command and posted to the consulate in Miami. Over the ensuing months, there were recurrent clashes and crises but García Godoy survived them successfully.

Finally, on 1 June 1966, under the supervision of UN and OAS missions, the elections took place. To the general surprise, Juan Bosch received only 39 per cent of the votes and the contest was won by the man who had preceded him in office in 1960–62, Joaquín Balaguer. The new President took office on 1 July. The IAPF withdrew from the country on 21 September.

*   *   *

P. CALVERT: *Latin America, Internal Conflict and International Peace*, Macmillan, London 1969.

G. CONNELL-SMITH: *The Inter-American System*, Oxford University Press, 1966.

R. LOGAN: *Haiti and the Dominican Republic*, Oxford University Press, 1968.

A. F. LOWENTHAL: *The Dominican Intervention*, Havard University Press, 1972.

NINTH HAMMARSKJÖLD FORUM: *The Dominican Republic Crisis*, Oceana Publications, Dobbs Ferry 1967.

J. SLATER: *Intervention and Negotiation, The United States and the Dominican Crisis*, Harper and Row, New York 1970.

Nigeria 1966-70

NIGERIA was "perhaps the most artificial of the many administrative units created in the course of the European occupation of Africa".[1] A large country, six hundred miles in either direction and with some fifty million inhabitants, the numerous minority tribes were dominated by three great peoples, different in language and in most other aspects of their traditional cultures: in the north, which amounted to four-fifths of the area and half the population of the country, the Moslem Hausa-Fulani; in the west, the Yoruba; in the east, the Ibo. The latter, generally reckoned the most enterprising and progressive, dwelt in large numbers outside their eastern homeland.

The British organised the country as a federation of North, East and West and the federal territory of Lagos in 1954, and as such it became independent on 1 October 1960. Part of the Western Region, inhabited by some of the minority tribes and by Ibo, was detached to form a Mid-West Region in August 1963.

The Federal President was Nnamdi Azikwe, an Ibo and a politician of great astuteness. Among other leaders, the most powerful was a traditional potentate, the Sardauna of Sokoto, Sir Ahmadu Bello, Prime Minister of the North. He had the allegiance of the Federal Prime Minister, a northerner, Sir Abubakar Tafawa Balewa, and was the senior partner in an alliance with the Western Prime Minister, Chief Samuel Akintola.

The country, while giving a mature and stable impression internationally, was managed and held together by tortuous, behind-the-scenes bargaining by its leaders, and not without considerable tension and trouble. Southerners resented the permanent majority of the more numerous northerners in the federal legislature and their grip on the central government. The Eastern Region disliked parting with a high proportion of the growing oil revenues of the East for the benefit of the rest of the federation. The others, for their part, resented the prosperity and modernity of the Ibo, thought them arrogant, and feared creeping domination of the country by them. In 1963, there was a crisis in the Western Region. In the same year, there was general dispute over the results of the population census, followed by an Eastern Region boycott of the federal elections (December 1964). In 1965, the troubles of the Western Region came to a head with

---

[1] Lord Hailey, *An African Survey Revised, 1957*, Oxford University Press, 1957, p. 307.

accusations that the regional elections (October) had been manipulated by the Government, followed by continual outbreaks of violence.

In January 1966, President Azikwe was away in Britain, convalescing. On the night of the 14th–15th, a group of army majors and captains mounted a *coup d'état* simultaneously in Lagos, Kaduna (capital of the North), Ibadan (West) and, apparently, Enugu (East). Their declared aim, as so often elsewhere in the world in the late 1950s and 1960s, was to rid the country of "the corrupt politicians". They slaughtered the Sardauna, Balewa and Akintola and various other notables. Within a few hours, the Commander of the army, Major-General John Aguiyi-Ironsi, had gained control of the situation in Lagos, and on the following day (the 16th) the Deputy President, with the assent of the Cabinet, suspended the ordinary government of the country and handed over power to him. The *coup* collapsed in the other capitals and the leaders were arrested. General Ironsi appointed a military governor to each region.

In the southern regions of the country there was popular rejoicing at the sweeping away of the old order, but in the North there was straightaway some suspicion that the whole affair was an Ibo conspiracy to seize control of the country. It was noted that almost all the officers who had led the *coup d'état* were Ibos; that, though arrested, they were not punished; that of the high army officers killed, only one was an Ibo; that there had been no killing in Enugu; that General Ironsi himself was an Ibo. Northern suspicions deepened as Ironsi sought to improve the constitution of the country for the future by abolishing the federal structure. On 24 May, he decreed that Nigeria was henceforth to be a unitary state. Instead of regions, there were to be groups of smaller provinces. He further decreed on the same day that the higher civil service of the country would be unified. The first of these measures seemed likely to result in a reduction of the standing of the Hausa-Fulani in the central government; the second, in the domination of the administration of the whole country by Ibo officials, including the North.

In the last days of May, riots and killing of Ibos began in Kano in the North. After a lull, during which Ironsi maintained his policy, a group of northern army majors and their northern soldiers mutinied in Abeokuta and Lagos and the other capitals on the night of 28–29 July and slaughtered Ironsi and many Ibo officers. Then followed three days of prolonged argument among the northerners on whether the North should secede or whether Nigeria should be preserved. Finally, the decision went against secession. Lt.-Colonel Yakubu Gowon, Chief of Staff under Ironsi, a northerner but from a minority tribe and a Christian, was proclaimed head of state and supreme commander.

Gowon was acknowledged in the West and Mid-West and gained some popularity there by releasing Chief Obafemi Awolowo (Yoruba) and Chief Anthony Enahoro (Ishan, Mid-West) imprisoned in 1963. In the East, on the other hand, the Ibo military governor appointed by Ironsi, Lt.-Colonel Emeka Ojukwu, refused to acknowledge Gowon. In the following weeks, the breach between the Ibo and the northerners widened further. There were continuous negotiations among all the regions on the form of the constitution, including a conference of the civilian politicians at Lagos in mid-September, at which, after first favouring a confederation, the northerners argued for a federation. The East's delegation wanted a confederation.

Meanwhile, there was continuing violence against Ibos in the North and retaliation by them. The explosion came on 29 September. Several thousand Ibos and others from Eastern Region tribes were massacred. In one of the great migrations of the world since 1945, about one million Ibos and others fled from the North and about half a million from the other regions to their homeland in the East.

At what point in the following months Ojukwu finally decided on the secession of the East remains uncertain. In a speech of 30 November, Gowon rejected the East's idea of confederation. Moreover, as a concession to the minority tribes (perhaps especially as a blandishment to the minority tribes in the East) he adopted the idea, hotly disputed at the Lagos Conference, of dividing the North and East into smaller states. More was to be heard of this the following spring.

In the interim, on 4–5 January 1967, Gowon and the military governors, including Ojukwu, came together at Aburi in Ghana to thrash out their disagreements. They discussed at length, in an informal style, the composition, status and powers of a central authority for the country. There was rough agreement on ideas put forward by Ojukwu, amounting to a loose confederal structure. Afterwards, however, Gowon and his advisers made no progress in giving detailed, workable shape to this. Ojukwu denounced them for delaying.

On 10 March, Gowon issued a decree which, while strengthening the powers of the regions, provided that the Supreme Military Council might declare a state of emergency in any region and take the necessary action with the assent of only three out of the four military governors. On the 31st, Ojukwu announced the appropriation to the Eastern Region of federal revenues (except oil) and federal corporations. The Supreme Military Council declared in response a blockade of the Eastern Region.

All this time, Gowon and Ojukwu had been competing for the sympathy of the minority tribes and the Western and Mid-West regions. By the end of April, Gowon had persuaded the North to accept the division of North and East into smaller states. In the course of May, he appears to have gained the upper hand in the struggle for Western support, though possibly Ojukwu believed that this would change in the event of Eastern secession.

On 27 May, Ojukwu obtained the mandate of an Eastern Consultative Assembly to proclaim the independent state of Biafra. On the 28th, Gowon took personal power from the Supreme Military Council, declared a state of emergency and simultaneously announced the division of Nigeria into twelve states, Lagos, Western, Mid-Western, six in the old North, and three in the old East, of which one (the East-Central State) was the Ibo homeland. On the 30th, Ojukwu proclaimed Biafra.

In the war which followed, the first major episode was a struggle for the revenues paid in London by the oil companies, British Petroleum and Shell. The Biafrans, able to stop eastern production of oil, demanded that 57 per cent be paid to them and that the rest be suspended; the Nigerians, threatening to blockade the export of oil, demanded that the revenues be paid to them as usual. The companies apparently offered a "token payment" to Biafra of £250,000 (1 July); the Nigerians declared a blockade (2nd); and the British Government prevented the payment.

On 6 July, the Nigerians advanced into Biafra from the north and on the 26th from the south, the coast, also. On 9 August, the Biafrans made a counter-thrust in the centre, into the Mid-West state, deeply divided between the Ibo and the other tribes. Military resistance was negligible, and by the 17th the attack was careering onwards towards Lagos and Ibadan, lightly defended and in uproar. But the column was a small one; it was checked; slowly it was pushed back. By early October, the Mid-West state was under Nigerian control; the northern thrust had taken the Biafran capital, Enugu (4 October); the southern advance continued; and the Biafrans had been beaten back to the Ibo heartland in the centre of Biafra.

Now and for two years, the war became one of attrition, with blockade, some bombing, slow Nigerian advance against bitter resistance, starvation and disease in what remained of Biafra. The resistance of the Biafrans was fortified by a deep fear of massacre, which was further sustained by the speeches of their leader, Ojukwu, and which the counter-promises of Gowon could do little to allay.

Internationally, the struggle was given vast publicity, assisted by the public relations organisations hired by the two sides. Most governments favoured non-intervention. Britain, the country with the deepest sentimental and investment interest, uneasily maintained its traditional supplies of light armaments to the Nigerians. Various sections of the French Government, and President De Gaulle himself, sympathised with the Biafrans and French arms went covertly to them.

The United States Government, while favouring Nigeria, was content to leave the initiative to the British and embargoed arms supplies to either side. The Soviet Union, having had no foothold in Nigeria until 1966, signed technical assistance agreements with the Ironsi regime, and now supplied fighters, bombers and artillery to the Nigerians. China seized on this example of unholy solidarity between the capitalists and the Russian Communists and castigated them all in the cause of Biafra.

In Africa, Rhodesia and South Africa showed sympathy for Biafra, as did Portugal; but most of the members of the Organisation of African Unity, fearful as always of the chaos which might ensue if the continent's inherited borders were called in question, supported the continued unity of Nigeria. At their annual summit conference in September 1967 (at Kinshasa) they appointed a Consultative Committee, but its spirit was not neutral and it did not visit Biafra.

The Nigerians were, in any case, opposed to international mediation, fearing that this would enhance the standing of Biafra. On these grounds, and because the OAU was held competent, there was little movement at the United Nations. Similarly, the efforts of the Commonwealth Secretariat to bring the two sides together, which came to a climax in September 1967, proved fruitless.

In April–May 1968, the morale of the Biafrans was boosted by recognition by Tanzania, Gabon, Ivory Coast, Zambia and Haiti. They also had the sympathy of Ghana. The motives of these states were various but one element, especially it seems in the case of Tanzania and Zambia, was concern at the sufferings of the Biafrans and the belief that the gesture might put pressure on the Nigerians to negotiate. In the event, the Nigerians accepted African mediation but, apart from this, at the Kampala Conference (May–June) inspired by the Commonwealth Secretariat and the further conferences at Niamey (July) and Addis Ababa (August) arranged by the OAU Consultative Committee, there was no weakening in the attitudes of the antagonists. The Nigerians insisted that, before a cease-fire, the Biafrans must renounce secession and accept the division of the country into twelve states. The Biafrans would not agree.

The sympathy of much world public opinion for the sufferings of the Biafrans had meanwhile become a force to be reckoned with. In Britain there was growing unease and agitation against arms supplies to the Nigerians. Responding to Biafran fears and propaganda on the threat of "genocide", the British Government took the initiative in the setting-up of an Observer Team in Nigeria to accompany the Nigerian forces, consisting of representatives of Britain, Canada, Poland, the UN and the OAU (August 1968). The International Committee of the Red Cross and various churches organised relief supplies to the war-stricken areas, but in continual argument with both sides, the Nigerians fearful of the element of recognition and support of the Biafrans, the Biafrans fearful that the Nigerians might turn the relief-supply openings to their military advantage.

In this way the war dragged on through the rest of 1968 and 1969. The fighting was assisted by a handful of mercenaries on either side. In May 1968, the Nigerians took Port Harcourt, in September, Aba and Owerri, but then their "final offensive" ground to a halt. The following April (1969), they took the temporary Biafran capital, Umuahia, but the Biafrans recaptured Owerri. Peace efforts at the Commonwealth Conference in London (January 1969) were fruitless, as were efforts through the European Economic Community (March) and by the Vatican (July), and Biafran appeals to Switzerland and other European neutral states (November), and renewed Ethiopian proposals (December).

At last, at the turn of 1969–70, Nigerian military pressure, but still more, the blockade of war supplies, starvation, disease, and the waning of hope, ended Biafran resistance. The Nigerian forces began to break through in the final days of December 1969. On 11 January 1970, Ojukwu gave authority to surrender to the Biafran Chief of Staff, Major-General Philip Effiong, and left the country. The surrender was completed on 14 January. Thereafter, the worst fears of the Ibo were unfulfilled and the work of reconciliation began.

* * *

J. DE ST. JORRE: *The Nigerian Civil War*, Hodder and Stoughton, London 1972.

A. KIRK-GREENE: *Crisis and Conflict in Nigeria, A Documentary Survey 1966–69*, Oxford University Press, 1971.

R. LUCKHAM: *The Nigerian Military 1960–67*, Cambridge University Press, 1971.

J. MACKINTOSH and others: *Nigerian Government and Politics*, Allen and Unwin, London 1966.

S. PANTER-BRICK (ed.): *Nigerian Politics and Military Rule, Prelude to Civil War*, Athlone Press, London 1970.

W. SCHWARZ: *Nigeria*, Pall Mall Press, London 1968.

K. POST: "Is there a case for Biafra?", *International Affairs*, January 1968.

Hong Kong 1967

THE population of the British Crown Colony of Hong Kong in 1967 was some 4 million, including about 1 million refugees from Communist China. Most of them lived on the island of Hong Kong (ceded by China in 1841) and in Kowloon on the mainland opposite (ceded in 1860). The much larger but mostly mountainous New Territories behind Kowloon (leased from China for ninety-nine years in 1898) were comparatively sparsely populated. In the 1950s and 1960s, the Colony enjoyed a great manufacturing and trading boom but this still left the great majority of the population living in crowded conditions with bad housing and low wages.

Out of these general economic conditions, particular issues arose which touched off disturbances in 1966 and, far more serious, in 1967. On 5–6 April 1966, there was disorganised rioting over rises in ferry charges. The events of 1967 began with a dispute over pay and conditions in a Kowloon factory. Moreover, general economic conditions played some part in the spread of sympathetic strikes and in the availability of demonstrators and rioters.

At the same time, it seems clear that general economic conditions were not the crucial factor in the events of 1967. The majority of the population appear to have been more or less opposed to the riots and demonstrations. The hundreds of trading associations in the Colony expressed their support for the authorities. In these years, the general sentiment of the population, intensely aware of the Colony's vulnerability on the doorstep of China, was averse to trouble and indeed was apathetic towards political activity of any sort. Even after the shock of the events of 1967 and the intensification of discussion and effort by the authorities to improve living conditions, only a quarter of the electorate voted in the Urban Council Elections of 1969. The driving-force behind the events of 1967 was the militant section of the local Communist Party, influenced by developments in China at that time.

The Great Proletarian Cultural Revolution which began in China in the autumn of 1965 may be summarily described as the mobilisation by a section of the Chinese leadership around Chairman Mao Tse-tung of bands of young Red Guards and older Red Rebels charged with re-generating the revolutionary enthusiasm of local party leaders and the people. The disorder, deliberately created, extended from the beginning of 1967 to industry and the Army and, perhaps becoming uncontrolled, led to clashes between Red Guards, Rebels, still more extreme Maoists,

265

workers, peasants and army units, culminating in a major confrontation between extreme Maoists and the local military in Wuhan in July 1967 and thereafter slackening in intensity.

This ferment in China spread to Communist parties abroad under Chinese control. In Burma, Cambodia, Indonesia, Laos, Malaysia, and Thailand, they demonstrated and harangued and distributed *The Thoughts of Chairman Mao*, provoking ill-feeling, and sometimes counter-demonstrations and clashes. One of the first territories to be affected was the Portuguese Overseas Territory of Macao, like Hong Kong, on the doorstep of China. Early in December 1966, the local Communists staged riots in support of demands amounting to complete effective power there. In January 1967, the Governor conceded these demands.

In April 1967, it was Hong Kong's turn. In the last days of the month, in a Kowloon factory making plastic flowers, a dispute came to a head over low pay and sweated labour conditions. The management dismissed the workers involved. The trouble spread in Kowloon and, on 6 May, to Hong Kong island. The Communists organised demonstrations, including processions of school-children and students, petitioning the Government to exact confessions and apologies from the factory managements concerned and to punish them. As the police sought to control the movement of demonstrators, outbreaks of rioting began.

The extent to which the Chinese Government ordered or approved or was willing to push the situation which now developed, was a matter for judgement by the Hong Kong Government and the British Government at the time and still remains uncertain. On 1 May, the Chinese leadership had patched up the differences between those leading the Cultural Revolution and those doubtful or opposed, and had appeared in seemingly renewed solidarity (temporary, as it turned out) at the Peking May Day celebrations. Propaganda in support of the Hong Kong demonstrators and generally hostile to the British authorities began. On the 15th, the Chinese Government publicised Five Demands: that the Hong Kong Government immediately accept the petitions of the demonstrators, that all those arrested be released, that those responsible for fighting against the demonstrators (the Hong Kong police) be punished, that their victims be compensated, and, finally, that guarantees be given against similar incidents in the future.

As a general consideration to set against these possibly ominous signs, there was the long-standing tolerance of the Colony by the Chinese rulers, explained by Western commentators primarily in terms of its economic value to them. They gained several hundred million dollars' worth annually of foreign exchange by trade with and through the Colony. In the period preceding the Cultural Revolution, Sino-British relations had been correct, if not cordial. The Chinese had raised certain issues concerning the Colony such as the fact that United States personnel spent leave there from the war in Vietnam and that the United States Navy used the harbour, but this seemed to be for propaganda purposes only. There were difficulties in pressing this grievance further in that the Soviet Union made use of the harbour in sending war supplies to North Vietnam.

On balance, the British concluded that the disturbances were partly a spillover from the Cultural Revolution, as the British Foreign Secretary, George Brown, put it, and partly an expression of local problems which must be tackled in future; the aim of the Communists was to humiliate them rather than to end their rule in Hong Kong. They took the line in response to China's propaganda that the demonstrations were an internal affair of Hong Kong and that law and order must be restored. As further evidence of their determination, they sent a commando-troop carrier (HMS *Bulwark*) to take up position in Hong Kong harbour.

The demonstrations and outbreaks of riots continued unabated through mid-May, and on the 21st the Hong Kong Government declared a curfew, and on the 23rd emergency powers against inflammatory publications and seditious propaganda. The immediate response was still more violent rioting and strikes throughout the Colony. Over the next few weeks, however, the tactics of the authorities and in particular the police proved capable of containing the rioting. As the organisation for protection against intimidation proved its effectiveness, the workers began to return to the factories and the campaign of strikes began to collapse.

On 8 July, a serious incident occurred at Shataukok on the border with China, with or without the knowledge of the Chinese Government. Five Hong Kong policemen were killed by machine-gun fire and a mob of about a thousand attacked the police post. Some 550 British and Gurkha troops were thereupon sent to give added security along the border. In the city itself, a new phase began. On 13 July, bombs were used to blow up several police stations and to kill a popular Chinese radio broadcaster. Bomb explosions and bomb scares through the planting of dummy bombs multiplied over the next few days. On 20 July, the Hong Kong Government took further emergency powers, and in a massive operation the police arrested several hundred known or suspected militants.

Bomb incidents continued in great numbers over the following months but none the less the sense of crisis died away. In Peking, on 22 August, the authorities allowed a mob to burn down the office of the British *chargé d'affaires* in retaliation for the banning of three Hong Kong Communist newspapers and the arrest of some members of the staff. This, however, was the last major episode. By the end of the year, the affairs of the Colony had returned to normal.

K. Hopkins (ed.): *Hong Kong, The Industrial Colony*, Oxford University Press, 1971.

J. C. Hsiung: *Ideology and Practice, The Evolution of Chinese Communism*, Pall Mall Press, London 1971.

R. Hughes: *Hong Kong, Borrowed Place, Borrowed Time*, André Deutsch, London 1968.

R. J. Lifton: *Revolutionary Immortality, Mao Tse-tung and the Chinese Cultural Revolution*, Weidenfeld and Nicolson, London 1969.

The Far Eastern Economic Review, Issues of May to July 1967.

The Arab-Israeli War 1967

THE hostility between the Arab states and Israel which had caused war in 1948 and 1956,[1] intensified once again from 1965 onwards as a result of raids by Arab guerrilla groups across the borders of Israel. The main source of the guerrillas was the Arab refugees who had left Palestine at the time of the establishment of the state of Israel in 1948 and who now numbered 1·3 million in Syria, Egypt, Jordan and Lebanon. The main sponsor of the guerrillas was Syria. Egypt, at this time, while as hostile as ever to Israel, was doing little to push the quarrel and was deeply involved in the civil war in Yemen in rivalry with Saudi Arabia;[2] Jordan remained especially vulnerable to Israel and found the refugees dangerous and troublesome guests; Lebanon had always been the least bellicose of Israel's neighbours. In Syria, on the other hand, a *coup d'état* in February 1966 brought to power a Baathist government, extreme alike in its social doctrines, its antipathy to Western influence in the Middle East and its hostility towards Israel. It made no secret of its support for the most prominent of the guerrilla groups, Al Fatah. The raids on Israel became heavier and more ambitious in scope.

Israel's response, as in earlier years, was punitive counter-raids, of which two were particularly heavy. On 13 November 1966, it mounted an infantry and armour reprisal attack on the Jordanian village, Es Samu. On 7 April 1967, the most serious border clash since 1956 occurred when Israeli aircraft attacked Syrian artillery positions which had fired into Israel and, in the ensuing air combat, shot down six Syrian aircraft.

These episodes were followed as usual by Israeli warnings to the Arabs that further attacks would be punished by further counter-attacks. Renewed attacks and fresh warnings in the first fortnight of May raised tension to extreme heights. Egypt was later to claim that at this point Israel massed troops near the Syrian border. There seems to be no evidence that this was so though in view of Israel's warnings, some action on its part was likely. In any case, President Nasser of Egypt had special grounds for making some sort of demonstration at this point. During the raids and counter-raids since 1965, he had been militarily inactive apart from a defence agreement with the new regime in Syria (4 November 1966); he had been taunted by Jordan and Syria with sitting safely behind the

[1] See pp. 48–9 and 124–8.
[2] See p. 229ff.

269

United Nations Emergency Force[3] making bellicose propaganda while they took the blows from the common foe; he was in danger of losing prestige with the Arab masses at home and abroad.

On 14 May, Egypt put its armed forces on the alert and moved army formations towards the border "in support of Syria". As they reached the border, the Egyptian Commander-in-Chief requested UNEF to withdraw in that area (16th). When the Egyptian Government itself repeated this request on the 18th, the United Nations Secretary-General, U Thant, ordered withdrawal from Egypt. He was much criticised by Western commentators for failure to temporise further but replied that the position of the force was untenable in view of the host country's request for withdrawal and the movement of its troops. On the 19th, Egyptian troops occupied Sharm el Sheikh overlooking the Tiran Straits. On the 22nd, President Nasser announced that from the 24th, the Straits would be closed to Israeli shipping bound for the Israeli port of Eilat.

Israel had long made plain that it would view such a move with the utmost gravity. One of its reasons for invading Sinai in 1956 had been to maintain freedom of passage through the Straits and it had resisted heavy United States pressure to withdraw until it received United States assurances on this point. In a published *aide mémoire* to Israel of 11 February 1957 the United States had declared that it "believes that the Gulf (of Aqaba) comprehends international waters and that no nation has the right to prevent free and innocent passage in the Gulf and through the Straits giving access thereto". Israel accordingly viewed Egypt's closure of the Straits not simply as a blow to its commerce but as a deliberate defiance of itself and the United States and a challenge to its whole existence. Either it must counter the move successfully or it must admit that Egypt and Syria aided by the Soviet Union had at last won the upper hand over it.

In the preceding weeks, as the crisis developed, the United States had been busy urging restraint on all concerned. Its policy in past years had been to seek to maintain a balance of armaments between the two sides and to persuade the Soviet Union to limit its support for Egypt and Syria for fear of renewed war in the Middle East, perhaps involving a confrontation between the two super-powers. In the present crisis, the crucial aspect from its point of view was the attitude of the Soviet Union. What this attitude was and how clearly it was conveyed to the two sides and to the United States is not yet fully known publicly. It seems, however, that though Soviet public statements in the first half of May were as unreservedly partisan as ever, the Soviet Government, at least in the last stages,

[3] A force of 3,800 men stationed in Egypt by the Security Council after the 1956 war along the border with Israel and at Sharm el Sheikh near the tip of the Sinai peninsula (see p. 128).

urged caution on Egypt and Syria. It seems, in particular, that Egypt's closure of the Straits was announced without consultation with the Russians.

As to what could be done to counter Egypt's move, the United States showed some interest in a British scheme for creating a consortium of maritime states which would declare their belief in a right of free passage through the Straits and attempt to get this right established. However, the scheme aroused little general enthusiasm among the maritime states. In the Middle East, meanwhile, war fever was intense. The broad drift of President Nasser's speeches was: war is coming, Egypt will not be the first to attack, Israel will at last be crushed. Enmities between the Arab states were covered over. Israel had striven hard for the neutrality of Jordan, but on 30 May Egypt and Jordan signed a five-year defence agreement whereby the Jordanian Army would come under Egypt's command in the event of war. This *rapprochement* may have been the crucial factor in Israel's decision that it should strike without further delay. Popular pressure within Israel in favour of strong action, mounting steadily for some months, was now heavy. On 1 June, a Government of National Unity was formed in which General Moshe Dayan, the hero of the 1956 Sinai campaign, became Minister of Defence. On 4 June, Iraq joined the Egypt–Jordan defence pact.

On 5 June, Israeli aircraft attacked the main airfields in Egypt, Jordan, Syria and Iraq, destroying a large part of their air forces. With control of the air assured, the Israeli army advanced rapidly on Egypt and Jordan and subsequently on Syria. The Egyptian High Command announced (6th) that British and United States aircraft had taken part in the attacks and it has been speculated that this was an attempt to compel Soviet intervention. In the event, the announcement (later stated by Egypt to have been due to mistaken radar readings) led only to an embargo by Arab oil-producing states on oil exports to Britain and the United States (which lasted until 1 September 1967). The two super-powers made use of the "hot line" between the Kremlin and the White House to reassure each other that they did not wish to become directly involved in the war. Soviet warships in the Mediterranean were presumably able to verify the facts regarding British and United States aircraft.

This was the limit of United States–Soviet understanding, however. As the Israeli armies continued their advance into Egypt, Syria and Jordan, the UN Security Council met in almost continuous session. The United States wanted non-partisan cease-fire resolutions; the Soviet Union wanted resolutions calling for a cease-fire coupled with a vigorous condemnation of Israel and the demand that it immediately withdraw to the pre-war lines. Compromise cease-fire resolutions were passed on 6, 7 and 9 June but with no effect. The fighting ended on each front only when Israel had attained its objectives. It took from Jordan the eastern half of Jerusalem and the territory on the west bank of the river; from Egypt, Gaza and the whole of the Sinai peninsula; and from Syria, the Golan Heights commanding the border. Jordan accepted a cease-fire on the 7th, Egypt on the 8th and Syria on the 11th.

Little progress was made subsequently towards converting the cease-fire into a political settlement. Israel declared that it was ready to withdraw from occupied territories provided this formed part of a peace treaty ending the twenty-year state of war between itself and the Arab states. The Arab states demanded unconditional withdrawal. Disagreement between the United States and the Soviet Union prevented united pressure on the two sides.

At the request of the Soviet Union, an emergency session of the UN General Assembly opened on 17 June and lasted till 18 September. It failed to adopt any of the four resolutions proposed by the Soviet Union, Yugoslavia, Albania and the Latin American states. Two resolutions calling upon Israel to desist from measures in Jerusalem prejudicial to an eventual determination of its status were, however, passed (4 and 14 July).

The Security Council met again on 8 July to discuss the frequent violations of the cease-fire across the Suez Canal. On the suggestion of the Secretary-General, it accepted a "consensus statement" by its President that it favoured stationing observers from the UN Truce Supervision Organisation in the Suez Canal sector to report on violations (10 July). The observers began to take up position a week later and, for a time, the periodic bombardments across the Canal ended. The Canal itself, declared closed by Egypt at the onset of the war, remained closed.

After further months of strenuous diplomacy inside and outside the United Nations, the Security Council adopted on 22 November a British compromise resolution calling for an Israeli withdrawal from occupied territories; an end to the Arab state of war with Israel; respect for the territorial integrity of all states in the area; a just settlement of the Palestinian refugee problem; and freedom of navigation in the international waterways. The Security Council also directed the Secretary-General to appoint a special representative (he appointed a Swedish diplomat, Mr Gunnar Jarring) "to establish and maintain contacts with the states concerned". However, as reflected in this choice of words, the states concerned were not even in agreement on the manner of treating with one another. Israel did not favour United Nations mediation; it wanted the Arab states to accept direct discussions. The Arab states, for their part, would not give this degree of recognition to Israel.

R. and W. CHURCHILL: *The Six Days War*, Heinemann, London 1967.

M. HOWARD and R. HUNTER: *Israel and the Arab World, The Crisis of 1967*, Adelphi Paper 41, Institute of Strategic Studies, London 1967.

W. LAQUEUR: *The Road to War 1967*, Weidenfeld and Nicolson, London 1968.

A. LALL: *The UN and the Middle East Crisis 1967*, Columbia University Press, New York, rev. ed., 1970.

E. O'BALLANCE: *The Third Arab–Israeli War*, Faber and Faber, London 1972.

M. RODINSON: *Israel and the Arabs*, Penguin Books, Harmondsworth 1968.

C. YOST: "The Arab–Israeli War. How it Began", *Foreign Affairs*, January 1968.

O. YOUNG: "Intermediaries and Interventionists, Third Parties in the Middle East Crisis", *International Journal*, Winter 1967–68.

Czechoslovakia 1968

AFTER the Second World War, Czechoslovakia was governed by a coalition in which the Communists held a strong position. In February 1948, a Communist *coup d'état* led to a Soviet-type government under President Klement Gottwald, succeeded in power in 1953 by Antonin Novotný (First Secretary of the Communist Party from 1953 and President as well from 1957). The turmoil in Poland and Hungary in 1956 had little visible effect in Czechoslovakia. Not until the spring of 1967 was it evident that the Novotný regime was under heavy domestic pressure.

The clearest grievance was the economic condition of the country. By the early 1960s the rate of growth of living standards had fallen below that of even Poland and Hungary. Much of the blame for this was attributed to the running of the nationalised industries according to political criteria which cut across administrative and technical efficiency. Moreover, since 1948, Czechoslovakia's international trade had been directed mainly to the Soviet Union and the Communist bloc instead of its traditional markets in the West. There was a widespread belief that prices for the country's exports were kept artificially low. A confession of the failure of the centralised economic planning was seen in the abandonment of the Third Five Year Plan (for 1961–65) in 1962.

In the autumn of 1963 Czechoslovak economists began discussions on ways of rectifying the deteriorating economic situation, the suggestion being made by some that elements of a market economy ought to be introduced. A compromise, suggested by Professor Ota Šík, Director of the Economic Institute of the Academy of Science, aimed to replace over-detailed planning by a more flexible approach, and reforms on these lines were adopted by the Party Central Committee in January 1965. However, they aroused considerable opposition from supporters of centralised planning and it was not until the beginning of 1967 that major economic reforms were actually introduced.

Central planning was retained but was to concentrate on the long-term. Managers of individual enterprises were to be given increased powers and the criterion of their success was to be ability to sell at a profit rather than mere increase in the volume of production. Prices paid for exported goods were to be foreign market prices, while internally prices were classified as either free, semi-free, or fixed. These reforms quickly ran into trouble, however. Prices rose steeply because of the general scarcity of goods. The belief began to strengthen that alterations in the economic system were inadequate without wider liberalisation in the manner of running the country's affairs.

A related issue was "freedom of expression". It was in newspapers and journals and novels that the first public stirrings against the Novotný regime were heard. At the Fourth Czechoslovak Writers' Conference, 27–29 June 1967, an open split developed between the writers demanding freedom to write what they wished, and the Party delegation led by Jiří Hendrych, which stressed the need for loyalty and non-interference in political matters. There were also attacks on the Party's monopoly of power and on the Government's anti-Israel policy during the recent Arab–Israeli War. In disregard of Hendrych's views, a resolution was passed condemning censorship and calling for the establishment of contacts with Czechoslovak writers abroad.

In response, on 30 June, in an address to the graduates of the Party College in Prague, Novotný defended the Party's achievements and warned the writers that deviation could not be tolerated. On 3 July, Jan Beneš, a writer, and Karel Zámečník, a student, were tried on subversion charges. Pavel Tigrid, a journalist who had taken United States citizenship and lived abroad, was also tried *in absentia*. All were found guilty and heavy sentences were passed. In September, the *Literarní Noviny*, the Writers' Union Weekly, was placed under the control of the Minister of Culture and Information by a decision of the Central Committee and its editorial board was replaced by Novotný nominees.

Czechoslovak students were also discontented with the rigid paternalistic system the Communist authorities had imposed upon them. This culminated in a clash in Prague between students and police on 31 October 1967. Known as the "Strahov Incident", it was triggered by the failure of power supplies but had much deeper causes. The vigorous way in which the police halted the demonstration caused a public outcry.

The third great issue in the country was ethnic. Czechoslovakia's short history had been constantly troubled by the fact that the Czechs and Slovaks were two distinct peoples. Officially the Novotný regime was said to have solved the "nationality problem" by treating both groups alike, but in fact the regime was controlled by the Czechs and, in its early period, several Slovak Communists had been purged, and Slovak demands for modest federal rights were condemned as "bourgeois nationalism". The majority of Slovaks had, it seems, by 1967 long lost all confidence in Novotný.

It was thus against a background of collapsing conservative morale that the Party discussions took place during the autumn and winter of 1967–68 on the economic situation and the role of the Party. Both the ten-member Praesidium and the Party Central Committee were involved. During these discussions, on 8–9 December, Leonid Brezhnev, the Russian First Secretary, came to Prague. He seems to have accepted that the majority of the Central Committee had turned against Novotný and not to have exerted any pressure on his behalf.

There is some evidence that Novotný planned a military *coup* against his opponents but failed. On 5 January 1968 it was announced that he had resigned as First Secretary and that the Central Committee had elected in his place Alexander Dubček, First Secretary of the Communist Party of Slovakia. Dubček visited Moscow at the end of the month and consultations were also held with the governments of other Eastern bloc countries.

On 22 March it was announced that Novotný had also resigned from the Presidency and on 30 March General Ludvík Svoboda was named as his successor. A new government was appointed, with Oldřich Černik as Prime Minister. On 5 April, an "Action Programme" was approved, outlining Czechoslovakia's "road to socialism". Press censorship was to be relaxed and rehabilitation was promised to political prisoners. The leading role of the Party was confirmed but it was to be responsive to demands from below. Freedom of assembly and organisation were accepted and minorities were to be protected. The economic reforms were to continue. In foreign affairs it was stressed that friendship with Russia and other Communist countries remained the basis of Czechoslovakia's foreign policy and the country would continue to support "national liberation movements" in the world. In sum, socialism was maintained but, in the Programme's phrase, it was to be "socialism with a human face". Reforms were not to be merely imposed from above; there was to be an element of popular control. There was to be not merely liberalisation but "democratisation".

The "Action Programme" caused deep concern in Russia and Eastern Europe. In his talks with the Soviet and other Eastern European leaders, Dubček had sought to reassure them that he was in control of popular demands and especially that the country would remain loyal to the Eastern security system, the Warsaw Treaty Organisation. Doubts on these counts about Imre Nagy were believed to have been the prime causes of Soviet intervention in Hungary in 1956. These assurances did not, apparently, satisfy the other WTO leaders. It seems that they saw "democratisation" as undermining the authority of the Communist Party and thus posing the gravest possible threat to the internal cohesion of the other authoritarian regimes in Eastern Europe, particularly in East Germany and Poland. The fear was, it seems, that the East Germans, the Poles and the Hungarians, and even the Russian people, would urge that the Czechoslovak experiment be applied at home. Moreover, Czechoslovakia's position as "the dagger in the heart of Europe" made it of vital strategic importance to the WTO and meant that the other WTO leaders could not countenance the risk of Dubček losing control of events.

Throughout the spring and summer there were continual exchanges between the other WTO countries and Czechoslovakia, with mounting pressure to halt the changes on the one side and determination on reform blended with firmness and efforts at reassurance on the other. On 23 March the WTO countries (except Rumania) met at Dresden. Then followed the promulgation of the "Action Programme". On 4–6 May, Dubček and other Czechoslovak leaders had talks in Moscow. On 8 May, Ulbricht of East Germany, Kadar of Hungary, Gomulka of Poland and Zhivkov of Bulgaria met in Moscow without Czech participation.

From 30 May, WTO military manoeuvres were held in Czechoslovakia. Dubček had agreed to "staff exercises" but the manoeuvres included large armoured and infantry contingents. On 1 June, the Czechoslovak Central Committee called an Extraordinary Party Congress for 9 September but coupled this with a statement reaffirming adherence to socialism and the leading role of the Party. On 27 June, a manifesto entitled "Two Thousand Words" by a group of eminent Czech intellectuals called for action to maintain the momentum of reform. The military manoeuvres were due to end on 30 June but the Soviet troops were withdrawn slowly and "air defence exercises" took place along the Czechoslovak border. On 14–15 July, the five WTO countries opposing Czechoslovakia met in Warsaw and agreed a letter condemning the situation in Czechoslovakia as "unacceptable to socialist countries". Czechoslovakia replied on the 18th reassuringly but firmly.

From 29 July to 1 August, the Politburo of the Soviet Party and the Praesidium of the Czechoslovak Party met at Cierna Nad Tisou (on the Czechoslovak–Russian border). This was followed on 3 August by a conference at Bratislava of the Central Committees of Bulgaria, Czechoslovakia, East Germany, Hungary, Poland and Russia. The communiques issued at these meetings contained only generalities but it was widely supposed that a compromise had been reached. Shortly afterwards, the last Russian troops left Czechoslovakia.

On 10 August, the new draft Czechoslovak Party Statutes were published in preparation for the forthcoming congress. They asserted the right of an outvoted minority to continue to adhere to its views and introduced secret ballots for Party elections.

On the night of 20 August, WTO units from Russia, Bulgaria, East Germany, Hungary and Poland invaded Czechoslovakia. At the request of their government, the Czechoslovakians offered no forceful resistance, although passive resistance was widespread. Dubček, Černik and others were arrested and secretly taken out of the country. A "Worker and Peasant" Government was announced, but appears to have had only a fleeting paper existence.

Externally, strong opposition to the invasion came from Yugoslavia and Rumania. Both had previously given support to the Czechoslovaks. President Tito had visited Prague on 9–11 August and President Ceauşescu on 15–16 August. Both felt their own countries to be threatened by the WTO action and both immediately placed their forces on alert, making known their intention of resisting if invaded.

The Soviet Union accused the Western powers of having been involved in a "counter-revolutionary plot" in Czechoslovakia. In those countries, the reaction of the public to the invasion was one of outrage but governmental response was restrained. The strongest protests came from Britain and France. The United States Government condemned the invasion but at the same time wished the current *détente* with the Soviet Union to continue.

The United Nations Security Council met on the evening of 21 August. A resolution condemning the invasion was vetoed by Russia. Algeria, India and Pakistan abstained. Later a resolution concerning the safety of Czechoslovak leaders was debated but no vote was taken and the matter was not referred to the General Assembly.

On 27 August the Czechoslovak delegate requested the issue be withdrawn from the Security Council agenda. Four days previously President Svoboda had arrived in Moscow and on 26 August agreement was reached. Dubček was to remain First Secretary and the WTO forces were to be withdrawn. Censorship was to be restored and the leading role of the Party reasserted.

On 3–4 October, further Soviet–Czechoslovak talks were held in which the latter agreed to "step up efforts to raise the leading role of the Communist Party, intensify the struggle against anti-socialist forces, take the necessary measures to place all the mass information media at the service of socialism and reinforce the Party and the State organs with men firmly adhering to positions of Marxist-Leninism and proletarian internationalism". On 16 October, a treaty was signed allowing for the temporary stationing of Russian troops on Czechoslovak territory. On 17 April 1969, it was announced that Dubček had resigned as First Secretary and had been replaced by Dr Gustav Husák, the leader of the Slovak Communist Party.

*   *   *

G. GOLAN: *The Czechoslovak Reform Movement*, Cambridge University Press, 1971.

R. REMINGTON: *The Warsaw Pact*, The MIT Press, Cambridge (Mass.) 1971.

R. REMINGTON (ed.): *Winter in Prague, Documents on Czechoslovak Communism in Crisis*, The MIT Press, Cambridge (Mass.), 1969.

H. SCHWARTZ: *Prague's 200 Days*, Pall Mall Press, London 1969.

P. TIGRID: *Why Dubček Fell*, Macdonald, London 1971.

P. WINDSOR and A. ROBERTS: *Czechoslovakia 1968*, Chatto and Windus, London 1969.

Z. ZEMAN: *Prague Spring*, Penguin Books, Harmondsworth 1969.

Index

(Chapter headings are indexed in bold type)